The

Christian Contemplative Journey

~

Essays on the Path

By Bernadette Roberts

Published by ContemplativeChristians.com
December, 2017
P.O. Box 164202
Austin, TX 78716

The Christian Contemplative Journey: Essays on the Path
© 2017 Bernadette Roberts. All rights reserved.

First published in 2007 by Bernadette Roberts as *Essays on the Christian Contemplative Journey*.

Library of Congress Cataloging-in-Publication Data

Roberts, Bernadette (1931 – 2017)
The Christian Contemplative Journey: Essays on the Path
ISBN-13: 978-0-692-98721-6

p.cm.
1. Spiritual life – Christianity. 2. Contemplative Journey. I. Title.

BV 4501.3.H33 2017

20100

Printed in the United States of America

ABOUT THE COVER IMAGE

"THE MONK" is used with the kind permission of Brother Mark, an artist of the Camaldolese Hermitage on the Big Sur, California. For many years it was on sale in their bookstore, but now is out of print.

CONTENTS

The

Christian Contemplative Journey

~

Essays on the Path

PREFACE

This is a collection of short papers written over the last twenty-five years. They were written in response to various issues that came up and passed along to friends. Since each piece has its own explanation, no further introduction is really needed. The only piece originally intended for a book was "The Spiritual Journey Recapitulates the History of Religion". With no time to do the research, only the thesis was salvaged. Still waiting in the wings is a book, The Fallacy of Reincarnation, which took almost a year and five-hundred pages before the computer crashed. This book is still in its old dos format on 5x5 disks. God only knows if there will be time to unravel this mess. Basically, family affairs are all time consuming. Yet nothing guarantees keeping one's feet on the ground like family life, and more especially, five beautiful little grandchildren.

Although other papers were written over the years, there has not been time to include them here. There hasn't even been time to proofread the ones that were included, so the reader is bound to find grammatical and typo errors. Please excuse these and be assured they will be caught and corrected before the next printing. As it stands, there was only a single week to put these essays together, it was either do it now or put it off another year. Already this project was delayed a year due to family concerns – not only births, but the recent death of my closest friend, my sister Marge. Another never ending delay is due to the computer itself. Trying to get it to obey has consumed more time than all the writing I've ever done. Just last week my friend, Ric Williams, a university computer-science instructor, took a look at my computer and said, "I've never seen anything like it!". Somehow I've managed to set precedence in computer problems. (He bravely left me his expensive IBM ThinkPad to grapple with – or mess up.)

There is only one thing I would like to remind the reader who manages to plow through these essays. There is nothing in my background that remotely prepared me to address people into Eastern religions or philosophies. I've read the books – one of the first being Fr. Raimundo Panikkar's translation of the Vedas – and while I see truth in these religions, I also see the truth that is lacking. Indeed, I see profound, even critical differences. Because of the numerous people I've met over the years who are into the Eastern religions, I've been somewhat forced to address the issues they bring up. This fact could not but color some of the papers I have written; it explains why some of these essays include my perspective on the Eastern belief systems. Always keep in mind, however, I never had the experiences they talk about, never shared their practices and goals, do not share their view of soul or self, and find their terms totally foreign. In short, my views represent but one Christian contemplative looking East, and this, after the fact – meaning, there is nothing there for me.

Following the publication of my first book, nothing was more surprising than the number of people I heard from who, spiritually at least, had moved East. These last twenty-eight years I'd say eighty percent of the people I meet (with Christian backgrounds) have gone East in search of a deeper spiritual life. Though knowledgeable and well versed in the Eastern religions, with few exceptions, my impression is that few seem to have gone beyond a first grade understanding of Christianity. This has been a continuous problem: how to communicate the Christian journey to those who know nothing about it, and who can only translate it according to the terms and beliefs of the Eastern religions – mainly Hinduism or Buddhism.

By the same token, how can they expect someone to understand their Eastern perspective who knows nothing about it – apart from some books? This has all been an unwelcomed business. This problem has totally delayed what I initially set out to contribute to the Christian journey. Instead of adding to our knowledge of the completed journey, my time is spent going over its most rudimentary Christian background. Thus after one retreat, when people were commenting on the talks, one lady said, "Well, all I know is that you are a good spokesperson for the Catholic Church!" Of all the things anyone could have said, this was the most shocking. Teaching the Faith would never have gotten on my list of life's accomplishments — I'd sooner spend my life in a cave. But this illustrates the approach one has to take when there is no background even to begin understanding the Christian contemplative journey. At least you have to know the Faith!.

Recently I received a letter from Fr. Raimundo Panikkar, a well-known writer and scholar in the field of East-West dialogue. He is not only genetically half-and-half, but is a spiritual melding of East and West. In his letter he made the remark that Christianity has come to a crossroads whereby it can no longer go it alone, but needs the other world's religions to go forward. Considering my own East-West dilemma, his remark struck home, perhaps it was even prophetic. There is no denying people seeking a richer spiritual life have gone East. This means they are not only translating the East to fit their Western paradigms, but turning around, they are looking at Christianity though Eastern glasses, a perspective and understanding colored by the whole Eastern paradigm and belief system. Fr. Panikkar seems to have no problem with this, in fact, he holds out for a type of theological reconstructionism which I, for one, regard as impossible. My view is that the East can never honestly come West. All that has come West is a Western version of the East. It's too late for anything else. Let me give one example of why I think so.

Years ago I met the head honcho of a Zen Buddhist community (Tassahara in Carmel Valley, California). He told me this story. One day they were all sitting silently in the zendo when the Roshi (I think his name was Gallacurchi or something like that) suddenly stormed into the hall, stomped up to the platform, pointed his finger at them and shouted, "You are all looking for God! That is not Buddhism!" Then he stormed out again. The man said they just looked at one another with raised eyebrows — knowingly, that is — and went back to their silence. They knew the Roshi was right, he had said the truth. They were indeed looking for

God – call It what you will. This makes one wonder if the West can ever import authentic Buddhism and Hinduism. There is no getting away from the West's Judeo-Christian background. And then there is the Indian who told me "You cannot convert to Hinduism, you can only be born a Hindu" – so much for espousing a religion you can never be part of. No, the West can only import so much, it will never import it all.

In ending, nothing I've written was ever intended for all the good people in other religions. Everything was intended for those immersed in Christianity's long tradition of the contemplative life. My writing was solely intended to lend some clarity to this spiritual journey, more especially, living out its unitive state. There is still much more to be written, many issues to address that have never been adequately covered or even brought up. Although the journey itself is timeless, yet how it has been understood and presented down the ages has ever varied according to its contemporary milieu. (I think the short piece I wrote on "Apatheia" illustrates this). At any rate, my next project is to put into writing what, until now at least, has only been available in short form on tape or CD, "A Passage Through Self". I have always regarded this as my definitive, most complete contribution to the subject, an entire overview of the contemplative journey from beginning to end. I don't know how or when there will be time to write this – just now I received an ad from the Alzheimer Foundation and Neptune Society – but God willing, time will be sufficient for the task. I once read a brief biography of this distinguished man, but I can't find it now. I do know, however, he is about 88 and lives in Spain where he was born. After being ordained a Jesuit he went to India to research his heritage – I think one of his parents was from India. As a theologian, I think he was involved in Vatican II, but afterwards became renowned for promoting East-West dialogue. He has written a number of books and numerous articles, the most memorable being The Trinity and the Religious Experience of Man.

Because I disagreed with his final pages I wrote at length about some of its issues, but never sent it on. He also wrote The Unknown

Christ of Hinduism; Worship and Secular Man; Christophany, the Fullness of Man, and others books. His publishing company recently sent me his last book, but being in Spanish, I couldn't read it. Early on, however, I first heard of him when reading his beautiful translation of the Hindu Vedas. Although a great scholar and prolific writer, what makes his works special is not only his unique insights, but his unique vision of "reality" – its threefold dimension of the divine, the cosmic, and the human. I believe all his books in English are published by Orbis Books, Maryknoll, N.Y. I never met the man, but in the 1980's someone sent him one of my books, which is why I have a few letters from him. I even received a card last year announcing the Golden Jubilee of his ordination. As a theologian he is somewhat a modern Meister Eckhart, only without Eckhart's shock-appeal. Though I disagree with some of his views, I nevertheless hold him in the highest regard. If we have anything in common besides the Trinity, it is the problem of getting across God's greatest Mystery – Christ. As I've always said, "the truth of Christ is unbelievable, literally unbelievable".

OUR SPIRITUAL JOURNEY RECAPITULATES THE HISTORY OF RELIGION

OUR SPIRITUAL JOURNEY RECAPITULATES THE
HISTORY OF RELIGION

From our biology classes we might recall the catch phrase "ontogeny recapitulates phylogeny". As this refers to the human species, it points out that the embryonic development of each human being recapitulates the evolutionary process of the human species as a whole. From a single cell and its particular elements, the development of each individual passes through the entire history of the emergence of the human species. Thus, in the development of the individual, there is the repetition of its phylogenetic history, each one recapitulating the whole developmental history of mankind.

Transposing this biological theory to man's spiritual development, we find a similar phenomenon. Namely, that the spiritual development of each individual recapitulates the progressive development of man's various religions. Where, in a matter of months, a single embryo covers millions of years in the evolution of mankind, so too, in a single life-span the spiritual development of the individual recapitulates the key revelations on which man's religions were founded. Thus our spiritual journey recapitulates the history of the world 's religions.

Whether or not this biological theory is factually true makes no difference to our thesis. Our interest is in the "principle of recapitulation" for which biology provides an analogous theory.

From the beginning of human history God has revealed Himself to man. Although the fullness of God is present in every revelation, the nature of this fullness is only progressively revealed until man is prepared to understand its all-encompassing reality. This progressive revelation is not only the history of man's various religions, but this same progressive revelation can be found in the spiritual journey of each human being. In this way the process of each one's spiritual development is a recapitulation of God's progressive revelation to all men.

In making our spiritual journey, we tend to overlook the larger historical religious context of the milestones we encounter along the way. Usually, we unknowingly take for granted what, at one point in the history of religion, was a major breakthrough of God's revelation. Few people, however, see their individual experiences in its broader historical context, much less grasp its significance, like we might by studying phylogeny.[1] My hope is that by pointing out the correlation between individual experiences and the key revelations of our religions, we can better appreciate and understand the diversity of God's revelation to man. This is not only a way to better understand our various religions, but understand the variety of our individual experiences as well. By making this correlation, everyone can place their journey in a much larger context than would otherwise be warranted.

Origin of Thesis

I derived this thesis, first of all, from a backward look over my own experiential journey, and secondly, from tracing the key revelations of various religions to see if there was any key revelation I could not relate to at its original level. What I came upon was a remarkable convergence of the individual's path and God 's key revelations — as far back as I could trace them at least. Though I could not relate to the historical and cultural outgrowth of these religions, I could nevertheless see where the original revelation arose and how, over time, it had become increasingly distorted and, possibly, even lost. That the original becomes misunderstood often happens when it passes from the individual recipient to the group.

---

[1] The biological definition of this phrase, sometimes called the "recapitulation theory", is that an organism passes through successive stages resembling the series of ancestral types from which it has descended so that the ontogeny of the individual is a recapitulation of the phylogeny of its group. Thus the term "ontogeny" refers to the course of development of an individual organism, while "phylogeny" refers to the development (or evolution) of the whole group-species, family, or genetically related group of organisms. ("Phylum" refers to a common descent or direct line of descent within a group from a single point of origin).

For the group, revelation is primarily hear-say, understood intellectually at best, emotionally and culturally at worst. This is all the more reason the original revelation needs repeating down the centuries and in every age. This repeatability lends revelation more credence than warranted by a 'one-time-only' revelation occurring thousands of years ago. Indeed, it is only because these revelations are part and parcel of everyone's journey they are still with us today.

The continuity of religions' key revelations, then, is not due to any scholarly means of transmission, books, talks or hearsay, but to the fact these revelations are continuously being repeated – recapitulated – in the history of man's individual journey. Nowhere is this continuity of revelation more evident than in the lives of saints and holy people revered as models and inspirations in their respective religions. Without this experiential continuity, revelation would become no more than an intellectual concept or idea, a memento of a bygone era, or simply degenerate into legend and myth. So the advantage of focusing on individual development is that it reveals the uniqueness of religion's key revelations without being obscured by the diversity of its cultural and unoriginal overlays.

Having come upon this convergence between God's historical revelations and their encounter in everyone's journey, it was obvious to me, at least, man's true spiritual journey is, in fact, a recapitulation of the key revelations on which our world's religions were founded. Thus in our individual journey, we miss nothing God has ever revealed to the whole of mankind.

Individual vs. Group

When we say the spiritual journey recapitulates the history of religion, we do not mean it recapitulates the chronological record of historical events. What is recapitulated is God's original revelation, more especially, as it applies to the spiritual development of the individual. Thus our focus is primarily on the individual and not on historical groups or events. In the history of religion it seems its foundational revelation is always given first to an individual, which then becomes known to a group. So while the historical time and setting of these revelations are important to know, yet the breakthrough of every revelation always starts with the individual.

What we look for in man's spiritual development, then, is a religion's key revelation. This revelation, however, must not be confused with the religion's historical development or its extraneous accruements in the course of history. By "accruements" I mean the philosophy, theology, rituals, and cultural overlays that often identify a particular religion. Although these factors are the practical and cultural outgrowth of revelation – or what develops in the living of a particular religion – our present focus is on the revelation itself minus its cultural overlays.

The reason we find a religion's most authentic history in the individual journey is not only because the light of revelation is first hand, but because this same light, filtered through a group or social prism, becomes diffused according to each one's level of reception. It is this diffused diversity of interpretations that has divided our religions into numerous sects and denominations, sometimes to the point where the original is no longer reflected at all. This is why the spiritual history of the individual yields a clearer view of revelation than its fragmented, secondhand accounts.

In this matter it is well to remember that a religion's history is always traced to individual founders – Moses, Christ, Buddha and others. Although the history of religion plays out on two levels, that of the individual and the group, to overlook the individual for the group is a mistake. Too often the group takes on a mentality and spirit of its own quite apart from the revelation that brought it together. Group-think is one of the surest ways a revelation can become unrecognizable, and why, without repeated revelation, it can be lost altogether.

So our purpose here is not to outline the history of man's various religions – about which so much has been written already – but to focus on God's primary revelation as it came to various groups through singular individuals. The concern is not with an academic or intellectual understanding of our religions, rather, our focus is the experiential path of the individual as it reflects the key revelation of our enduring religions.

Definitions

The key terms used in this paper are "religion", "God", and "revelation". Because these terms are so entwined, however, they cannot be defined apart from one another. Nevertheless, we will say something about how these terms are used in their present context.

Every revelation has two sides: God the giver, man the receiver. Putting the two sides together, we have "religion". Thus we might think of religion as a single coin. As the giver of revelation, God's side is both the act of revelation and "what" is revealed, while man's side is the receiver and experiencer of the revelation. Thus God, or "what" is revealed, is the objective side of religion, while man and his experience is its subjective side. Because the history of our religions are equally the history of God 's revelation, the terms "religion" and "revelation" are all but synonymous. Thus the title of this paper might just as well have been "the spiritual journey of each individual recapitulates the history of God's revelation to man".

Religion

Since I hold there is no authentic religion without revelation, my definition of religion is limited to "God's revelation to man". Had God not revealed Himself we would not know God exists and, consequently, no authentic "religion" would exist. Whatever man can discover on his own has no need to be revealed, only "that" which is truly transcendent to man must be revealed to him. Thus "God" is "that" which can only be revealed. "What" is revealed, then, becomes the keystone of a religion and, as such, is the primary focus of our thesis.

Religion might also be defined as a life based on a specific revelation. Thus it can be regarded as the way a particular revelation is lived and perpetuated. But while revelation is first and foremost experiential, religion is usually the intellectual medium that conveys and passes it on.

However, as already noted, where revelation is passed on solely by way of intellectual concepts – with its endless diversity of interpretations – it soon becomes obscured and corrupted. Only through repeated experience is a revelation continuously verified and perpetuated.

God

Since God is not revealed as a concept, thought, idea or image, neither can God be grasped or defined as such. In experience, God is not our ideas and thoughts of God; indeed, thought and experience are two totally different dimensions, two different modes of human knowing. It is because we cannot pass along an experience of God, however, that we have no choice but to convey God in the objective form of words, concepts, descriptions, images, and so forth. This is unfortunate because God in experience is neither how the mind knows or thinks of God. It is only in the absence of experience the mind tends to rely on words and concepts for its truth. This is why, in the effort to convey a revelation, the language must be honed to as accurate an objective statement as possible, otherwise the revelation can be overwhelmed with subjective intrusions. So although experience and intellect both refer to "how" we know, each implies a different means of knowing. For our present purpose, we are using the term "God" in its more experiential sense, not its secondary or intellectual sense.

As far as names go, God has no name, thus the term "God" is not a name. "God" simply designates (points to) the ultimate mystery of existence – as far as man can go, or beyond which, he knows of nothing that exists. Actually the term "God" is one of the broadest, most unexclusive terms man ever came up with. All other terms – like "light", "energy", "source", "bliss", "love", you name it, – are all exclusive terms describing an individual 's experience of God, terms, however, that are not what God is. Nobody knows "what" God is, we only know "that" God is – and this, by revelation alone. As it is, the term "God" is so universally open-ended it is unlikely any two people in history have ever had the same rapport, experience, notion or understanding of the term. At the same time, everyone knows it refers or points to the ultimate mystery of all that exists. Those who avoid the term invariably suffer a deep seated prejudice or anger against somebody or something, after all, they can't be against a God they never encountered. Their problem is not with God, but with people, maybe some overbearing religious parent – who knows?

We can define God, then, as "That" which can only be revealed – "only", because of himself man cannot come upon God. Where there is no revelation I hold there is also no true religion, but instead, mere philosophy, speculation and myth. Without revelation no certitude is possible, not even the certitude God exists. We might add, "That" which is revealed never identifies Itself by the term "God" or says anything at all. The term "God" is man's term for "That" beyond which nothing exists.

Revelation

"Revelation" is central to our thesis. Because I have much to say about it, I will leave its major characteristics for an appendix and only give its barest definition here. The dictionary defines revelation in broad terms as: a disclosure to man of something he did not previously know. But since this could apply to anything man has yet to learn, it will not do for our purposes. My use of the term "revelation" is restricted to a first-hand "seeing" or "knowing" God.

By "seeing" we do not mean sensory or visual sight, and by "knowing" we do not refer to any mental faculty. Rather, it is God's gratuitous disclosure of Himself to man as opposed to any truth man can come upon, see or know, on his own. Revelation is thus a key experiential knowledge not otherwise accessible to human experience. (I exclude from authentic revelation any kind of paranormal experience – visions, voices, all such phenomena – see Appendix). It is also the disclosure of Truth, a Truth not merely for the individual recipient, but a universal Truth for all peoples of all times. It is because what is revealed is "Truth" (another term for "God") it is continuously repeated down the ages as part and parcel of man's journey. It is a mistake to think God has only revealed Himself to a few privileged people in a bygone era. On the contrary, God reveals Himself to everyone past and present.

Since the key revelation of each religion is also the end or goal to be realized, whatever this revelation is, will dictate the means of getting there. Thus, for example, if the revelation is God-in-nature, man seeks God there; if, however, God is revealed as immanent or within man himself, then a more inward path will be required. If, on the other hand, the revelation is the utter transcendence of God – beyond nature and ourselves – then a more outward path is required. In this way the key revelation not only dictates the goal to be attained, but the path to be taken to reach that goal. The reason different religions have different goals and paths is due solely to their different revelations.

As to why there are different revelations and not just one, keep in mind God is not an aloof impersonal monad or an enclosed entity – a static "something". God's revelations are different because the nature of God is dynamic, all-inclusive and multidimensional. Like a finely cut diamond, we have to see all sides if we are to truly know God. There is also the fact that the fullness of Truth is only gradually revealed. "See God and die" indicates the fullness of God's revelation is incompatible with earthly existence, thus a gradual accommodation is required. Indeed, it is the constant need to integrate and accommodate progressive revelations that constitutes the essence of our spiritual journey.

We can discount God's different revelations being due to the particularity of individuals. Over the ages, vastly different people have come upon these same revelations-young-old, male-female, learned-illiterate, happy-sad, and so on. God is no respecter of persons. Though recipients will have different experiences and descriptions, yet, "what" has been revealed is the same across the board. Finally, we should not forget that what is important about any revelation is what we learn from it – learn of God, that is. The experience itself (our reactions, thoughts and feelings) is not relevant – "experiences" merely come and go. It is the knowledge, the Truth of God given in revelation , that is important to our life and journey.

To summarize our definitions: "revelation" is God's disclosure of Himself to man. Thus "God" is "That" which is revealed – can only be revealed. This gratuitous revelation is the essence and foundation of man's "religions". Without this, I hold no authentic "religion" is possible.

The Nature of Spiritual Development

The key to spiritual development is neither biological, intellectual or psychological. Rather, the key to spiritual development is the encounter with revelation, in particular, the central revelation of our major religions. It is the breakthrough of these revelations into soul and psyche that is responsible for authentic spiritual change and transformation. Without this supernatural intervention, man's development goes no further than his limited natural resources.

Today there is a tendency to mistake the natural development of the psyche or consciousness for the true nature of man's spiritual journey. People have not only made the case that the spiritual journey depends upon one's psychological maturation, but even made it synonymous with it. Yet there is nothing particularly spiritual about consciousness or its natural development, and no study of psychological development has disclosed this fact. So there is nothing to back up the claim there is anything autonomous or developmentally natural about the spiritual journey. Thus Freud's deepest probing of consciousness revealed little more than a bundle of sexual drives and survival instincts hardly different from animals. Though Jung was more optimistic, his collective unconscious revealed a myriad of biologically inherited mythical archetypes man could neither control nor transcend. No, the study of man's psychological development has never yielded an inspiring picture of man, much less assured him of any transcendent destiny or reality.

The goals and norms of psychology may even be diametrically opposed to the requirements of spiritual development. When the spiritual goal is lowered to focus on the psyche – one's own consciousness or self – instead of on God, then we are being led in a direction opposed to authentic spiritual development. Only total dedication to God's revelation can bring us to the final destiny God intended for man. Anything less only stunts and retards human development.

So revelation is the key factor in spiritual development; it is the cause of the soul's transformation and subsequent change of consciousness. Since man's soul is open-ended we do not know how far it is destined to develop, or to what extent the Maker will expand its original limits. But just as we did not make ourselves or choose to be human, so too, we cannot limit ourselves to our ordinary biological and psychological dimensions.

Although no one can travel many paths or live all religions at once, nevertheless, the key revelations or central truths of various religions may be encountered within a single journey, even encountered without going outside one's traditional path. Should these key revelations not be found in our path, then of course it would be necessary to go outside to find them. But where they are part and parcel of the path, the need to go outside does not arise.

As usually happens, however, even when we encounter these revelations in our own tradition, we may not realize they are key revelations of other religions as well. With some knowledge of other religions, however, we may see these revelations in the larger context of our world religions. Thus one advantage of pointing out these key revelations, is to see our individual journey in the larger context of God's timeless revelation to all men.

We should also keep in mind that within any given religious group, there always will be individuals privy to revelations beyond the group itself. Because God's revelations are not restricted by any group, no individual can be deprived of encountering all God's revelations. Two examples that come to mind: the Egyptian Pharaoh who made his case for One God and was put down by his people; the Jewish philosopher, Philo of Alexandria, who came upon the Trinitarian nature of God, also deemed unacceptable to his group.

We can even find evidence of a trinity in Hinduism and Buddhism long before Christianity. The point is that everyone, regardless of their religion or belief system can come to know the furthest reaches of God's revelations, know them long before they become known (accepted or rejected) by a particular group.

Historians of religion would not agree with this, of course. Giving no credence to God's revelations, they have no choice but to search for a religion's origin in indigenous myths, legends, cultural ethos, philosophy and so on.

Where they find similarities they theorize there must have been some contact between totally disparate and distant religious groups. It never occurs to them that the origins and similarities between religions derive from the same revelation given in every age throughout the world. Indeed, God's revelations are as old as man.

Three Variables Inherent in the Journey

The journey is made complex by the interaction of three variables. The first is God's different revelations; the second is the ever-changing human recipient and variety of his experiences; the third is the movement of the path with its stages and major turning points. The interaction of these variables does not permit us to attach a specific time-line or chronological age to the journey. Despite this complexity, however, I intend to adhere to the journey's sequential nature.

The first variable, God's progressive revelation, is due, as we shall see, to God's own dynamic inner nature. God is multidimensional, multifaceted – infinite. Although no revelation withholds God's fullness and truth, the progressive nature of revelation is also due to our own undeveloped "eye" required to see God's fullness and Truth.

We may also lack the spiritual strength to endure this fullness – remember, for the unprepared "see God and die" is a profound truth. So even though God's revelations vary – no two are alike – the variability is both on God's part and our own as well.

The second variable of the journey is our ever-changing self, the recipient of revelation. Because self, with its ever changing thoughts, feelings and experiences is such an obvious fact, we need not spend time pointing out the dynamics of its variable nature. We change day to day, year by year, hopefully, always growing both intellectually, psychologically, and, by the grace of God, spiritually. The good news, perhaps, is that God does not wait for any of this. He does not wait until we have mastered the ABC's, have a college degree, or managed to keep ourselves quiet for more than a minute. None of this means anything to God. Whatever God's chosen moment, His revelation has nothing to do with our developmental state or anything going on in our lives. God waits for no one, and by the same token, no one should wait for God, but do their best at all times, for no one knows the day or the hour.

The third variable is the spiritual path itself. This path is the line of travel between ourselves and God marked by revelation, irreversible turning points and major milestones. In the act of creation we are set in motion with the goal, not simply to exist, but to move toward an ever higher, greater End. So inherent in the divine act of creation is a dynamic movement that will not end until the journey is completed. When the end is reached no further movement is possible – because the energy that put us in motion has been consumed in the living of it. This continuous movement is a major variable of the spiritual path, indeed, it is the path itself.

Different religions, of course, have different paths because they have different revelations. Since the revelation is also the goal to be realized, it automatically sets up the path to that goal. Thus, for example, God revealed in or through nature automatically draws one toward nature, whereas God revealed imminently within one's self automatically draws one inward. While the two are not incompatible, their priorities, practices and envisioned goals, are nevertheless quite different.

We should also add, while making this journey there is no awareness of being on any "journey", no sense we're getting any place at all. There are only two points on this seemingly pathless path when we can actually look back and see a path in retrospect. On the Christian path, one such point is after arriving at the egoless Unitive State. Here we can look back to see the distance (and difference) between then and now. If we look ahead, however, we see no further progress possible on earth – in this, however, we are mistaken. Once the Unitive State has been thoroughly tested and lived to its fullest potential, the Unitive State falls away completely – as Christ put it, "It is finished". Now, no further movement is ever possible. From this vantage point we can see the entire path from beginning to end, a vista we could not have seen before; an end we could never have even suspected.

In summary, the variables that complicate the journey are: 1. the height, depth and breadth of God gradually revealed to us; 2. the ever changing self; 3. the movement of the path with its ever expanding perspective, experiences and stages.

The True Nature of Integration

Before we go over the diversity of God's major revelations, it is important to point out that integrating these revelations is not within our own power. It goes without saying, if all revelations were the same or identical, the need to integrate them would not arise. The need arises because they are different, yet equally True. Because the knowledge (or better put, "the knowing") conveyed in every revelation is totally new and unassimilated, it raises questions as to how it fits in with all that went before – our previous knowledge and experiences of God. Thus we ponder the relationship between "what" has been variously revealed, and ponder our relationship to them as well. How are we to account for these different revelations, each engendering a different knowledge of God, each a totally different experience? Initially, they seem to point us toward a different end or goal to be realized. Could one be higher or truer than the other? To which should our singular love and desire be directed?

Like seeing parts of a puzzle without seeing the whole, we cannot envision the outcome ahead of time. Seeing parts without the Whole is, in my view, an unreported dilemma in everyone's spiritual journey.

More often than not, a part is mistaken for the Whole. Such a premature conclusion, however, may only close the door on a further revelation. As it stands, our efforts to integrate different revelations into a Whole can never bring about any true or authentic integration. We can intellectualize all we want, study, ask around, even guess and hope, yet no conclusion will last or satisfy, much less yield an honest or lasting certitude. All we can do is be patient and pray God to resolve the dilemma – which God will do with a further revelation. Until God steps in, all we can do is submit to not-knowing, incertitude, and our own helplessness in this matter.

It is up to God, then, to integrate his own revelations. As we move up the spiritual ladder, everything that went before is gradually integrated and assimilated into each new step. It goes without saying, while a lower rung of the ladder can be integrated into a higher one, a higher rung can never be integrated into a lower one. And since we cannot know what is higher until we come to it, we cannot incorporate what we do not know. Even if we have heard of a higher rung, it remains pure hearsay, and like all hearsay, what we "think" it is, is not IT.

Speaking of higher and lower rungs, this is not a reference to higher and lower revelations. Since all are God, there is no inequality in these revelations. As these rungs regard our journey, however, the path can be envisioned as moving vertically or in stair-step fashion. Thus one revelation builds on another so there is no such thing as one-static-revelation, which not only limits God, but implies no growth for man. As these revelations are understood historically, however, or as the core revelation of various religions, the path moves horizontally. Put together, both vertically and horizontally, the sequence of revelations represents God's progressive revelation to mankind.

The reason for pointing this out is that on a purely intellectual basis, people are always attempting to integrate their experiences with a bookish knowledge of the journey. The inevitable result, however, is a hodgepodge of misconceptions and wrong conclusions. This is what I call "forcing the fit". Like pouring a liquid quart into a pint container, not only will most of it be lost, but we end up with the same pint container we started with. Nothing has been gained while the new or further revelation has been totally lost – spilled out because it didn't fit.

There is no greater cause of the watering down and eventual loss of authentic revelation than attempts to prematurely incorporate or integrate a higher rung of the journey into a lower one. Unknowingly – even knowingly – people do this all the time. More often they are writers on the spiritual journey who have never lived it.

In conclusion, the term "integration" as used in the context of our spiritual ascent does not refer to any rational or intellectual activity on our part. Instead, as we move through the journey, God alone will integrate and unify all knowledge and experiences until, ultimately; they converge in the fullness of God's revelations.

God's Major Revelations

What follows is an outline of the major revelations that mark both the stages of the individual journey and the advent of various historical religions. My original intent was to fill in the outline with examples of religions for which a particular revelation was pivotal or central to its belief system. In researching these ancient religions, however, I found such a plethora of data and examples, the job of writing it all down, including the sources, became too time consuming. Although it would have expanded this piece to book-length, no amount of data is essential to the thesis. After this I decided to expand the outline, based less on man's various religions, than on the individual's journey, but this became too autobiographical and was ditched as well. In the end, I cut the original outline down to the essentials of the thesis, leaving to others, perhaps, the more scholarly chore of filling in the relevant data.

The problem of putting any revelation into words is that it tends to concretizing the ineffable and make into a concept what, in Itself, is non-conceptual. But this is the risk everyone takes who writes on spiritual subjects. I believe, however, that everyone has in themselves a "truth censor" able to detect truth beyond mere words and concepts. Also, in going through these revelations, keep in mind the focus is not on the experiencer (who could be anybody) or the experience itself (which comes and goes), rather, the focus is solely on "That" which is revealed.

A final note. Despite the successive nature of revelation, no revelation cancels out a previous one. To the contrary, each successive revelation expands the previous one. Thus no authentic revelation is ever nullified or superseded, each is the Truth of God.

Foundation of all Revelations

There is in every human being a "knowing" that ever remains pre-intellectual and pre-conscious. The mind has no access to this knowing. It can never be grasped by the intellect as a piece of knowledge. We do not even know how we know this "knowing" exists. Though this "knowing" is ever present, it is not a feeling or experiential "presence" of any kind. It has no aura of the mystical or supernatural. This knowing is simply "there", yet nowhere in particular. To say it is "in our very bones", is an apt metaphor for its inherent nature.

Though speaking of this knowing makes it a piece of knowledge, it can never be that. While people can affirm this knowing, they cannot say how they do so. Thus speaking of it to others, I have been met with both instant recognition and total denial. So despite its universal nature, this knowing is recognized by some and not by others. Of course, when hearing of this "knowing" everyone automatically wonders "what" this knowing knows.

Yet the only answer that would satisfy the mind is something that could be intellectually identified or grasped, which is not what this knowing knows. What this knowing knows is never available to the intellect because it never arose from the intellect in the first place. It is a totally different type of knowing. Indeed, there is more to ourselves than we know!

Basically, what this knowing is, is the Creator's knowing its creation and creation knowing its Creator, simple as that. It is not a knowing about something or of something, it is simply an innate subjectless, objectless, knowing. I believe this knowing is inherent in every act of creation and participates, in some measure, in God's own knowing.

I might add, this knowing is close to what I define as "faith" (which is not belief). I regard this knowing as the ground of faith, a faith inherent in everyone regardless of whether they recognize it or not. This knowing then, is the ground and foundation of all God's revelations. It is not only prior to them, but in the end, ultimately participates in God's own divine knowing.

God In Nature

Who has not had some memorable experience in the great out-of-doors? In a quiet moment mundane cares disappear as the surroundings and vistas impinge on the soul to fill and uplift it. No description can do justice to such moments. Call it beauty, wonder, peace or whatever, these experiences in nature transcend our words and descriptions. There is probably no more universally shared experience than man's experiences in nature. Those with a more contemplative bent will seek them out, and in doing so, will come to know their possibilities for spiritual growth. What one gleans from these experiences will exceed all knowledge that can be gained any other way. As the first steps of our journey, then, we will speak of two revelations where nature is God's medium.

Omnipresence

"All Present" or "Everywhere" throughout creation. Since there is no place God is not, God is no place in particular. God fills all space, cannot be pointed to, or become a visual object of focus. This is an Imageless, all-pervasive "seeing" apart from what appears. Because this revelation lacks the particular, it is global in nature, a non-particular presence, more in the order of an experiential knowledge than a discrete "experience".

Because It defies being seen as an object or as residing any "where", this mystery seems to be more present in open vistas than in enclosed places. Our initial encounter with this Omnipresence is thus tied to the more formless elements in nature – earth, sea and sky – rather than any particular form in nature – flower, rock or whatever. At times it may seem to be the mystery "in" which all things exist; at other times, it seems to flow "through" all that exists.

Then again, Its prominence may be such that nature becomes but a backdrop for Its Presence. But these are subtle distinctions for which everyone will have their own report.

God's Omnipresence is man's first and most universal revelation. I'm convinced people see It all the time, only they don't know this or recognize It. This is why, at some point, it may be revealed to them. It can happen, however, that before we become conscious of this mysterious Omnipresence, we have been so taken up looking for God elsewhere that we missed this Presence completely. Then too, we may soon forget this seeing in favor of some trivial pursuit.

Because this sighting (Omnipresence) is so simple, it seems to be all but innate. Because it is so simple, however, it may even be objected this cannot be called a "revelation". But what makes it a revelation is the sighting, the recognition, the absolute certitude which is ours forever. We often hear people excuse themselves from going to Church with, "Oh, God is everywhere." Yet they've never seen God-Everywhere and merely believing it cannot, and has not, produced this seeing. Seeing this truth is a grace in itself.[2] Something else. To see and know God's omnipresence is, in my view, the true nature of "contemplation", or what it

---

[2] Needless to say, there has to be something in the receiver capable of seeing God 's Omnipresence. As to the true nature of this inner eye on God, it turns out to be the same "eye" whereby God sees creation and creation sees God. The "eye", then, does not belong to us at all.

means to "contemplate God". This is an outward, external gaze at the formless, aloof, ever present mystery of God everywhere. From a purely sensory stand-point, it's like looking at nothing. It is a gaze at the mystery of what lies behind, throughout or prior to, the sensory world. I stress this as an "outward" gaze, because seeing this Omnipresence can never be an inward gaze.[3]

Religions Founded on this Revelation

As to religions founded on this key revelation, the first that comes to mind is the initial "sighting" of a mysterious "flow" permeating all existence. In Chinese this "flow" is the Tao, the goal being to become one with this flow. To do this, they reasoned their physical body had somehow to become "spiritualized", and many of their practices were geared to this end. (I'm reminded here of St. Paul's reference to the resurrected body as a "spiritual body"). From my readings of this religion, however, it seems its present day adherents have gone so far afield that the original can be regarded as lost altogether. Still, if the group religion lost the original, its founding revelation is as true today as it was in the beginning.

The second example that comes to mind is the central belief of the Greek Stoics. Though regarded as a philosophy rather than a religion, within the stoic enclaves their goal, doctrines and practices were as religious as any cult today. Their name for this Omnipresence was the "Logos" – which today might translate as the "Intelligent Designer" of the universe.

The Logos was not some intelligence standing above or behind

---

[3] Some theologians have divided contemplation into two types: natural or "acquired contemplation", and supernatural – a special grace in other words. (The term "acquired" is unfortunate because if the faculty to contemplate was not innate or God-given it could not be acquired). I have no problem with these theological distinctions except they only apply to beginners. The proficient have no need to acquire anything. Infused contemplation is their second nature, part and parcel of their whole being. To tell the truth, I do not think many people understand the true nature of "infused contemplation", including theologians.

the universe, however, but was immanent in the universe and in each person as its intelligent, generative or creative power. The Stoics' goal was to establish themselves in unity with the Logos by achieving a state of "apatheia", a profound interior state of imperturbability where reason (intelligence or Logos) could run the show instead of their passions. With research, I'm sure other religions could be found where the revelation of God's Omnipresence was its key or founding revelation.

God Immanent in Nature

Closely aligned to Omnipresence but still a step beyond, is God's mysterious presence in or within nature itself. Where Omnipresence was global and never focused on the particular, this revelation requires the particular. This is where the object of visual focus fades into the divine or the divine emerges from it, overshadows it – however the case may be. Thus where God's Omnipresence is global, aloof and impersonal, God Immanent or within nature is particular and personal. It is personal because this epiphany is a deliberate showing or manifestation of God to us. It's as if God wanted us to see Him and wanted us to know He sees us. So from this revelation we learn God is not only "in" nature, but wants us to know It, know Its personal presence.

This revelation will have various descriptions not only due to the particular visual focus – be it the sea, cloud, tree, flower, or whatever – but because it can range from subtle to brilliant. It could even stand one's hair on end. Its common denominator, however, is that it is formless, non-sensory, totally outside oneself. Its "personal" aspect is neither close nor intimate, but more in the order of someone suddenly being pointed out in a crowd by the Almighty – that momentarily stuns the brain. Afterwards we don't know if we should be flattered or afraid, afraid of "what" God really is. (There is something about every revelation that alerts us to the utter disparity between God and man. It makes no difference how close God is or how God may inundate us with overwhelming love, always the disparity is obvious.)

There is another experience worth mentioning. While not the original revelation of God-Omnipresent, it nevertheless awakens us to a Mysterious dimension of nature beyond ordinary existence. In this experience our whole being seems as if dissolved – become lightsome or buoyant – into a transcendent dimension of nature, a delightful and utterly fulfilling state of existence. The true nature of the delightful "Medium" in which nature exists and seems to drift, is the Omnipresent.

Immersed in Its mystery as part and parcel of nature, there is no sense of being one with anything; in fact, whatever "we" are, could be anything, it didn't matter. What matters is the Omnipresent mystery in which all things exist, virtually a heavenly dimension of existence (For myself, I was convinced the elements of matter existed in this marvelous dimension and that this was their everyday experience). What we learn from this experience is that somehow nature itself exists in God. Thus not only is God Omnipresent throughout nature, but nature itself is immanent in God.

Religions Founded on This Revelation

The revelation of God's Omnipresence and Immanence is the origin of all man's "Nature Religions", so called because the focus is on God's presence in nature. Religions that grew up around these particular revelations can be found in every age, and are as much alive today as ever. There especially comes to mind those indigenous tribes who witness to the "Great Spirit" in nature. From this revelation we can find sects from sun-worshippers to forms of animism. I also think this is the origin of polytheism – the various gods representing the various forces in nature. Much of this diversity is due to the circumstances of the original revelation – did God seem to emerge from fire, sun or moon? It could be anything in nature. In some of these sects the goal is placating an awesome Spirit through various forms of sacrificial offerings; in other sects, the goal was becoming one with this Spirit.

In the hands of a group these revelations are more open to the corruption of the original than all other revelations together – a noted example being human sacrifice. Then, of course, there is pantheism –

belief the material universe is the Almighty Itself. Because it is possible to weave elaborate spiritual and metaphysical systems around a true revelation, it is important to see through these mythical accruements and ritual elaborations and to recognize the original.

A particular myth to be dispelled is the belief that these religions originated solely from man 's ordinary observations of nature. Not true. Not only are the founding revelations of these "nature religions" important first steps in man's spiritual journey, but on some level most people can relate to them. Not only is nature a medium of God's revelation, God is both Immanent in nature and Omnipresent throughout it – the very source of its existence. So regardless of later corruptions, originally these religions are products of God's revealing presence in nature.

Integration of God's Omnipresence and Immanence in Nature

Initially no particular need arises to integrate these two revelations. We take for granted the unseen Omnipresent deigned to show itself as Immanent, an epiphany that only acts to further verify God's presence in nature. In time, however – and perhaps with repeated experience – we increasingly ponder the difference, for these are, in fact, two very different ways of seeing and knowing God. A problem only arises if we try to integrate these two revelations on an intellectual basis. Thus if we conclude God is Omnipresent because God is Immanent in nature, we tend to eliminate God's Omnipresence. Or the other way around: to conclude God is Immanent because of His Omnipresence, then the Immanent becomes lost. Keep in mind, one is not the other. To be present in something is to be enclosed, located and particularized, whereas to be present everywhere, has no enclosure, no location, can never be particularized. Also, where the former is personal, the latter is relatively impersonal. While both revelations can be awesome in their own right, they are nevertheless totally distinct. They are not just two different experiences or even just two different revelations; rather, God's Omnipresence and Immanence are two totally different aspects of God.

God Immanent in Man

Up to this point God was revealed outside ourselves, but here now, arising from a hitherto unknown center in ourselves, God reveals Himself. Experiential reports vary from this being a quiet disclosure to a powerful infusion. To communicate "that" which has been revealed, people use different terms, such as the sudden appearance of "light", "spirit", "power" depending on the dynamics of the experience. The common denominator, however, is that it arises from the depths of our being, a mysterious space or center that, till then, we never knew we had. Above all, we know this dynamic Presence is not ourselves. It is its own cause deliberately revealing Itself to us. Although this Presence is utterly personal to us, it is also totally independent of us, has a life of its own. In short, this Presence is totally "other".

Like every revelation, "that" which is revealed admits of no mental image, does not speak or identify itself. Although we intuitively know God – indeed, what else has access to the core of our being, our life, our existence? At the same time, however, "that" which is revealed may not be in accord with what we had ever heard or learned about "God". Like every revelation, "that" which is revealed does not match our previous ideas and concepts, much less any image (including those from the Bible) we may have formed of God.

Although the initial revelation may seem to fade, the Presence remains. If prior to this time we had looked within ourselves we probably would have encountered nothing more than our thoughts and feelings. From here on, however, a look within is an encounter with this indwelling Presence. In time there is no need to look within, because there develops an automatic "feel" for its presence, a knowledge as certain as our own existence. From time to time this presence draws attention to itself, not by way of words or through our mind, but solely by its central, interior timely "movement" that informs and enlightens.

By comparison, this revelation may seem to pale all previous revelations, yet initially it seems to enhance those that have gone before.

Now we are no longer outside observers of God's presence in nature, but also experience God's presence in ourselves. There is a difference however. Whereas God's presence in nature is more objective and impersonal, God 's presence within is more subjective and personal. In time this raises a certain dilemma – how are we to integrate these different revelations?

Religions Founded on this Revelation

The revelation of God's Immanence (within ourselves) is the key revelation of Hinduism. This is God "in the cave of the heart", the center of being – the "Atman". The goal of this religion is to discover this abiding Truth within one's self. Though God-Immanent is also found in Christianity, it is not its central revelation. A major difference between the Hindu Atman and God-Immanent in Christianity, is that for the Christian, God-within is "other" than one's self, whereas for the Hindu, Atman is one's Self – "thou art that".

So where the Christian has a personal rapport with God-Immanent, the Hindu has no rapport with Atman, its presence is simply an impersonal, universal truth. If we grant that both religions have the same revelation, to account for the difference, it follows that once you believe Atman is your self, then there is no one left to relate to – no relationship with God possible. Christians familiar with God 's interior Presence, however, neither regard this Presence as themselves nor could regard It as impersonal. Still, both religions affirm God-Immanent or God within us. [4]

One corruption of God 's Immanence, however, is the attempt of an individual to be taken over by this interior power or spirit – to literally become possessed by it – one form of Shamanism, at least. To this end man has invented various techniques to forget himself, his own exist-

---

[4] While the Hindu Absolute (known as "Brahman") may not be "God" as understood in Monotheism, nor "Atman", the Holy Spirit of Christianity, nevertheless, my interest is in the original revelation of God-Immanent, not its philosophical, psychological and theological overlays.

ence via drugs, incantations, rituals and much more. To a lesser extent, we have accounts of people attempting to become "mediums" of this indwelling presence, accounts probably as old as man. Then there are those who claim "special powers", which is all but endemic in our religions – Christianity no exception. In this respect, the revelation of God's Immanence is risky. It is the only revelation that lends itself to religious charlatans – power hungry deceivers, all in the name of God, of course.

Integration of God's Omnipresence and Immanence in Man

God-Immanent has a central locus in ourselves, a Center we can know and experience. On the other hand, God-Omnipresent has no locus, but seems to flow freely through all that exists. Thus we look inward to find God-Immanent and look outward to see God-Omnipresent. Seemingly, the difference between these two revelations is between the particular (Immanent) and the universal (Omnipresent). While these revelations are not opposed, their differences pose a particular quandary: how can both be God? What, exactly, is their relationship to one another? And which one should be the primary focus of our love and trust?

The only way this quandary can be resolved is by yet another revelation, which revelation is the momentary coming together of Immanent and Omnipresent in their all but explosive union into a singular, brilliant Whole. This "Whole", however, is totally outside ourselves and beyond nature as well. It has nothing to do with either one. While this temporary merging resolves the initial quandary – in that we now know it is the same God inside as outside only two different experiences – yet this resolution leaves a new mystery in its wake. This is the mystery of the united "Wholeness" of God, a wholeness seemingly beyond both Immanent and Omnipresent.

Unknown to us this resolution – the true relationship between God-Immanent and Omnipresent – is setting us up for yet a further revelation. For right now, however, we are content to love and trust both God-Immanent and Omnipresent, knowing they are essentially the same, only two different ways of knowing, seeing and experiencing God.

No amount of intellectual thought and inquiry can bring about a true or lasting integration of God's different revelations – nor the different experiences they engender. Since these were not engendered by reason, neither can they be resolved by reason. If anything can throw us off track it is a premature, seemingly rational resolution of thinking we can resolve a mystery not of our own making. In this matter people can become so sure of their own resolutions they unknowingly close the door on the furthest reaches of the journey.

God Transcendent

This is the revelation to die for. A revelation beyond nature, self, all creation, seemingly, beyond all other revelations. By "beyond" I mean It neither touches us or anything in this world – just seeing It stops the brain, and it may take weeks to regain any interest in ordinary living. It is life changing in that, in the deepest sense, one can never set mind or heart on anything in this world again. For its spectacular nature and the change wrought, this revelation is like no other. Though only a passing glimpse, Its traces remain forever. In truth, this is God utterly and absolutely Transcendent.

The sole "personal" aspect of the Transcendent is Its obvious will that man see and know It exists. And not only know It exists, but that It cares enough for man to reveal Itself to him. Because it does not touch us in any way, however, the Transcendent remains somewhat aloof and impersonal. Yet it engenders a love and gratitude that wants only to live eternally with this vision, have it always – die for it.

The problem with a transcendent God is Its inaccessibility. All the previous revelations revealed God-with-us (in some fashion) and thus we could always find God in nature, in ourselves – everywhere, in fact. But as God is truly Transcendent, apart from moments of revelation, we live without the Transcendent's continuous personal presence. Seemingly totally detached from creation, we cannot approach It of ourselves. Thus, between God's Transcendence and our mundane lives there seems to be a void, a void, however, we long to pass over.

Religions Founded on this Revelation

The revelation of one transcendent God is Judaism's bequest to the world. Without this revelation there would be neither Christianity nor Islam. This is not only the transcendent God of Abraham, Isaac and Moses, but the God of Jesus and Mohammed. Of these three Monotheistic religions, however, only Judaism and Islam hold solely to the revelation of God-Transcendent. Although in Judaism God is utterly personal – read the Torah or Old Testament – yet theoretically, at least, Judaism holds God to be absolutely transcendent with no link between Creator and the created. With no intermediary, however, we ponder how an utterly transcendent God can reach man or what hope man has of reaching God. God's absolute transcendence can create such a chasm between God and man as to lend itself to agnosticism, the next step being atheism. While both Judaism and Islam have cults that more or less adhere to God's being both Immanent and Transcendent, these cults have never been regarded as orthodox or mainline.

Despite an essential chasm between man and God, Judaism bequeathed to the world a God who personally cares for man and everything He created. Perhaps no religion offers a more personal give-and-take between God and man than Judaism. So despite its belief in God's utter transcendence, in practical reality, God is not all that transcendent. It's unfortunate the term "mono" (as in Monotheism) is used for belief in God. Though no doubt "mono" was used to distinguish it from the many gods of Polytheism, it is hard to escape the purely numerical, quantitative implications of "mono".

Not only does "one" distinguish it from other "ones", it can be taken for a singular solitary entity, a detached, impersonal monad. Certainly this doesn't promote any genuine rapport or love between God and man – in fact, "mono" promotes nothing for man at all. Given the infinite mystery of God, "Theism" would have been a sufficient term.

Integration of God Immanent and Transcendent – A Dilemma

If the revelation of God-Transcendent had cancelled all previous revelations, no dilemma could arise. But such is not the case. With this revelation, the dilemma is not only two different revelations and experiences of God – Immanent and Transcendent – but two different ways of knowing God. Thus these two revelations pose different directions for seeking God: the Immanent focuses us inward, the Transcendent outward (and upward). In which direction then, is our journey? Do we seek God within ourselves or beyond ourselves? The question is this: if God is truly Transcendent (beyond all creation) then how could the Immanent presence in us be God? And if it is not God, then "what" is It?

While initially the Transcendent may seem to supersede the interior Presence, it by no means overshadows it. On the contrary, the Transcendent heightens the interior Presence. The Immanent not only knows the Transcendent, but uplifts us to it, even alerting us to its occasional sightings. It is as if the Immanent is "that" in us that recognizes the Transcendent. We have no doubt there is a connection between the two, but what is it? What is the true relationship between God Immanent and God Transcendent? Unless the nature of this relationship is revealed, we have no way of knowing, and without this knowing our journey is at an impasse – literally directionless.

When the Transcendent and Immanent are considered separately, each gives rise to a different way of knowing God and, consequently, a different perspective of man and the world. Each gives rise to a different rapport with God – or no rapport at all. Thus a totally Transcendent God leaves man pretty much on his own, for which reason man needs a system of God-given laws by which to live. On the other hand, for a God who is solely Immanent, there is no transcendent reality at all – at best, God only "transcends" mere visual appearances. Then again, from God-Immanent, it is just a step to identifying it as the Reality of all that exists – including one's self. But this is how, when God-Immanent and God-Transcendent are considered separately, each becomes the basis of two different religions.

It is also why, based on their specific revelations, religions have different views of man and the world, different views of God (personal or impersonal), different experiences, and totally different paths. As noted before, whatever the revelation is, so is the goal, and so goes the path that lies between.[5] By experience, however, we know these revelations are not totally separate, we know there is some mysterious link between them. The dilemma, then, is finding out the true relationship between them. Ultimately, the sole resolution possible is the indescribable revelation that follows.

God Immanent-Transcendent

In simple but inadequate terms, this revelation is like "seeing how God works". Although the mind cannot grasp "what" is seen – in any revelation – this knowing and seeing is ours forever. As best it can be put: God's inner nature consists of different manifestations (aspects, functions?) distinct in themselves, that when revealed to man, are distinctly different experiences of God. It was as if God was composed of different dimensions and functions that nevertheless work as an undivided whole. To the recipient of this revelation all that matters is what is learned, namely: God-Immanent and God-Transcendent are the one same God with different aspects, manifestations, and consequently, different revelations to man. With this truth all previous differences, questions and quandaries are resolved. We are left with the marvel of God, and the marvel of sharing His Truth with us.

No Religion Founded on This Revelation

I do not know of any religion where the revelation of the Trans-

---

[5] It is a paradox that the utterly Transcendent God in Judaism is held to be a "personal" God, while the close Immanent God in Hinduism (Atman-Brahman) is held to be "impersonal". Offhand, we could think it to be the other way around. The difference, of course, is between a God who exists outside and beyond creation (Judaism) and a God who is all that exists (Hinduism) – you cannot be "personal", after all, if you're the only one around!

cendent-Immanent is unique to that religion or constitutes its central revelation. While this revelation is included in Christianity – even imperative to it – it is not, however, its central or key revelation. This revelation, however, is so vital and important I do not see how anyone could go further in their journey without it. I find it inexplicable that nothing has ever been said of it. Without this revelation man is at an impasse, an either/or option: either go solely with God-Transcendent (as in Judaism), or solely with God-Immanent (as in Hinduism). With this choice the two (Transcendent and Immanent) become mutually exclusive. As said before, it <u>is because each is a separate revelation that each became the founding revelation of two different religions.</u> So the reason this present revelation of Transcendent-Immanent is so important is because it is a far more complete revelation of God than either God-Immanent alone, or God-Transcendent alone.

As it stands, instead of realizing the Immanent and Transcendent are two discrete revelations, reference to God's Immanence and Transcendence are taken for granted as merely two interchangeable terms. The thought is that although God is Immanent in creation (as its source of life and existence) God is nevertheless Transcendent to creation. Thus God's Immanence is equally a reference to God's Transcendence. While this is true as far as it goes, it falls short of recognizing the distinctive Transcendence of God that is not immanent in creation at all. On the contrary, creation is in the Transcendent, creation is not in the Immanent. This is why, to regard God-Immanent as indistinct from God-Transcendent eliminates or totally ignores God's utter Transcendence to creation – an ignorance that can lead to some erroneous views of God. At any rate, the Immanent and Transcendent are not interchangeable and not the same in God, not the same in creation, and not the same in ourselves.

The distinction between Immanent and Transcendent then, is not due merely to man's different experiences of God, nor even due to two different revelations of God, but rather due to the fact God-Immanent and God-Transcendent are distinctions inherent in the very nature of God. Without this key revelation of God as both Transcendent and Immanent there is no going forward in our journey, and as to why this is so, we will explain as follows.

A Dilemma

Due to the above revelation an inevitable crisis arises. Despite the marvel of God Transcendent-Immanent, this revelation never revealed any eternal oneness between God and creation, more especially, between God and ourselves. To illustrate the nature of this crisis let us imagine that creation is an empty vase where the air on the inside is God-Immanent and the air on the outside is God-Transcendent – the same air, only experienced differently by the vase. Now take away the vase, smash it, and the air (God) goes right on, only without creation. Without an eternal relationship or oneness between God and creation (or the air and the vase), man must face the terrible truth he is but a temporary disposable container that someday will crumble and disappear. [6]

Just because God is immanent in creation does not mean God has any oneness with creation – after all, God is not "enclosed" in anything. So too, because creation exists in the Transcendent is no guarantee it will stay there forever – created from nothing, it could go back to nothing. Also, the fact man has an immortal soul guarantees no eternal oneness with God – since the soul could just as well go to hell. No matter how we look at it, without the knowledge and assurance of an eternal oneness with God no human being could find true happiness either in this life or in heaven. But if this is the way things actually work (no eternal oneness with God, that is), why would God bother to reveal himself to man? Why would God want man to know and love Him if, in the end, it all came to naught? No, if God is to have any true meaning in our life there has to be an eternal link between God and man.

---

[6] God Immanent-Transcendent can also be illustrated with a balloon, where the air (God) on the inside is the same air as on the outside – hence God Immanent-Transcendent. Seemingly the balloon (us) is in God at the same time God is in the balloon. Yet pop the balloon, and it's all over for us, though not for God.

But what is this link? Does it even exist? And if so, what could it be? Because God Transcendent – Immanent revealed no such link, if one exists then it remains unknown – remains to be revealed, that is. What cries out for the following revelation then, is our very life, our eternal life with God.

God Transcendent-Immanent-Omnipresent

This is the revelation of God's threefold oneness: Transcendent - Omnipresent - Immanent. Here we see and know how creation's eternal "link" to the Transcendent and Immanent is the Omnipresent. Thus our true oneness with God is neither the Transcendent nor Immanent, but God-Omnipresent. The term "Omnipresent", however, is inadequate because its reference is solely relative to creation whereas, in Itself, It is far more than this. Its mysterious presence in nature is what the Stoics called "Logos", the cosmic generating, governing principle and reason imminent and active in all reality. So the Logos, or God's Omnipresence, is the "vessel" (like the vase) that both contains the Immanent and eternally dwells in the Transcendent. The Logos not only brings together the Transcendent-Immanent, but is creation's eternal "link" to the Transcendent-Immanent. In short, creation's true oneness with God is the Logos and thus the Logos is our true oneness with God.

It can rightly be objected that this threefold revelation of God is purely relative to creation and that without creation (or prior to it) we don't know the inner nature of God at all. This is true, without creation there would be nothing and no one to whom God could be revealed, no one even to know God existed. But there's no use pondering what God would be like if we didn't exist. The fact is, we are here now, thus the question of God's nature prior to creation is totally irrelevant, and especially for God who is stuck with us now.

Religion Founded on This Revelation

The sole religion founded on this revelation is Christianity. This same revelation, however, is reflected in writings of the Jewish mystic, Philo of Alexandria, a contemporary of Jesus – who knew nothing of the man. What Philo saw in his own scriptures, was the Stoic's notion of the Logos; which was Yahweh's presence and manifestation in creation. So too, when speaking of "that" mystery of God that became Incarnate, St. John begins his Gospel, "In the beginning was the Logos" – "Logos" being the term used for Christ's divinity. The incarnation reveals God's oneness with creation, and were this not true, the Logos could not have become incarnate. [7]

The same revelation, however, is reflected in the ancient Hindu Trimurti, more especially in Brahman's three-fold sat-cit-ananda (being, knowing and bliss). There is also the Buddhist's triple body of Buddha – possibly more applicable to the nature of Christ than the Godhead Itself. Because these religions had no monotheistic background and predated Christianity, their understanding of a trinity is very different than that of Christianity. Yet who knows the original revelation of these religions? Obviously, the ancients were on to something as regards the true nature of the ultimate Mystery – whatever they called "It".

No doubt research would yield other reflections of this Trinitarian revelation. Quite apart from any revelation, however, God's Trinitarian nature is reflected in the three dimensional nature of matter itself – the height (Transcendent), depth (Immanent), and breadth (Omnipresent) of matter, a unique reflection of God Itself. As it stands, however, Christianity is the sole religion for which the Trinity is its key founding revelation. Without this revelation Christianity would not exist.

The Trinity

A word on the Christian Trinity. The term "Trinity" defines God's nature as three distinct but inseparable modes of existence with a

---

[7] While this term "Cosmic Christ" may have more meaning to a Christian than "Omnipresent", yet for non-Christians, the term "Cosmic Christ" is not only exclusive to Christianity, but it is not, in fact, the original revelation of God's Omnipresence.

common essence. Nobody knows the "what" of God's essence, but we do know the "nature" of God's existence, because it has been revealed. Each mode of God's existence has its own unique manifestation, which, when experienced by man, is a singular revelation and a unique way of seeing and knowing God.

It was only when studying other religions, however, I realized the Trinity was a remarkable integration of all God's revelations to man, a virtual summary and recapitulation of our historic religions. I know of no other revelation of God that brings together and includes all God's revelations. Thus the Trinity provides us with an entirely new view of God's on-going revelations in the process of everyone's journey.

Something else to ponder. Had the revelation of the Trinity been given at the outset of man's journey, with no previous revelations, what would have been its meaning or understanding to man? What place would It have in the journey of someone, say, just starting out? In my view, without the background of God's previous revelations (God Omnipresent, Immanent and Transcendent), the Trinity wouldn't have much impact, certainly not its proper understanding.

Without some experiential background wherein God's gradual revelations act to answer man's ultimate questions and resolve his spiritual dilemmas, the Trinity remains no more than an obscure belief – for some, no more than a mental construct. Possibly this is why the Trinity is all but foreign and ungraspable to the majority of Christians. For many, the Trinity has no central place in their life or journey. This is regrettable, because without the centrality of the Trinity there can never be a full understanding of Christ, never.

Conclusion of God's Major Revelations

My search for the key revelation of man's religions did not turn up any foundational basis other than the revelations presented here. All religions can be traced to the revelation of either God's Omnipresence,

Immanence, Transcendence or a combination of these. In my view, everything of essence man knows and experiences of God falls under one or more of these key revelations.

Each of these revelations is not only a major step and turning point in the history of religion, but equally a major turning point in each one's journey. While there are many other subtle revelations and turning points, here our focus has been solely on the key revelation of our various religions. The order in which these revelations have been presented is, I believe, the sequence in which they were revealed. This does not mean, however, the individual will recognize them in the same order in their journey. More often than not, it is only after the fact one recognizes their journey had a specific sequence. Thus no one knows where they are on the path until a rare vista allows them to look back on the path traversed. In writing this piece, my hope is that people will be able to look back and recognize God's ongoing revelation in the course of their own journey.

Although the perspective of the journey presented here may seem like an inter-religious endeavor, this is not its primary intention. The goal is to point out how every major step in our journey is due to the breakthrough of a key revelation of God, and why, without this breakthrough, we go no further in the journey. To say we only progress as far as revelation permits, means that our spiritual development waits for revelation and not the other way around. It is because revelation leads the way we can affirm that the spiritual journey recapitulates the history of God 's revelations.

As to the more inter-religious application of this perspective, on an experiential level it enables us to integrate, understand and appreciate various religions in a way not possible on a purely intellectual level. Solely from a scholarly or cultural perspective, our profound religious truths often appear incompatible or contradictory, whereas, encountered on an experiential level in the process of the journey, different religions can be understood as the progressive stages of God 's on-going revelation.

The Christians Journey Recapitulates the Revelation of Christ

Up to this point our focus has been man's journey in light of God 's revelations as the keystone of our world's religions. Now, however, we would like to focus on the individual 's journey in light of God's singular revelation in the Person of Christ. Not only does our journey recapitulate God's revelation to man in general, but recapitulates the journey of a single Person as well.

We have already seen that God's triune revelations were around long before Christ came on the scene. Although Christ brings these revelations together, it cannot be said he revealed God to us – God had already been revealed – rather, what Christ revealed to us was man himself. Thus he revealed man's essential oneness with God, path to God, and man's ultimate destiny with and in God. In short, Christ reveals God's plan for man from beginning to end. He reveals what man is to God, how much man means to God, and how God wants us to live with Him on earth and in heaven. Thus it could even be said that the primary focus of Christianity is not on the revelation of God, per se, but rather on the revelation of man. The center of this focus, of course, is the incarnate Logos, Christ.

Perhaps the major phenomena peculiar to Christianity is Christ's on-going revelation down the ages, all over the world, in every culture and to people in other religions, even to die-hard atheists. The varied accounts of these revelations would fill tomes. Though few people have St. Paul's encounter with Christ – of being knocked off his high horse – the accounts range from the extraordinary to Christ's formless emergence in utter silence. This is always an unexpected surprise, and one not always greeted with joy and delight – indeed, it can be utterly disconcerting and go against the grain. One thing is certain, however, it can never be forgotten.

I'm convinced that were it not for this on-going revelation of Christ (even as we speak), Christianity would not have outlived the days of the Apostles. That Christianity is alive today, and always will be, is solely due to Christ's continuous revelation to us. In some ways this repeated, phenomenal revelation is Christianity. For those who respond, of course, this is the beginning of their Christian journey. All that went before, including all Gods' revelations, are but a preparation for this take off.

Another phenomena peculiar to Christianity is that Christ never pointed out a path, taught any how-to's or left any rules, he didn't even tell *us* to follow him – imitate or get in line. Instead he said, "*I am the Way*". But how can a person be a "way"? What does this mean and how does it work? What it means is that: *the "way" it went for him is the "way" it goes for us*. Thus it means we have to recapitulate or re-live his own human spiritual journey, to live and experience life with God just as he did. This is a "way" of transformation, a transformation into Christ Himself. So just as Christ gave his whole life over to the Transcendent – whom He called His "Father" – so too do we.

We are also to live in oneness with God-Immanent, what He called his "Spirit". Like Christ, we are to love God with our whole heart, mind, soul and body, a path of love requiring a total giving of self, even unto death. Anything held back is self, anything given, is God's. Thus as we decrease, God increases – the more empty of self, the more room for God. Our journey, then, is one of ever changing proportions: less self, more God, until in the end there is no-self at all. It has been replaced by Christ and all He is.

Christ confronts us with a mystery of God that can never be taken for granted, a mystery that a Christian will spend his whole life coming to know. Because Christ is the mystery into which we are being transformed, we cannot fully or totally know Christ ahead of time or before our transformation is complete. It is the gradual unfolding of this mystery that constitutes the Christian path of transformation. It is also the unfolding revelation of God's plan for mankind, a plan that has been in place from the beginning.

In making this journey we might keep in mind the fact that Christ never knew Christ – certainly not the way we think we know Him.

So while Christ may be "other" to us, for the living true Christ, there is no "other" Christ. If, then, we are to truly recapitulate his spiritual life, Christ must never be "other" to us – because Christ was never "other" to Himself. When St. Augustine said, "God is closer to us than we are to ourselves", he could only be speaking of Christ. Christ is too close to ever be an object to us, be it an object of the senses, mind, or any level of consciousness – why? Because Christ is closer to us than our very selves. This is why the human Christ always pointed us to His Father and never pointed to himself. [8]

What was "other" to Christ was the Transcendent (Father), and in like manner the Transcendent Father is "other" to us. It is by keeping our eyes on the Father – as did Christ – we recapitulate Christ's interior life. God-Immanent or indwelling Spirit is never, of course, wholly "other" to us.

Indeed, in the Unitive State this Spirit is virtually our "other half", without which, no one is ever a whole human being. So from beginning to end what the Christian journey is, is the unfolding of God's greatest mystery, Christ, and our transformation into Christ. What follows is not a detailed account of the entire journey, but a brief summary of the major revelations of Christ in the unfolding of the journey.

---

[8] I once heard a Priest tell his congregation their behavior in Church amounted to idolatry. They exhibited no awareness of the Presence of the divine Christ in the Eucharist. It is not hard to get the impression Christians worship a totally human person, the historical Jesus, a man in heaven they hope to see one day. Christianity has always walked a fine line between idolatry and Truth, but such was the risk of the Incarnation.

Christ's Revelations

Unitive Revelation [9]

From conception, the human Jesus lived in a state of oneness with God. Thus our journey only catches up with him when we too have come to what, in Christian terms, is called the "unitive state". The knowledge that we have come to this abiding state requires a specific revelation, one always preceded, however, by a descent into the black hole in the center of our being – seemingly, the hole of our own nothingness and utter helplessness. All God has done, however, is replace our self-center or ego with Himself. Yet His Light blinds us so we see only darkness – which we mistake for God's absence.

Not only will God be revealed as the deepest center of our self and the very source of our being, but the immediate result of this revelation is the knowledge that the "old" person we were (up to this moment, at least) is gone forever and a new person has arisen. A new person, however, known only to God.[10] (Responsible for this change from the old to the new is a radical change of consciousness. We can never go back to recapture our "old" egoic consciousness simply because there is no ego anymore. Self has been replaced by a new center, a divine Center

---

[9] John of the Cross reminds us there are three ways we are, and can be, united to God: 1) A natural union – God sustains our very existence thus everything that exists is united to God. 2) A supernatural union – God's special presence in the soul by grace, a virtual sharing of God's own divine life. 3) A "mystical union" – God effecting a radical and permanent change in the soul itself. It is this revelation of "mystical union" or "Unitive State" we are speaking of here. Some people have also called this "Transforming Union" and "Mystical Marriage".

[10] This new person is the "true self" – "hidden with Christ in God" as St. Paul put it. No doubt Paul's reference to death of the "old person" and rising of the "new Person" was this same unitive revelation, since nowhere else in the journey is there any such experience. It is a great mistake to compare this to Christ's death and resurrection. Christ was born in the Unitive State ever conscious of his profound oneness with God and it was this unitive consciousness that "died" in Christ – literally the death of God. (St. Paul's reference to the "old" and "new person" referred to Baptism, which is but the beginning of our journey into Christ).

– hence the "new" consciousness.) This unitive revelation then, begins a whole new consciousness and way of experiencing life, a life of oneness with God.

The unitive revelation is not, in itself, a revelation of Christ. Intuitively, however, we identify this state as the same state in which the man Jesus lived his earthly life, the same human experience of oneness with God. In this unitive state, however, there are several surprising and important revelations of Christ. Because the divine Center is like a light, we cannot see a line between God and ourselves, cannot see exactly where we leave off and God begins. Thus we may ponder "just what is His and what is mine?" We may also question, "What exactly is "that" in me that is one with God?" A surprising answer to this question is: "that" in us, which is one with God, "that" is Christ. It is a surprise to learn it is not we, ourselves, who are one with God, but rather, Christ, only Christ. This is a mystery because this is not the Christ we "thought" we knew, but the Christ we do not know – the "unknown Christ".

Another revelation is when we realize the burning love we experience for God is beyond us, and that of ourselves we could never generate such an enormous love. Here the surprising revelation is that "that" in us that loves God is not our self, but rather, it is Christ's own love of God. This, then, is how our transformation goes, punctuated with unflattering revelations for self, but at the same time, the surprised unfolding of the mystery of Christ. Obviously Christ is replacing self – not taking it over, not replacing it with some other self, but rather, gradually rendering it totally unnecessary.

The Market Place – A Major Turning Point

Without encountering this major turning point there is no going further in the journey. No literature on the spiritual journey, however, mentions this strategic point. Instead we have been led to believe that arriving at the unitive state is as far as one can go in this life. While it is true that the "inward" journey is finished – there's no going deeper than the Deepest center of our being (God) – yet, from this point on, we are either at a standstill or the journey must turn around and go outward. Since there is nothing wanting to the unitive state – nothing that can either be added to or subtracted from it – what more in this world is there to attain? We have it All. But if we cannot have more or less of God, we can, nevertheless, have more or less of self, and that's what lies beyond this turning point.

While the unitive state is the beginning of a new life, yet it is a life that remains to be tested and lived – lived to the end – literally, the ending (falling away) of the unitive state itself. The over-riding desire is to equalize the love we have received from God by giving with no return – getting nothing back, that is. Thus the goal of this new life is to live with nothing in it for ourselves. Prior to coming to this state it was not possible to live an egoless life for God, but here now, in the egoless unitive condition, finally we can truly give without getting anything out of it for ourselves. So long as any "divine experiences" persist – ecstasy, bliss or whatever – there is something in it for us. Thus the only way to live with nothing in it for ourselves is to have no more such experiences, indeed, no more "experiences" of God at all. Basically we don't need them anymore because they cannot add to what we already have, God Himself. But even though we may want to forfeit all such experiences, only the Giver can take them away. It is God's withdrawing all divine experiences that constitutes the "turning point". If this does not happen, there is no going further in the journey, not in this world, at least.

Although this withdrawal is abrupt and bewildering, at the same time, there is Christ; Christ who forfeited the glory of God to be one of us, totally human, that is.[11] His choice has become our choice: to fully accept our humanity, live with God amid the mundane affairs of the world no different than anyone else, with nothing in it for ourselves. (Needless to say, this is not a forfeiture of the unitive state. In being human Christ could no more forfeit his oneness with the Logos than we

---

[11] Christ is unique in that he *chose* to be human. How many people, given a choice, would do this? Most people would rather be divine. Indeed, many people on the spiritual path are honestly seeking their own divinity.

can). For the incarnate Christ the Unitive State was but a beginning (he was conceived in this state), but it was not his ending. Thus Christ had further to go, and now we are ready to go with him.

As to how life in the marketplace goes or where it leads, we need only look to Christ. The way it went for him is the "Way" it goes for us. It will lead to the death of the whole Unitive State – self and God. And beyond this? To Resurrection.

Death

Without a thorough understanding of the Unitive state, a state that has been totally exercised, tested and lived through, there can be no understanding of the true nature of Christ's death. His death is the falling away of the entire Unitive State, literally, the death of God and self in one fell swoop. With this goes every experience man has of "life", "being", "energy", "feelings", even the experience of body and soul, it is a complete wipe out. Such was the true nature of Christ's death, and such is the only true death-experience man will ever know. That this event took place on a Cross was God's way of dramatically demonstrating this Truth (the true nature of death) to the world for all time. Thus everyone ponders the great mystery of Christ's death, literally the death of God Incarnate.[12]

Following this event the body obviously remains – literally the walking dead – and thus the sole question that arises is "What is the true nature of "this" that remains?" Since only God knows, only God can reveal it.

Resurrection – Logos

The Resurrection is not the body coming to life, rather it is the

---

[12] The true saving act of God was not the physical death of the man Jesus, the true saving act of God was the Incarnation. This singular act was God-awful, beyond any human experience of suffering, beyond any human description. As terrible as Jesus' physical suffering, it cannot be compared to what was endured in the Incarnation.

answer to the question: "What is the true nature of "*this*" (body and soul) that remains – remains beyond self and all its human life experiences?" The answer is the revelation of the true nature of Christ. First and foremost it is the revelation of the Logos, the "Form of God" – Form of the Formless. Second, it is the revelation of the Logos' oneness with creation – a union of Divine Form and created form. Third, it is the revelation of the Logos' unique union with man (human nature) – the Incarnate Christ. So what is the Resurrection? Christ said it, "I am the Resurrection". Thus Christ is what Resurrection is, and Resurrection is what Christ is.[13]

There is no revelation of Christ more definitive or complete than this. Christ is no longer a mystery, but an unbelievable Truth, "unbelievable" because the human mind with all its intelligence and reasoning can never get hold of the Reality that is the true Christ. Something else learned in this revelation: "only Christ dies and only Christ rises". But who can understand this? It seems this too is beyond the grasp of the human mind.

Pentecost – Holy Spirit

After his Resurrection Christ promised to send us his enlightening Spirit. This event is the descent of what I call a "Cloud of Knowing" – so-called because it is the reverse of a much earlier experience, a descent of a "Cloud of Unknowing" which heralds the onset of the Passive Night of the Spirit.

As to this cloud of "Knowing", nothing can be said of it. Because it is without knower or known, it can only be called "Knowing". It is not a way-of-knowing and cannot be grasped by the mind, intellect or thought. It does not fall into any category of experiential knowledge and

---

[13] Earlier in life I could not make sense of St. Paul's saying that without Christ's Resurrection our Faith was in vain. My Faith did not depend on Christ's (or my own) physical return to life, but rather, on Christ's divinity for which I did not regard His Resurrection as "proof". But here now, with the revelation of the Logos, Paul was indeed correct. What the Resurrection is, is the definitive revelation of the Logos Incarnate – Christ.

does not even have a physical location – such as in our head. There is absolutely no way to account for this Knowing, we could not even say it knows "something". Furthermore, no one could claim it as his own or even as a gift. The sole concern of this Knowing is ultimate Truth, the Truth of God and God's plan for man – his life, journey and ultimate destiny. It has nothing to do with anything else.

While this is a genuine Pentecost, it is not that experienced by Christ's Apostles. Though it was the same enlightened Knowing, their active conscious minds, being unable to grasp this transcendent Knowing, expressed it as so much babble. But if the human mind cannot grasp this Knowing, it nevertheless remains, and with this indescribable "Knowing" the Apostles went forth. While the dynamism of this descent of the "Cloud of Knowing" is obviously the "Spirit", yet Its gift or the Knowing imparted, belongs to the Logos, not to the Spirit. Thus what the Spirit gave the Apostles was Christ's own Knowing – "We shall have the mind of Christ".

Ascension – Transcendent

As if dissolved in a glorious Air, the body literally experiences itself being vaporized. This revelation is quite simple: the true nature of the glorious Air that pervades every cell is the glory of the Transcendent – "that" in which the Logos eternally exists. This, then, is the body's heavenly existence.

Unfortunately, the Biblical account of Christ's Ascension has left some people with the impression Christ rose so high in the sky He couldn't be seen anymore – as if heaven were in outer space somewhere. Because the body is immortal, people think heaven has to be a physical place. But this is not true. Heaven is God's "dimension" of existence, not ours. (I use the term "dimension" as opposed to "place" because God is not confined to any "place", nor are those in heaven. So too, just as God is not a "where", heaven is not a "where"). As the account says, Christ disappeared in a cloud, was "taken up", literally disappeared into air. So heaven is neither up, down or around, but a totally different dimension of existence, a dimension not available to the senses. (The senses, after all, are not privy to the ultimate Truth of anything, which is why they are of no use in heaven).[14]

So what the Ascension reveals is this: whatever physical elements remain – after death let's say – they dwell in the state of unutterable Glory, the Glory of the Transcendent – "Father", as Christ called Him. Thus the Eternal Form of God, the divine Christ (into which all has been transformed), is pervaded by the Glory of the Father.

Conclusion of Christ's Revelation

There is only one way to know what Christ meant when he said he was the "Way, the Resurrection, the Truth and the Life", and that is by recapitulating his own human spiritual journey. Since no revelation can be validated ahead of time or before it has occurred, we only come upon Christ's truth when we have relived or recapitulated His same truth. Thus Christ validates each stage of our journey after we have come upon this same stage in His own journey.

In this way it could be said Christ follows us, it is not we who follow Christ. It is only by reliving or recapitulating the original we can verify its Way and Truth. In making this journey, then, Christ not only validates our experiences, but in turn, our experiences validate his own. Thus validating Truth works both ways.

There is more to Christ than given here. We have said nothing of His Incarnation and continued presence with us – the Eucharist. Going over the Christian Path, however, is but another illustration of how our spiritual journey recapitulates God's revelations to man. In this case, God's unique revelation of Christ.

---

[14] After death, regardless of the earthly status of the body or what other people see with their senses, the body knows and experiences the glory of the Transcendent – and this, even though people may be looking at a decaying corpse. What we see (mere appearances) does not and cannot give us the ultimate Truth or Reality of anything, not of God, not of man, not of anything that exists. Relying on our senses for truth is fodder for magic and myth.

Conclusion of Thesis

Altogether we have traced God's unfolding revelation from birth to death and beyond. The ability to view our journey as a recapitulation of the key revelation of our world's religions has certain advantages. It not only recognizes God's revelation in different religions, but enables us to understand our experiences in a wider context. To think God only revealed Himself to individuals within a certain group at a certain time in history puts an unwarranted restriction on God. Nothing can keep God from revealing Himself in every age whenever and wherever He will. Unless we realize this on-going revelation, instead of moving forward in our journey, we spend it nostalgically looking backward to bygone eras and dead individuals. No, God is no less with us today than from the beginning.

Another advantage of understanding different religions by way of personal experience, is that the true unity of religions cannot be based on theologies and philosophies, but rather on the living encounter with its revelations. As someone once noted, recognizing the unity in our religions will not be brought about by its respective pundits and theologians, but rather by its mystics. This is because our religions are first and foremost revelatory or mystical, whereas intellectual statements of revealed Truth lack the experiential reality of a lived encounter.

A certain disadvantage of this thesis, however, is that an authentic convergence of religions can only take place at the most inclusive or final stage of revelation. Since an initial revelation cannot integrate or incorporate a later one, any premature convergence is incapable of yielding the fullness of Truth. Since we cannot know or come upon what has not yet been revealed, a synthesis based on anything less than the final revelation cannot disclose the fuller reaches of the journey. Thus a premature integration results in one religion submerging or subsuming another under its own revelation thereby making all religions irrelevant but its own. Instead of seeing how each different revelation ultimately makes its way to final Truth, the tendency is to collapse these differences into sameness as mere "semantic" differences. Leveling all revelations to sameness, however, indicates nothing more than intolerance of plurality and the inability to recognize God's on-going revelations.

From the beginning of man, everyone has been born into some belief system or religion. For those who are faithful to its founding Truth, God leads them forward to encounter the fullness of His revelations and this, regardless of their group affiliation. Thanks to God alone, no one is stuck at any particular stage. Thus within any group there will be individuals who have gone all the way with God – though it would be rare to hear from them since they would not be recognized by the group. While I can think of numerous examples, the point is that God is no respecter of groups, nor limits anyone because of their group affiliation or religion.

Although the stages or revelations we have outlined can be criticized as having been written by someone in the Christian tradition, this same exercise can be undertaken by anyone experienced in any religious tradition. Indeed, we need to know how the key revelation of man's religions are encountered and verified in the journey of each religious tradition. It would be helpful and insightful then, if those in other religions undertook this same task to give an account of how their journey recapitulates and includes the revelation of other religions. The only requirement, of course, is that it be an experiential account, not merely an academic exercise. Philosophizing and second-hand information have no validity in the sphere of revelation. We can only speak of revelation (Truth) as it comes to us personally, because this is the only way to recognize authentic revelation in any religion.

Since no one can live all religious paths at once, and since the present account stems from the experiential path of a Christian, the hope is that those in other religions might take up the challenge to give an account of how the unfolding of their journey was the unfolding of God's gradual revelation to all men. By doing this, whatever bias or limitation is found in one person's presentation will be compensated and enhanced by the testimony of others. What is more, such an account would further illustrate this thesis, namely, *that everyone's spiritual journey recapitulates the history of religion or God's revelation to one and all.*

A Note on Revelation

The Nature of Revelation

My definition of revelation is strictly limited to God's disclosure of Himself to man; as such, it constitutes a genre of its own. Of all man's graced, supernatural experiences, revelation is in a class by itself. The reason God must be revealed is because God transcends creation, is beyond man's earthly dimension of existence. Since it would be impossible to see God and *not* know God, the definition of revelation is that of a particular "seeing" and "knowing". There seems to be some aspect of the soul reserved for God alone and to which only God is privy.[15] There is no name for this mysterious aspect of the soul, in fact, we have no idea what it is. All we know it that it has nothing to do with what we know of the faculties of soul – senses, intellect, consciousness, memory, etc. By its very nature, God's revelation stuns these faculties, bypasses them altogether. Thus revelation comes and goes before the faculties can even react. All post reactions and responses are totally our own, ourselves, our faculties. So although we use the terms "seeing and knowing" these do not refer to anything visual or intellectual. Because of this, revelation cannot be compared to any other human experience. As said before, it constitutes a genre of its own.

Characteristics of Revelation

Revelation is Universal Truth. A universal Truth we cannot come upon of our own accord. No one and nothing can reveal God to us but God Himself. Revelation is God's deliberate gracious act of making

---

[15] While it is tempting to regard this unknown aspect of the soul as the soul's "center", this turns out not to be true. Any experience of a "center" (be it the ego or the divine) is due to consciousness, thus the center is always self or the center of the psyche. Take away consciousness or self and there is neither center nor a circumference – no interior life whatsoever. So all along, "that" in us which sees and knows God is God – the Logos to be specific – and not our self or consciousness. Christ, after all, said only He could reveal the Transcendent and Immanent to us, and in turn, only the Transcendent – Immanent could reveal the Logos to us. This is the way the Trinity works in us.

Himself seen and known to man. Thus God alone is both the Cause, as well as "What" is revealed – the revelation's sole content, that is. The universal Truth revealed is that: God exists; God has revealed Himself to us; God thus wants man to know God and to know God cares for us.

Revelation is non-intellectual, non-conceptual, non-sensory. Revelation shatters all previous knowledge of God – all our notions, concepts, images and whatever. God is something else entirely. Those most likely to question whether or not "What" is revealed is God (or can be called "God") are those who have preconceived ideas of God – which most people do. A revelation, however, shatters all that. We can never go back to our preconceived notions with their cultural, theological and rational overlays. This is another reason why revelation changes our lives, we cannot go back to any hear-say or bookish view of God.

When we say God is "unheard" of, we mean no words can convey the Reality that is God. All we can do is think and talk about God – just as we are now. Because revelation shatters all we may have heard about God or associated with the term "God", we may ponder if what we have heard is the truth of What we have just "seen". Initially there may be some disconnect, indeed, there is nothing like a revelation to get us questioning our beliefs and all we've heard about God. Always, however, we go with what we know and have seen, not with what we have only heard or read about.

If someone asks if "What" is revealed can legitimately be called "God", our answer is this: "What" is revealed never identifies itself in the subjective "I am God", or "I am this or that". Revelation is always wordless. Thus God is not a "subject", but is totally beyond our human faculties with all its names and labels. The human term "God", then, is simply an expression for what can only be revealed. While it may be true that when speaking of this revelation to others unfamiliar with the term "God", some other culturally familiar term might be used to convey "What" was revealed, yet today, living in a Judea-Christian culture, the only term that fits "What" is revealed, is "God"- though not "God" known to the intellect , but rather, God known in revelation.

Having said this, however, following a revelation, our minds may have a lot to question, not about the revelation itself, but what it means to us; how it fits in with what we already know of God – or what we still need to know. While every revelation answers a major human question, it also tends to raise another. One thing is for sure: the revelation will change our life forever.

Revelation is non-interpretable. Revelation is not an unknowable experience on which we project our understanding and interpretation. If this were true, revelation would be pointless because it could be anything the recipient thinks it is. In this case, objective Truth could never reach man or be known by him. The very idea of God waiting on man's interpretation to "get it right" is absurd. God does not depend on man's interpretation for any Truth whatsoever. He does not reveal Himself "hoping" man will recognize Him. Furthermore, revelation stuns the thinking, interpretive mind. As said, revelation comes and goes before it even can be thought about. Thus identification of "what" is revealed admits of no human interpretation – it's simply too late for all that.

Revelation, then, is not a product of putting two and two together or imposing our ideas and understanding. Rather, "What" is revealed stands independent of the recipient; It is Its own immediate identification. Like seeing and knowing a light when turned on, the light does not say, "I am a light", "I exist", or "this is a light". There are no two steps involved – one seeing, the other knowing – because merely to see is to know. Thus knowing God is inherent in the revelation itself. It conveys Its own existence totally undistorted by the mind of the recipient. For this reason revelation is contentless, Itself being the content, and thus revelation is non-interpretable.

Revelation causes an irreversible change in the recipient. Revelation effects a change in the soul, the whole person in fact. We can never be the same again because we cannot go back to not-knowing or not-having seen for ourselves. I cannot think of any other abiding certitude man can have in this life. Compared to this certitude even death is uncertain. What immediately follows revelation is an overwhelming desire to see It again, know It better. Thus we seek a life worthy of this revelation, ponder how best to pursue it, search or go after "that" which has been revealed. I stress this "follow-up" to revelation because without it, there's no going any further in our journey. (In my view, God reveals himself to everybody, only some people don't "follow-up", and therein lies a huge difference).

Revelation is consistent. Though revelations are progressive they never negate a previous revelation or contradict it. If one asks how to account for God's different revelations, keep in mind the different natures of God and man. For the Infinite to be revealed to the finite, the Unlimited to the limited, requires some degree of proportionality, a proportionality not made possible by nature, but by grace.

Thus as spiritual growth enlarges our capacity to encounter the Infinite – to see, know, and bear the Truth – we are also being prepared to see and know more of God, hence the progressive aspect of revelation. In Christianity the term "heaven" for man 's final estate is the recognition that man's purely natural life on earth cannot sustain the fullness of the Godhead, not at least and survive on earth. Thus the final goal of the journey is to effect a supernatural change in man's nature so as to sustain the ultimate revelation of the fullness of God – which is what heaven is.

What Revelation is Not

It is unfortunate the term "revelation" has been used to identify so-called "mystics" who claim God speaks to them, dictates words, or gives them visions of this or that. There is absolutely nothing supernatural about these paranormal experiences. They are neither a sign of sanctity nor the cause of it. In fact, they have nothing whatsoever to do with holiness or genuine sanctity. Those I have in mind are not only New Agers, but Christians generally regarded as saints and mystics.[16] Obviously, all such phenomena fall outside my criteria and definition of authentic

---

[16] Here I think of all those feminine Rhineland mystics, plus Catherine of Sienna, Mary of Egrada, the recently canonized St. Faustina – a long list of women in fact.

revelation. Such phenomena are products of the unconscious, not the product of God, or even from God. John of the Cross, of course, would have us ignore them, give them no space in ourselves.

Book Two of his Ascent of Mount Carmel mostly deals with this subject. But where he thinks the devil may produce this phenomena, I see only the psyche. Similar to Jung 's conscious and unconscious arche-types, these phenomena are produced by the psyche and given a personal interpretation. Some people, of course, have asked if God, underlying the psyche, could not be the cause or source of this unconscious bub-bling forth?

One suggestion is that while God has indeed touched the soul or revealed Himself, due to a weak psyche, fragile emotions, a mentality giv-en to images and ideas, the recipient is overwhelmed and swept away by his own reactions. This would not be so bad if the recipient acknowl-edged this fact instead of claiming the content came directly from God – the usual claim. The real weakness of these psyches is a failure to "know thyself", that is, to distinguish God from self or psyche. And while the content may be relevant to a beginner, as his spiritual life deepens, this phenomena will eventually be seen for what it is – self oriented and self-produced. So even in those cases where God may have touched the soul, what bubbles forth is so much self, but not God.

For myself, even as a youngster I found these so-called "mystics" nauseous reading. I called it "cheap spirituality" – no depth, sickening sentimentalism, self-centered, boring (nothing new), seemingly reserved for the ignorant or weak minded. I never saw God in any of it. Besides, there is absolutely nothing they ever said or wrote we did not know al-ready. Nothing was communicated to them that was not on their minds already. So the only thing "revealed" was their own projecting minds, their personal inner words and images.

Furthermore, nothing is more evident in these so-called commu-nications than self. It would seem there is not enough in a truly "graced" communication to totally satisfy self. Thus to satisfy one's emotions and thoughts, the mind projects all kinds of things, a kind of spiritual self-absorption if you will. Those who hear God or somebody talking to them are only listening to their own inner voice – talking to themselves that is. In truth, however, God does not talk or have any image, thus whatever words and images we think are God, are solely our own – the mind's own anthropomorphic projections and nothing else.[17] People have no idea what a trickster the mind and psyche can be.

The paranormal is the manifestation of what a "trickster" self can be. Failure to see through this type of phenomena is an indictment not only of the recipient, but of those who believe them. It behooves everyone, then, to see through this ruse because it has entrapped many – like devotees making icons of these people. The bottom line, however, is that there is nothing more obvious in this phenomena than "self ". This alone is enough to discredit all such experiences.

Keep in mind, the authentically supernatural is a graced sharing of God's divine life with the soul. The focus, then, is not on our reaction – bliss, love or whatever – but on "that" which has revealed Itself. I am convinced anyone who experiences an authentic revelation automatically rejects the paranormal. By comparison, the paranormal is superficial, deceptive – cheap.

Although Jung used the term "numinous" instead of "spiritual" for man's more profound experiences, he was never clear as to the cause

---

[17] What does it mean that we were made in the "image and likeness of God" when God has no image and even forbade us to make images of Himself? Some people understand this prohibition to be against various works of art, pictures or statues depicting man's view of God. While such works are innocuous in themselves, what is really forbidden, however, is man's mental images of God, all of them inevitably anthropomorphic – indeed , how could they not be? These are the images that have to be smashed. No use burning icons and retaining the same anthropomorphic ideas and images in our minds. Because of the Incarnation, however, Christians need not apologize for depicting the humanity of Christ. As to depicting his divine nature (the Logos), no one seems to have any idea of it, thus, to my knowledge, no one has ever tried.

of these experiences, thus his use of the term is indefinite. Considering the psyche and the phenomena of which it is capable – illusions, delusions, visions, voices, reactions to drugs, alcohol, suggestion, etc. – there are a host of causes for the so-called "numinous". But then, these days the tendency is to mistake psyche for soul anyway, and consequently, mistake the paranormal and extrasensory for the supernatural. What sets a revelation apart, however, is that it is its own Cause, totally unrelated to any possible extraneous causes. The supernatural and paranormal are two totally different dimensions of man. Because they arise from different sources they are totally different experiences.

No doubt it is due to these paranormal experiences that religious authors, writing on the subject of revelation, always make a distinction between a "universal" revelation, intended for everyone, and a "private" revelation given to an individual solely for his own benefit or information. Since, however, my definition of revelation is limited to what is universally true, it admits of no distinction between its being given to an individual or intended for everyone. What is a universal Truth for one individual is certainly true for all individuals. That people are want to call all manner of paranormal experiences "revelations" is a complete misuse of the term.

In this matter, the question to ponder is whether we can legitimately make a distinction between authentic revelation (an objective universal Truth) given to an individual, and the same revelation (Truth) "intended" for a group of people. That Truth was ever intended solely for a lone individual is inconceivable. What is more, as a singular act of God, revelation is always given One-to-one, thus there is no such thing as a "group revelation". Any revelation experienced by a group would have to be the same experience given to each individual at the same time, yet there is no incidence of this on record – indeed, would that God had taken all the Israelites up the mountain with Moses! So even though a revelation may be "intended" for a group, it has always been given, first and foremost to a singular individual. Given this fact, it is somewhat of a misnomer to speak of a "group revelation" when it has never happened.

The final word on this issue, however, is that the divine Logos revealed Itself as a single Person. While this Truth is intended for all men, it was nevertheless revealed in and through the singular Person of Christ.

In conclusion, my definition of "revelation" is very restrictive. It is in this sense I have used the term in this paper. That other people do not agree, fine. But as regards this thesis, at least, any other interpretation of "revelation" will not yield the over-reaching view or understanding this writing presents. For the skeptic, agnostic or deist, of course, there is no such thing as revelation. Whatever exists beyond man has never revealed itself, but remains unknown and unknowable. Whatever be the cause or intelligence of an ordered universe, its nature precludes any such disclosure, it is utterly impersonal. This belief, of course, only locks man in himself, he is not open-ended – certainly not open to the revelation of the unknown. Such, at least, is the belief system of the agnostic, deist, atheist and others. They have locked themselves in.

A Personal Note

Were it not for the Incarnation I would have no great reason to value human beings of greater value to God than the flora and fauna. The evil of which man is capable makes me wonder why God doesn't wipe him out – why does God permit it? How can God stand it? Is man really worth it?   And what's in it for God – or for us? Nobody can wax more pessimistic about human nature than I can. There is only one solitary light that shines through, the only answer I know that has come directly from God, and that is the Logos' Incarnation.

This says it all. It's God's last word on humanity and what we truly mean to God. While I've never seen this act of God as saving man from sin, which goes right on, I do see this as saving us from despair and all it implies. The Incarnation is the Enlightener that reveals our human goal, our path and eternal life with God. Above all, the Incarnation is the ultimate proof of God 's radical love and care for mankind. If God loves man that much, then so must we.

So the Incarnation is my sole hope for man and the singular rock of my faith. There is no greater proof of God's determination that man know God's love, truth, and our final destiny in God. Indeed, no greater love could God manifest – could He create, undergo, even suffer for man than the Logos' Incarnation. Because of this God has what we might call a "self-invested interest" in man, a Personal interest, a real "link" with man. Responsible for our creation, we might even say God's reputation is at stake. (And let's face it, there aren't many success stories. Even the human Jesus, once he became known, didn't last more than three years). The Incarnation, however, was more than God's attempt to prevent man from becoming a total flop, a complete failure. By jumping into the fray God can now say: "Been there, done that, so let's get on with it, only this time, go the right Way". The Incarnation is all about this 'Way', and I, for one, know of no other way.

Admittedly I came late to the impact of the Incarnation. Earlier in life it held no meaning for me – even if it were true. I'm convinced this early obstacle was due to the traditional reason given for the Incarnation – the whole atonement theory. Even as a child it made no sense to me. Always, I thought of this theory as someone's attempt to make sense out of what was a complete mystery. To this day, I hold there is no truth to this theory. But if it was an obstacle for me, I'm sure it must be an obstacle for other Christians as well. To see the Incarnation engulfed in the fallacious aura of man's sins, God 's anger and demand for atonement, salvation from hell and damnation, casting out devils – that whole black story – is a crime against God. Not only is there no truth in it, it is a great disservice to God, worse even, than sin. Why? Because it works to undermine and discredit the whole truth and marvel of God's Incarnation. Christ has been so shrouded in error and wrong thinking by those who profess to know Him that, in my view, they know Him not.

/ 2 /

CESSATION OF SELF

CESSATION OF SELF

The circumstance that prompted this writing was an encounter with the editors of the "Laughing Man Magazine", who, in December 1985, contacted me for an interview. The interview was never published because as matters turned out, there was no agreement between us. The editors' insistence on equating Mr. Free John's "cessation of egoic contractions" with what I have called "the experience of no-Self," led to such a false and distorted view of the latter, it virtually eliminated no-Self from the spiritual journey altogether. Though I initially found their insistence and failure to understand somewhat curious, after looking over the books they had left, it became obvious their confusion arose because the no-Self event is not to be found in Mr. Free John's seven stage paradigm, which paradigm these gentlemen had accepted as the ultimate degree of truth a human being could realize.

When we hear of an experience that falls outside our usual frame of reference we are at a loss to explain it, and this was the situation of the interview. If through semantic ruses we reinterpret (or misinterpret) an experience in order to make it fit our paradigm, we only make it over into a different experience, an experience it never was in the first place. This is what happens when the no-Self event is interpreted as the cessation of the ego; by doing this, the true no-Self experience goes off the map, is eliminated from the journey, and becomes lost to the literature as well.

These gentlemen, however, are not the first to mistake the cessation of ego for the much later event, the cessation of Self. Until we have encountered both events, this mistake may be inevitable. Although modern psychology has raised our consciousness regarding the difference between ego and true-self, we are still a long way from understanding the difference between the falling away or transcendence of the ego-self, and the much later event, the falling away of the "true Self" and its oneness with the Divine – that is, the falling away of the entire Unitive or Realized Condition. Until we can get hold of this difference, we can never come to an understanding of the completed journey or hope to understand the true end of man's passage through human existence. [1]

Part of the problem is that no one can identify either the ego-self or the true Self until it has fallen away.[2] It is only in retrospect we recognize the old immature or superficial self and its "egoic contractions," recognize it in contrast to the "true Self" and the Transcendental Condition we have realized. By the same token, no one can know the ultimate nature of the "true Self" so long as they are living it, or are it. It is only when this true Self and its Transcendental Condition falls away that its ultimate nature is known by its absence. With this disclosure, the true nature of self is revealed as everything we experience – the psyche, the entire system of consciousness, man's entire dimension of experiencing and knowing, including his experiences of the Divine. As it turns out, the Divine or Absolute is beyond the experiencing self or consciousness. Until both of these events have been encountered, however, it would be impossible to get hold of the difference between the two.

It is my hope to someday put these experiences and their ensuing conditions side by side in order to clarify the difference, and, above all, to put these two events into the literature of the spiritual journey, where, at present, the latter event is totally absent. Mere philosophical statements of Final Truth will not suffice when it comes to mapping the experiential journey; such statements can be made by anyone no matter what their level of realization. Only exact experiential accounts can verify the perspective from which Truth is seen, and can attest to the degree that Truth has been realized in its fullness.

The journey to the egoless condition or state is a well-traveled path, one that has been amply articulated in our major religious traditions. What these paths have in common are the agonies and ecstasies of the

---

[1] In this paper the term, "Realized Condition" is used as synonymous with the following traditional terms: "Mystical Union", "Unitive State", "Transcendental Consciousness", "Transcendental Realization", etc.
[2] The "Laughing Man Magazine" (now defunct) was published by the community of Da Free John, an American guru later known as Adida Samraj.

transforming process, the transcendence or falling away of the ego-center, a radical change of consciousness, and the disclosure of an abiding oneness with the Divine or Absolute. Although the resulting Realized Condition is the mature state of man, it is not his final state or Condition. To come to the final Condition we must go beyond the Realized State, which is but a mid-point stage in our overall passage. At this mid-point, there will occur a major turning point in the journey, one so crucial that if it does not occur there is no possibility of going further or moving to the final cessation of self. We hear little about this turning point and consequently, little of the stage that lies beyond the Realized Condition and its eventual, unsuspected ending. Because we hear so much about the path up to and including the Realized Condition, and so little about the stages that lie beyond it, I propose to begin the following discussion at the point where our known traditional paths come to an end, and to focus instead, on those aspects of the Realized Condition that herald or initiate the major turning point of the journey. Afterwards, something will be said of the experiences that mark the true end of our journey or passage through consciousness.

The Major Turning Point of the Journey

Mr. Free John says well that in the Realized Condition the phenomenal, conditional self continues to arise. These arisings are the various movements of the conditional body, mind, emotions, life-energy, self-idea, and all relations. Whereas prior to the Realized Condition these arisings had been problematic or were seen as an obstacle to Realization, now they are "non-problematic" because the essential "self-consciousness or atman" has been "re-cognized or transcended as the focus of attention" so that "all conditions of self and its objects are tacitly or directly recognized IN the Transcendental Condition, Identity, Consciousness or Radiant Being IN which they are apparently and mechanically or spontaneously arising."[3]

Thus once we realize that our deepest unconscious self (or true

---

[3] From Mr. Free John's Nirvanasara or The Dawn Horse Testament.

Self) is one with the Divine, we realize that self originates and resides IN the Divine Ground, and that the arising self is a creative manifestation of the Ground – recognized even as the "play" of the Divine. Many Christian contemplatives have regarded this unconscious self as the Christ-self, the transformed or deified self. But whatever the terminology, the Realized Condition is the revelation of the true Self's oneness with the Divine, Divine Being IN ourselves and ourselves IN Divine Being.

In the Realized Condition, however, the conditional phenomenal self is not always arising; in a quiet meditative or contemplative state, the self does not arise because nothing calls upon it to do so. In such a silent state it is impossible to draw a line between the true Self and the Divine, or to say where one ends and the other begins. What is more, in the Realized Condition the continued awareness of self-existence is equally our awareness of Divine-existence; thus existence is given in a single, simple act of nondual awareness – which is the awareness of "being" prior to any arising self. Still, the phenomenal, conditional self, its energies, feelings, way of knowing and so on, continue to arise in response to the circumstantial conditions of mundane existence. In this way, the self is called upon to live, manifest and express itself in everyday ordinary life.

Naturally, if someone desired to keep the arising self to a minimum – the better to undistractedly enjoy the Realized Condition – he might choose a more reclusive life style, or stay out of the common marketplaces where the un-realized and un-enlightened do not know him from Adam. After all, nothing so calls upon the self to arise as does life in the common marketplace! For the recluse this means that the true nature of the Realized Self in its oneness with the Divine has little chance of becoming fully known. Its true nature can only be finally disclosed after it has confronted every possible and extreme condition under which the self could possibly arise.

Thus until the Realized Self (from which the phenomenal self arises) has lived to its fullest potential, it cannot possibly come to its own ending, which ending is heralded by the non-arising of the phenomenal self under the most trying and terrible of circumstances. In other words, at the beginning of the Realized Condition, the phenomenal, conditional self continues to arise in response to the changing phenomenal conditions of life, but at the end of the Realized Condition, the phenomenal self no longer arises at all – regardless of any phenomenal circumstance. Thus merely to Realize Self in its oneness with the Divine indicates neither the ending of self nor the ending of the passage.

Unless the Realized Condition has first been lived, exercised, tested and stretched to its fullest potential, this Condition is but a hollow capacity for life, a life that cannot come to an end so long as self or consciousness remains, or so long as self arises – no matter how un-problematic it may be. Let us just say that any Condition in which the phenomenal self continues to arise is less than a perfect Condition; the fact that self is non-problematic is not the issue, as Mr. Free John seems to imply in his writings. The self does not eventually fall away because it is problematic or bad, or because the realizer suppresses its arising (which is impossible anyway); rather, the self falls away because its potential for human existence – which is all self is about anyway – has been fulfilled, and there is nothing more within its dimension to be lived, experienced, known or realized. This is why the ultimate fulfillment of consciousness ends in no-consciousness and why the ultimate fulfillment of self ends in no-self. We cannot be finished with what has not, first, been lived or experienced.

Perhaps this is why those who come to the Realized Condition and live a reclusive life of sitting meditation or contemplation have never spoken to us of the further Condition of no-self and the falling away of the Realized Condition; quite simply, they have never truly lived out this Condition to its own ending. Instead, we are told the Realized Condition is the end of the journey and as far as we can go this side of the grave. We are told that self IS the Divine because in the silent meditative or contemplative state we can draw no experiential distinction between self and the Divine. The truth, however, is that in this state the self does not arise because nothing and no one calls upon it to do so! The slightest movement toward protecting ourselves from the arising phenomenal self, or maintaining a space where it does not arise, is a subtle form of attachment and clinging. Such an attachment or need for maintenance (practice), however, would not be indicative of the Realized Condition.

What is important to point out is that even when the "transparent, unnecessary, and non-binding" conditional self is not arising, it nevertheless remains as a potential for arising, as well as the simple act of awareness itself. Awareness of the Realized Condition is just what it implies — awareness OF. So long as there is any condition to be aware of, or so long as self is aware of its own condition, then there is awareness OF. The knowing self IS this simple, automatic, <u>unconscious</u> act of self-awareness; in the Realized Condition some people regard this as Divine awareness. Because this is awareness of self prior to the awareness of anything arising, this is thought to be the Divine's own awareness and therefore it is believed that the essence of the Divine is Consciousness Itself.

While I do not agree with this assumption (actually a philosophical belief), it would be pointless to argue the essence of the Divine because it cannot be grasped by the intellect and must therefore be left to silence. As to the true status of self in the Realized Condition, or as to how Divine it really is, there is no consensus within a single tradition, let alone across various religious traditions. As we shall see, however, this question has a way of eventually taking care of itself, when, at the end of the journey, self and the Realized Condition fall away. Thus it would make no difference if we thought the self was the Absolute, the immortal soul, the individual or phenomenal self, the unconscious "true self", or the Divine and self together, when, on completion of the passage, all these possible selves fall away in one fell swoop.

The point to be made is two-fold. First, in the Realized Condition self-awareness remains because it is the very condition of Divine-awareness (God-consciousness); without self-awareness there could be no Divine-awareness. Second, if given a chance in this Condition, the phenomenal conditional self will continue to arise. Thus one way or the other, or in both ways at once, in the Realized Condition the self remains; it has not ceased to exist, function, or to be experienced. What may be said to have ceased to function or exist are "egoic contractions" — the friction caused by self-will, self-desires and so on, as well as the cessation of self as the sole unconscious object of subjective reflexion. In the Realized Condition God-centeredness has replaced self-centeredness in such a way that the experience of "life" and "being" is equally the experience of Divine Life and Being. In this awareness God and self are given in the single autonomous and unconscious act of reflexion itself.[4]

With regard to the arising self, I agree with Mr. Free John that the arising self acts as a "reminder" of the Realized Condition. I would even go a step further and say that the more strenuous the conditions under which the self arises — the tragedies and crises of life — the more powerful and wonderful this "reminder" becomes. The wonder is not the arising self, of course, but rather the "threshold" of its spontaneous encounter with the Divine Center and its subsequent dissolving into a profound peace and equilibrium.

This reminder and dissolution is a joy in itself. There is no repression here, no attempt to keep the self (its energies, feelings and desires) from arising; rather, it is the continuous dissolution of these into the Divine Center that is the reminder and wonder of the Realized Condition. This is why, in the deepest sense possible, this Unitive Condition is said to be an "imperturbable" state. This dissolution is due, of course, to the absence of the ego-center. Instead of the arising self becoming stuck in its own (ego) center, the self now dissolves into emptiness, or

---

[4] "Reflexion" refers to the unconscious, automatic, spontaneous mechanism of the mind, the singular act whereby the mind bends on itself to know itself. By contrast "reflection" refers to the conscious recognition of the reflexive act as well as the deliberate act of reflecting on ourselves. Reflexion is thus self-awareness on the unconscious level, while reflection is self-awareness on a conscious level. The Realized Condition is the breakthrough of the divine into the center of consciousness resulting in the reflexive mind not only bending on itself (as object to itself), but equally bending on the divine. Thus consciousness is as aware of the divine as it is of itself, hence it is called a "unitive state". Self has not been concealed by this change of consciousness. The reflexive mechanism not only goes right on, but without it, there would be neither awareness of self or the divine.

comes to naught in the Divine-center. In this way the arising self virtually goes out of itself instead of being stone-walled in itself. (By "dissolution" I mean the arising self comes to an end-point or threshold beyond which it cannot go. This "point" is the threshold of the empty center where self meets or touches upon the Divine.)

But apart from Mr. Free John's affirmation of the arising self in the Realized Condition, another important fact he points out is the transient experience he calls "translation" or Bhava Samadhi (perfect Nirvikalpa Samadhi). He speaks of this experience as the Divine "outshining" the phenomenal conditional self, outshining all phenomenal existence in fact. Here Divine Being or the Unconditional Divine Self outshines all conditional arising so that in the end, It alone remains. He speaks of this as the final experience of his seven stage paradigm or the third stage of the Realized Condition. This outshining, however, is a transient or passing experience, which, if it were to become a permanent Condition, according to Mr. Free John, would not allow for continued earthly existence. Thus he says: *"The Ultimate Event of Translation (Which Necessarily Coincides with death or dissolution of the gross physical personality and every merely subtle or conditional form of the psycho-physical personality) the Objective Divine Star Will Appear, Steadily and Most Brightly. Then the Cosmic Mandala and Every Trace of the conditional personality will Dissolve in the Inherent or Subjective Brightness of Ultimate Recognition and Realization of the Divine Person."*[5]

Translation, then, or Bhava Samadhi, is the eventual outshining of the phenomenal arising self, the end of it, that is. In the Final Ultimate Condition, then, there is no arising self, but then the realizer would be dead, "dead" at least in medical terms – according to Mr. Free John. It seems not to occur to one who has had this Translation experience that it might be possible to go on living in this condition (Bhava Samadhi), wherein the phenomenal self is permanently outshined, or no longer arises. The reason this is not considered or is not seen as a possibility at this time, however, is because at this point of the journey the outshining of self is equally the outshining of all phenomenal existence – that is, the

---

[5] Da Free John, *The Dawn Horse Testament.* p. 638

senses close down together with self or consciousness. Obviously, there is no way man can get around in this world without his senses or without his bodily functions intact. What the Realizer does not seem to know, at this time, however, is that with a lot of living, this very possibility – the permanent cessation or outshining of self while still among the living – can become a great Reality.

Once consciousness (all self) falls away, it is realized that the senses are an entirely separate system from that of the psyche or consciousness, and that even without consciousness, the sensory and bodily system can continue to function. In the no-self condition, then, for the first time in life, man encounters "pure" sensory perception. Prior to this, and from birth in fact, consciousness had functioned in unison with the senses. This means that man can never experience "pure" sensory perception so long as consciousness or self remains, or so long as the senses function in conjunction with consciousness. But once consciousness falls away, the senses remain intact and life goes on. When the senses ultimately fall away (or cease), however, life in the human condition is no longer possible.

The experience we have been speaking of – Mr. Free John's Translation, Outshining, or Bhava Samadhi – is amply accounted for in the writings of many Christian mystics and contemplatives who have come to the Realized Condition. In the Christian tradition this experience is given various names, e.g., "Divine Rapture," or "Beatific Vision"; this is John of the Cross' "Transformation of Glory" or "Beatific Transformation" given to those who have already attained Transforming Union or Spiritual Marriage.[6]

As to how this particular experience is different from previous exalted experiences of the journey is a subject we will not go into at this time. "Ecstasy" as it is experienced at various levels of the path is a topic

---

[6] Stanza xxxix, *Spiritual Canticle*, John of the Cross. He speaks of these exalted experiences in other places as well, which experiences come <u>after</u> arriving at full Unitive transformation. Also see his book, *The Living Flame of Love*.

unto itself. What can be said, however, is that ecstasy in the Realized Condition is quite different than ecstasy in the egoic condition. In the Realized or Unitive Condition it seems to be an underlying potential, as if one bordered on this state continually or was standing on the fine line between the Realized Condition and the Beatific Condition (permanent translation or outshining). So, although we say ecstasy is a transient experience, it seems to be an inherent potential of the Realized Condition – unless, of course, we deliberately forfeit all such experiences.

What we want to call attention to is the fact that the mystics are in general agreement with Mr. Free John's view that this experience of Bhava Samadhi or Beatific Transformation could NOT become a permanent condition this side of the grave. This was the situation or condition John of the Cross was referring to when he repeatedly stated that there could be no permanent suspension of the faculties in this life, by "faculties" meaning consciousness, the conditional phenomenal self and all that goes with it.

It was this type of Divine onslaught that, according to John of the Cross, brought the Realizer to the point of wishing either to die in order that the Beatific Condition might become permanent, or, if not destined to die right away, to have no more of these experiences. This desire to die or to have no more of such experiences indicates not only the loftiness of the experience, but the experiencer's attitude toward the experience, an attitude that will give rise to the turning point of the journey.

What the contemplative learns from these lofty experiences is very great. For one thing, he learns that the passing experiences of Translation or Beatific Vision add nothing to the Realized Condition, a condition, which is now a permanent underlying abiding state, a state that needs no maintenance or practice. Because these passing experiences add nothing to his transformed condition, the contemplative realizes he has no further to go in this world; the inward journey is finished and the next step seems to be a final Divine or Beatific Condition which is not compatible with this world.

He also learns that the phenomenal conditional self is not only "outshined" in the Final Condition, but that all self-awareness, including the whole Realized Condition, is ultimately outshined. Here, there is neither awareness OF the Divine or awareness of the Realized Condition. There is only Light (a metaphor) and nothing IN the Light, no one seeing the Light, only "that" (as John of the Cross put it) which is beyond both the objective and subjective case. Clearly this experience reveals no self whatsoever. The Final Condition is void of anything or any experience that could be called "self"; in fact, the Absolute Condition is void of any statement or definition that could be given It. This experience reveals a great truth – namely, that every experience we call "self" is not eternal. Thus no matter how deified self may appear to be in the Realized Condition, it is nevertheless ultimately impermanent, and so, too, is the Realized Condition.

Although Mr. Free John makes a distinction between the true Self or Atman and the phenomenal conditional self (atman with a small "a" perhaps), without an arising conditional self, there could never be verification of the existence of any Atman at all. What verifies the existence of an Atman or true Self is its <u>potential</u> for giving rise to the phenomenal self-experience. When there is no longer any arising phenomenal or conditional self, there can no longer be any verification of an Atman or true Self. In other words, Atman is the potential for the arising conditional self (the conditional self did not arise from the Absolute), and thus without this arising there is no Atman or Self, nothing to be either distinct from, or identical to, the Divine. So what we learn from these Beatific or outshining experiences is that everything we call "self," including the true Self or Atman, pertains only to this life, to this human earthly experience, and with this insight we finally come to the imperative turning point of the journey.

I know of no other way of articulating this turning point than to put it in purely Christian terms. Having realized self's abiding oneness with the Divine, there is also the realization of Christ's self, his purely human self and its oneness with the Divine. At one time the divine Logos (or pre-incarnate Christ) "put off" absolute divinity in order to "put on" humanity, that is, to fully accept the conditional life of self. In like manner, the present turning point is the contemplative's full acceptance of the conditional, impermanent and non-eternal self and the "putting off" of the final Divine Condition.

This putting off, or having no more experiences of "outshining" or Beatific foretastes is accomplished by moving into the marketplace of the common man in order to fully live the conditional self. Live it in the Realized Condition of Oneness just as Christ lived it, giving away the self in the living of it with other selves. This means that the contemplative now seeks the maximum arising of the phenomenal self, which, as we have said, serves as a maximum "reminder" of its Divine Center. The degree to which we seek this maximum arising is proportionate to the speed with which we traverse this marketplace stage of the journey. (Many people do not realize that the marketplace is a necessary stage of the journey. Instead, there is the general belief that once we come to the Realized or Unitive Condition, this is the end of the line. This is a false or wrong view, of course).

The other way to go is to continue to relish and protect our exalted and blissful experiences of Beatific Outshining by keeping to our meditative, contemplative, or less distracting style of life – obviously, the reclusive lifestyle is more conducive to having such experiences. But actually, that would be the same as the butterfly clinging to his cocoon, the refusal of the Realizer to let go the raft once he has come to the other shore. In that case, there has been no complete acceptance of the phenomenal conditional self. Indeed, there cannot be full acceptance of self until and unless there is a "putting off" of the Final Divine Condition or heavenly state – total detachment from this experience, total surrender and forfeiture of it. This can only be done, however, by moving into the marketplace of ordinary life and becoming one with the unknown, unrealized and unenlightened. The marketplace means choosing the maximum opportunities and circumstances under which the conditional self can arise. This is the true challenge of the mature, Realized human being.

When we speak of "putting off" the Final Divine Condition we do not mean putting off the Realized Condition. Only the outshining experiences can be put off or kept at a distance. This is done by moving out of the conditions conducive to their occurrence and by seeking, instead, maximum opportunities for the phenomenal self to arise. We cannot, of course, put off the transformed or Realized Condition any more than the butterfly can return to its larval or caterpillar beginnings. There can be no return to the egoic or un-transformed condition; the Realized Condition is irreversible.

It has become our everyday experience of life and being. It is not dependent upon any particular experience, not even the outshining experience, which, as we have said, adds nothing to the Realized Condition. This means that the true Final Divine Condition can only become a reality after the Realized Condition has been lived to its fullest potential and thereby fulfilled its earthly mission of mature human existence. Man cannot begin to live fully until he has come to the Realized Condition; this is why the Realized Condition is a true new beginning, and by no means the end of the journey – as so many people seem to believe.

Another experience that abets the above forfeiture is that once the contemplative comes to the Realized Condition he no longer feels the need of his former practices or lifestyle. Once the goal of practice has been attained, these practices add nothing to his new state and may even be holding him back from the full expression of the Realized Condition. His interior, spiritual or psychological life is such that he feels nothing wanting, nothing more to be desired, nothing realized or attained; this fact alone, calls for a turning point. Prior to coming upon the Realized Condition the journey had been a movement inward to ever more profound levels and centers of union with the Divine. But having come upon the deepest Divine center – the Divine Ground, which is empty of all self – there is no further to go; we cannot go deeper than the deepest. Having come to this infinite Divine space, there is a sense of ending, after which the journey turns around and begins to move outward, to expand the human limits through going out to others. The Divine is not some tiny interior center; rather, it is a burning flame that radiates outward, thrusts us beyond ourselves.

Outside the Christian tradition I do not know how one handles this turning point or even if there is any recognition of this essential landmark. We find no evidence of it in the Hindu tradition and, consequently, in Mr. Free John's works.[7] Mahayana Buddhism, however, speaks of a point when the enlightened Bodhisattva puts off final Nirvana in order to save all sentient beings and, quite possibly, this is similar to the turning point we have been discussing. At least I see this particular point as the difference between Mahayana Buddhism and other "yanas" or Buddhist paths.

It would seem for both the Christian and Buddhist who come to the Realized or true Bodhisattva condition, there is the free, whole-hearted acceptance, even the embrace, of the human condition or arising conditional self, the living out of it in the common marketplace as one no different than his fellow man. It was this self or humanity Christ took on when he put off absolute divinity (Nirvana or the Beatific condition) in order to save man and show him the path to salvation, which path is our human passage through self or consciousness. We cannot put off Nirvana or Beatitude, however, until we have come to the Realized Condition of Oneness. A premature return to the marketplace would only result in the blind leading the blind.

We can now understand why, lacking this turning point or failing to understand its enormous relevance, some religious paths come to an end at the Realized Condition and regard this egoless state as the final

---

[7] It seems Mr. Free John's understanding of his experiences is according to the Hindu tradition. That self or Atman is the Absolute is a belief not subscribed to by any other religion. That he regards Gnosticism as the true Christian mystical tradition reveals a blatant ignorance of Christianity. No form of Gnosticism was ever regarded as authentic Christian Mysticism, not in its own day and not today. In its 2000 year history, no Gnostic was ever regarded as a Christian mystic. To call John of the Cross, Meister Eckhart, Teresa of Avila (to name but three) "Gnostics", is sheer ignorance.

condition or as far as man can go this side of the grave. Without this turning point (putting off Nirvana or Beatific outshining), we can understand why these religious paths say nothing of the further and much later experience – the ultimate cessation of self and the falling away of the Realized Condition. This is also the reason why the no-self event is invariably misinterpreted as the "cessation of the ego" – indeed, how could it be otherwise? If no-ego is as far as we have gone, there can be no understanding of what is meant by the "cessation of self".

Without this turning point and the stage that lies beyond it, there can BE no cessation of self. What it takes, then, to eventually come to this definitive cessation (which I know as the "resurrected" condition) is the forfeiture of Nirvana or Beatitude in order to enter the marketplace where self (true Self, Divine self, phenomenal self – all of it), our whole humanity, is lived fearlessly and selflessly to its dire end, an end that no one suspects ahead of time. It is only in the marketplace that the arising self in its Realized Condition has the opportunity of fearlessly encountering every conceivable experience of the human condition. In contrast, in the egoic condition self continually protects itself from all risky, fearful or unpleasant encounters. It is these encounters in the Realized Condition, however, that are the sole preparation for the eventual no-self condition. No other path leads to this end.

Beyond the Turning Point

There is so much to say about life beyond the turning point, an entire volume could be dedicated to outlining this little known path. This path or stage is little known because it can only be fully understood in retrospect, or after it has come to an end, an end heralded by the no-self event. Having arrived at the turning point we see no path ahead; unlike those going through the transforming process (the cocoon), the realized man (the butterfly) has no path. Thus he is virtually on his own to find a way – perhaps find a way to accomplish his mission in life. This mission, however, may seem to elude him at every turn because, in truth, he does not yet know the true end that lies ahead. As it turns out, the true goal or mission of the Realized Condition is to live the human adventure as fearlessly and fully as possible; without this, no one realizes their total human potential. Everything else we do in the Realized condition is secondary to this.

It was at this turning point that Christ appeared in the market-place. Although this was the beginning of his active mission, it was not the beginning of his Divine mission, which was to reveal through his own experiences (or the living out of the Realized Condition) the experiential path we too must follow. As we know, the living out of the Realized condition brought Christ to his death, the true nature of which was the cessa-tion of Self, followed by the resurrected condition, and then the ascen-sion. This was not only Christ's path, but the path he revealed to all of us as the path we too must follow, and as such, it is every man's path. If this is not the path originally designed for every human being, then Christ came in vain. As I see it, this path is man's total psychological-spiritual passage through self or consciousness, a passage through the human condition, our very life. Nothing so throws us off course as the Gnostic notion that Christ's experiential path was an esoteric path meant for saints, mystics, and a few privileged souls, a path that only Christ knew, a path no other human being could know or experience. When Christ told us to "follow" he was speaking to everyone. There is no other path that goes all the way; all other paths stop short of ultimate Truth.

Although it is not my purpose in this essay to go into the mar-ketplace stage that follows the turning point, or to follow the Realized Condition from its beginning to its ending, I will nevertheless touch on two major aspects of this stage that have bearing on the eventual cessa-tion of self. The first has to do with the fact that the Realized Condition is devoid of ego satisfaction, and that despite the profound underlying joy and imperturbability of this state, from the purely human side there is no deep joy coming from the phenomenal world or conditional self. Thus life in the Realized Condition is anything but perfect; we are really not "home free", as they say. The great joy we know in this state is solely the Divine, all other joys of life being relatively superficial in that they do not go this deep. And since we need nothing for ourselves that we do not already have, the way ahead can only be one of continuous selfless giving. Since nothing in this world can add to the Realized Condition, and since there is no ego-satisfaction possible (self-satisfaction, that is), this is not an easy life, as so many people tend to believe. Someone once suggested we call this stage the "night of self" (to follow John of the Cross' "night of the spirit") because it is such a totally selfless stage, or because there is no deep sense of self-satisfaction in it. Those who do not move into the marketplace, however, cannot understand this; they do not know how it works. In a quiet secluded lifestyle, the egoless conditional self rarely arises; instead, it merely rests contented and unknowable in Divine being — and there sits the realizer for the rest of his earthly sojourn.

An illusion to be dispelled, then, is that life after coming to the Realized Condition is some kind of blissful play-play. Those who move into the marketplace will not share this view of the arising self. The tragedies, heartbreak, and crises of ordinary life cannot be easily dismissed as Divine play-play, especially when they happen to us and not to someone else. (St. Therese of the Child Jesus, however, often thought of herself as "Jesus' toy".) Christ, however, revealed no crazy behaviors, he played no games with others. Although he saw the Divine in all things and in all people, his vision and mission was not that of Divine play in this world. We all know how his life ended in the marketplace.

Besides a life of egoless giving, the path through common everyday life is imperative for another reason. Everyone who comes to the Realized Condition has yet a major hurdle to overcome, which is the temptation to regard himself as some form of Divine God-send, a rare, privileged soul perhaps, or an empowered being. This temptation can take innumerable forms, its most extreme form being the realizer's belief that he, himself, is the Absolute. For sure, this is the ultimate delusion.

One explanation for these temptations is that although in the transforming process we had to deal with the archetypes of the personal unconsciousness, it is only in the Realized Condition that we can actually encounter (face to face) the archetypes of the collective unconscious, which seem to be the specific powers of the Realized Condition. In other words, it is because the self has realized its oneness with the Divine that these powers or energies always appear in the form of some Divine guise, savior, prophet, healer, martyr, saint, superman, any universal or "collective archetype". These are more than the ordinary roles man plays in his daily life; these archetypes are the various energies of the unconscious self that man, in the Realized Condition, is tempted to believe are akin to the very energies and powers of the Absolute. When we believe these are the Divine's own powers, and claim them as our own (which is all they are, anyway), we can see how the next step is the self's claim to BE the Divine.

We have to remember that in the Realized Condition the "true" self is often regarded as the Christ-self, the deified self, the Atman, and so on; we are not dealing here with any ego-self. Thus because the unconscious self originates in the Divine Ground and seems to share Its very life and being, we can see how it might be possible to mistake self's own energies and intuitive powers for the energies and powers of the Divine. The Divine, of course, has no such comparable powers or energies. In contrast to these experiences, the Divine is a "still-point", an absolutely unmovable Ground.

At this point, the task ahead, the hurdle to be overcome is to consistently see through these arising energies and powers, see them as only the unconscious self and not mistake them for the Divine. If we do not firmly resist or see through these temptations (which are rarely even recognized as "temptations"), we may fall into delusion and spend our lives playing out a false and often dangerous role – always a power-play of some type – a role more dangerous to others than to ourselves. Needless to say, if we fall into this trap we can go no further with the journey. No one comes to the permanent cessation of self unless every possible archetype (conscious and unconscious) has been seen through and totally unmasked for what it is – namely, the unconscious self, its various energies, intuitions, feelings, roles, masks, and so on. This is not a one-temptation situation, however. When an archetype fails to convince us we are a God-send or have God-given powers under one guise, it simply tries another. Thus we must eventually make our way through the whole collective unconscious if we are ever to go beyond it or get to the other side of the unconscious, which other side is the Divine beyond all consciousness or self.

The greatest protection anyone can have against these arising archetypes or energies is life in the common marketplace. Here no one sees us as any different from anyone else, nor have we put ourselves up as different from anyone else. The shared commonalty of the human condition has a way of setting aside all pretensions to the contrary. The only true difference between the realized and the unrealized is the difference between life with the immature self (ego) and life with the mature self (egoless), and all this implies. To see it any other way, or to make any more out of this difference is a tragic mistake, and one that may cost us the rest of the journey. It is the same Divine in all people, and the day we see this we can never again put ourselves above another.

It is interesting to note that shortly after Christ first appeared in the marketplace, he was tempted in this manner, and that shortly before Buddha's enlightenment, he too underwent a similar ordeal. These were temptations to seize power, to claim themselves as some form of the Divine, or set themselves above or beyond the common lot of men. It was only after they had put down these temptations they moved toward the permanent cessation of self – the cessation of that entire system of consciousness, with its conscious and unconscious archetypes. In a word, they ultimately went beyond all that could be called self or consciousness.

This stage of the journey (which lies beyond the Realized Condition) is not really covered in our contemplative literature, and thus no one seems to have a true understanding of the unseen, unknown path that commences once we come this far. Our various religious paths give the impression that the Realized Condition is the end of the journey. If we take a careful look, however, we find indications of a stage coming after the Realized Condition in both Christianity and Mahayana Buddhism. The latter speaks of a stage where the enlightened Bodhisattva "puts off" Nirvana and moves into the marketplace.

Though I do not think this has been well understood or articulated as a necessary turning point for the eventual cessation of self, philosophically, at least, it indicates the way towards this event. Although this same turning point can be found in the Christian contemplative tradition (one way to put it, according to St. Teresa, is the point at which there is no longer any distinction between Martha and Mary, the active and contemplative life, and the taking on of an "apostolic mission"), yet it has never been recognized or understood for what it is, never been seen as an imperative means to yet a further end. Thus the turning point and marketplace has never been given any emphasis apart from being the point at which the contemplative begins his active mission, usually some apostolic or religious mission to spread the Truth.

The point, so far, has been to show that an unseen path exists beyond the Realized Condition, and that a major turning point is required before anyone can start out on that path. Few people realize what it takes to live without self or consciousness; they do not understand the enormous preparation required for such an event. As the mid-point of the total journey, the egoless Realized or Unitive Condition begins the preparation for the final event. To ultimately go beyond all consciousness, self or psyche, the Realized Condition must first be lived fully and fearlessly.

So the first movement of our journey is a movement inward that brings us to the cessation of the ego or the Realized Condition. Shortly after coming to this Realized Condition there occurs a major interior turning point that begins an expansive outward movement. In obedience to this movement, we enter the marketplace as an unknown among unknowns. This expansive, undauntable movement gradually brings us to the true end of our passage, to the cessation of self and the falling away of the Realized Condition. Briefly now, we will say something of this latter experience.

End of the Realized Condition

The unforeseeable surprise of the no-self event is not the cessation of the phenomenal conditional self, but rather the dissolution of the

Divine Ground or Being – the cessation of the entire Realized or Unitive Condition. Now, when there is no Divine Ground or Being, there can be nothing in it, nothing arising from it, nothing identical to it – no self, nothing. The "Transcendental Fire" (Mr. Free John) or "Living Flame of Love" (John of the Cross) has gone out and taken self with it. Without fuel, the fire goes out; without self, there is no Divine fire. The Divine fire has finally consumed the self, and when this consummation is complete, even the Divine dies – the fire goes out.

Since the Divine Ground or Being was our deepest experience of "life" and "being", its sudden disappearance is the instant withdrawal of the entire experience of "life" and "being". This is why it is a true death experience and one justifiably called the "death of God". Not only has the Christ-self or true, unconscious Self disappeared, but more importantly, Divine Being or Ground (Source, Father and Spirit) has disappeared. (They disappear together because they were one anyway).

Obviously the Divine "play" is over, the curtain has rung down on self – "the veil of the temple is rent", "the ridge-pole is split", "the house of self has collapsed". Whatever we may have thought self to be – the Absolute, the eternal soul, the individual psychological self, the unconscious, no-self, or whatever – it makes no difference now; every experience these labels expressed is gone. Nothing remains that could possibly be called "self" or "consciousness". Discovering the true nature of "what remains", however, will be the revelation that lies ahead, a revelation that IS the Resurrection; a resurrection, however, that cannot take place so long as any self remains.

The no-self event then, is far more than the cessation of the conditional, phenomenal, arising self with its experiential energies, emotions, feelings and so on. This event is the dissolution or extinction of the Divine Being or Ground from which and in which the unconscious self (and consequently the conscious, phenomenal self) had arisen. In this experience the self has been outshined or consumed without physical or sensory death. While the sensory, phenomenal world remains, it is a life devoid of self or consciousness, devoid of any experience of life or being that can only be compared to the walking dead. Now, finally, it can be known what self was. The true nature of self is known; self is the totality of consciousness or the psyche, the entire system from the unconscious to God-consciousness.

So long as we are living it or are it, the true nature of self or consciousness is a mystery, an unknown like the Divine itself. For this very reason consciousness or self is often mistakenly identified AS the Divine. Perhaps the final and most tenacious illusion to fall away is the insistent belief that our experience OF the Divine IS the Divine. Although consciousness or self arises from the Ground – as does everything that exists – consciousness or self is not the Ground. As long as consciousness remains, however, it touches the Ground at the point or center of its origination, the center of consciousness or self. This touch or contact at the point of origin is responsible for man's experience of "life" and "being", which is consciousness' most basic experience of itself, its very existence.

By contrast, however, the Divine is <u>non-experiential</u>. It lies outside and beyond the dimension and experience of consciousness. Since consciousness is man's primary faculty or medium of experiencing and knowing the Divine, whatever consciousness experiences is <u>always</u> and <u>only</u> itself. Thus consciousness or self is the experiencer, the experiencing, and the experienced. This means that the Divine is the <u>non-experiential cause</u> of our experience (of the Divine), while the <u>effect</u>, the experience itself, is only our self.

Initially it is a shock to realize that all our experiences of the Divine (or our Divine experiences) had only been experiences of our unconscious self, and not really the Divine. Yet this very disclosure makes it possible to finally understand consciousness or self, to understand that it is the essence of our humanity, and as such it is responsible for the whole human experience and dimension of existence. This same experience works to bring us to our ultimate destiny in the Divine, which has been the Divine plan from the beginning. Man, then, can be defined as "that" which is making a passage through consciousness or self; when the passage is finally completed, there is no consciousness or self remaining.

This is why we say that the ultimate and final fulfillment of consciousness is no-consciousness, and the ultimate fulfillment of self – is no-self.

The no-self event is the extinction of the Divine flame, the disappearance of the Divine Ground of Being, the explosion and dissolution of the Divine center of consciousness (all consciousness). What remains is final Truth or the Absolute. This Absolute, however, cannot be located, focused on, pinpointed or pointed to; it is all and everywhere and nowhere in particular. It is no one, no- thing, no "being" and is beyond the one and the many. It can no longer be experienced as within or without, immanent or transcendent. Consciousness was responsible for this dichotomy, these were its experiences and the understanding derived from them. Beyond consciousness there is no interior, spiritual, psychological life or experiences. Then it is realized that the Absolute known to consciousness and experienced by it, while indeed "God", yet as the Absolute, exists beyond all self or consciousness. It is, in Truth, "Godhead". Thus the final dissolution into the Godhead necessitates the death of God, the death of consciousness or self.

As a piece of philosophy this truth may sound familiar, but final Truth is not a philosophy and can never be known or grasped by the mind. Also, Absolute Truth is not an experience; rather, it is the ultimate dimension or condition of existence. Those who merely restate a philosophical truth or speak to us in terms of a particular experience can always be spotted for their contradictions and errors. Thus we read of those who state a philosophy or truth and yet make experiential statements indicating they have not realized that truth. One rather prevalent example is the realizer who, after telling us of the All and Everywhere of the Divine, then points to himself as the Divine! Or perhaps he points within, or to a specific experience. Either the realizer is not aware of his own contradictions, or he hopes no one else is. Still, some people so believe in this realizer they manage to find explanations for his contradictions. This is how errors arise and how the journey or path is made crooked. This is how our traditions eventually become watered down and go off in all directions until, finally, Truth is lost altogether.

Who Can We Trust? Who Has The Final Truth?

Although it is true to say that in the end, Final Truth must be the same for everyone, yet the degree to which Final Truth can be realized or even understood this side of the grave, has been a question within our various religious traditions. Many people claimed to have realized Final Truth; but then, anyone can make this claim. But who among them are we to believe? Is there any criterion for recognizing the difference between one who has authentically realized Final Truth and one who is only reiterating a piece of philosophy, theology, or some esoteric experience? How are we to know if the realizer has actually gone all the way and completed the passage or is merely speaking to us from a lesser stage or level? In a word, what would indicate that someone had come to the Final Condition or had been in it, and then returned to show us the path?

To answer these questions we would expect everyone to propose the realizer or revealer in whom they had implicit trust and faith. Thus I propose to look first and foremost to Christ, who I know, and then to Buddha, as I see him. We look to them to find the criterion by which to recognize someone who has been in the Final Condition, revealed its Truth and shown us the way. Although followers of Christ and Buddha usually take their founder's ultimate status for granted, and regard their truth and experiences as the criteria for all who follow, yet the criterion by which they themselves (Christ and Buddha) might be known, has not to my knowledge, been investigated or questioned. We want to pin-point the specific criterion by which Christ and Buddha may be recognized as the ultimate realizers or revealers.

Apart from our own belief, faith, or personal revelation, is there anything in their lives that would indicate their Truth, and the Truth they revealed to us? In answer, the criterion I propose is somewhat unusual because it does not focus on their Final Beatific or Nirvanic Condition, much less on things blissful and ecstatic. Rather, it focuses on their particular experiential perspective regarding man and this world at the time they first became known to us, or first appeared in the marketplace. We must start, however, from their own beginnings, which were different, although I regard their endings as identical. To arrive at their mutual criterion then, I will briefly say something of their passage.

We have already spoken of the non-egoic, transformed or Realized Condition and the imperative turning point that begins the unseen path to a more perfect Final Condition. It was at this turning point that Christ first appeared in the marketplace, and Buddha, not satisfied with the Realized Condition, went off in search of a more perfect Final Truth. The next major event was the death and resurrection of Christ, and the grueling ordeal that preceded Buddha's enlightenment. In both cases there was the death of self followed by the Resurrected Condition (or Nirvana), a Condition which was obviously compatible with continued physical existence. Although Christ primarily spoke to us from the Realized Condition <u>before</u> his death, and Buddha taught from the Nirvanic (or resurrected) Condition <u>after</u> his an-Atman event, yet Christ wordlessly <u>manifested</u> in his death and resurrection the same truth <u>articulated</u> by Buddha. Following that event was Christ's Ascension and Buddha's Paranirvana – the onset of the ultimate Final Divine Condition – which was obviously <u>incompatible</u> with continued earthly existence. If the Final Divine Condition were compatible with man's earthly condition there would be no need for physical dissolution. Obviously man's final destiny is not in this world.

Since we have already said something of the no-self event and the truths discovered through this death and resurrection, we must now say something of the Ascension experience, which experience may also have been Buddha's "Paranirvana". It seems Buddha recognized the onset of this experience because he had predicted the time of his death, thus indicating prior familiarity with it. This experience is actually the revelation of the most Final Truth of all. Although neither Christ nor Buddha left us a description of this last earthly experience, Christ's manifestation of it speaks eloquently for its experiential reality – namely, his physical body evaporating into air, literally vaporizing.

Here the physical body experiences a dissolution into what might be called "Divine Air", as if this Divine Air had been released within every cell of the body or that the Divine Air was Itself the ultimate final reality of the physical body – the reality of all physical bodies. This experience is not the departure of a spirit or soul out of the body – nothing leaves the body. Rather, the Divine is revealed AS the reality of the body, the underlying mystery of all physical matter. (We might add that this experience has nothing in common with the much earlier experience of out-shining, translation, Bhavasamadhi or Beatific Condition; the difference is incomparable. The Ascension experience pervades every cell of the body).

What is learned from this experience is that the body and all matter dwells eternally in the Divine Condition and are not different from it. To some extent we came upon this truth before (between death and resurrection), in a different context, however, when encountering the dire void of all form.[8] This void-of-voids (Christ's "descent to the dead") was followed by the realization that the void IS absolute and thus form being void, Form IS Absolute. (I believe there is something similar to this in Buddhism). But next, in the Ascension (or Paranirvana) event, there is the further revelation of the Divine's Essence, which, as best can be put, is that matter or Eternal Form (the Logos or divine Christ) dwells in the ultimate Divine Condition.

This Eternal Divine Form, then, is the true meaning of the Mystical Body of Christ (and possibly the Triple body of Buddha – I am not sure of the proper term), which I regard as the Greatest of Great Realities and the ultimate Truth of Christ. But this event is not all. We have not yet come to the final criterion for recognizing someone who has been in this Unnamable Condition and either returned from it (as in Buddha's case), or initially came out of it (Christ's case) in order to reveal the path to us.

After the on-set of Ascension or Paranirvana there are two ways to go. Consciousness or self has already fallen away and now, either the senses permanently drop away, in which case, this Eternal Condition be-

---

[8] See Bernadette Roberts, *What is Self?*.

comes the Final Condition (Christ's case), or, there is a return to the resurrected or Nirvanic Condition (Buddha's case). But whether there is the initial move out of the Final Condition (Christ) or a returning from it (Buddha), the experience is the same; it is the most terrible and devastating of all possible experiences. Having to leave the Divine Condition and enter the world is so terrible and horrific the only word for it is "God-Awful" – meaning it is Awful for the Divine, and completely beyond man's capacity to withstand or understand. This coming out or down from the Absolute Condition into the human condition is the experience of Incarnation (not the same as re-incarnation where there has been some pre-existing being).

By sheer contrast to the Ultimate Divine Condition, earthly existence is a living hell, the world so ugly and hideous by comparison that the senses alone could not bear the burden. What then makes human earthly existence possible? The answer: consciousness or self makes it possible; it is possible only because consciousness veils the Ultimate Condition. This way man does not know and cannot see what he is missing, thus he settles for what he has, settles for what he sees, knows and experiences, settles for this world. Without consciousness, man or human existence would not be possible.

This initial coming into the world or return from the Ascension experience is the event and experience of Incarnation. In the case of Christ this was the initial putting off or coming out of the Absolute Condition; in the case of the Buddha it was a return from the Absolute Condition back to the resurrected/Nirvanic condition. This is the only true redemptive experience or act there is.

As a God-Awful experience it is a "God-Awful" act and one that cannot be compared to any other redemptive act or sacrifice on the part of man. This is a totally choiceless event – the dimension of the Absolute is beyond all our notions of willing, choosing, decision-making and so on. Beyond self or consciousness there is no choice, free will or any such acts. We cannot compare a Divine Act to an act of human will.

After this God-Awful return or descent from the Final Condition, what might be the first thing that such a one would say to us? "All is suffering," says Buddha in his first Noble Truth. Most people, of course, do not know that they are suffering and thus his view of the human condition has often been regarded as pessimistic. But if people do not know where Buddha is coming from, much less have they understood where Christ is coming from. Whence Christ's apocalyptic perspective on this world and his assurance the Kingdom of God is definitely <u>not</u> in this world? Christ and Buddha's view of man's condition has no other source or explanation than the Final Divine Condition from which they came.

Traversing the unspeakable void between the Divine and human condition was the God-Awful experience out of which arose their vision of the world, a vision of dire contrasts. Yet it was this unusual vision or perspective that gave them their saving mission and its urgency, and gave us, in turn, the paths to Final Truth that we know. This was the origin of the devastating world view with which Christ and Buddha began their earthly mission. They did not speak to us of Divine bliss, ecstatic states, radiant light or any of that stuff, rather, they spoke to us of our present condition of suffering and the way out of it, one path leading to the cross, the other path leading to the void; both going in the same direction.

Despite their devastating vision and difficult paths, however, Christ and Buddha were the most compassionate of human beings. They were wounded to their depths by the plight of man in sheer contrast to his Ultimate destiny. The charity and compassion that sprang from these wounds is not that of the ordinary man who experiences pity and sympathy when he sees others suffering. Rather it sprang from the disparity between man's Final Condition and his present earthly condition. To Christ and Buddha suffering was everything short of the Final Divine Condition; it was man suffering even when he does not know it – even when he thinks he is happy.

In a word, suffering IS the whole human condition. No one can know this fact or live with it, however, who has not first known the Final

Absolute Condition and emerged from that Condition into the relative hell of the human condition in order to save us all.

So the final criterion, then, of one who has gone all the way, knows Final Truth and reveals the true path, is one who speaks from the God-Awful experience of Incarnation. This particular perspective or vision cannot be found at any point in the journey because it is not part of the journey. This perspective arises prior to the journey as in the case of Christ, or once the journey has been completed as in the case of Buddha. Unlike others who speak to us in glowing terms of the Final Condition and bait us with blissful experiences, admitting no grueling ordeals that will stretch the human limits, Christ and Buddha revealed a radically different path that would have us put aside even our most blissful experiences of the Divine, put aside the entire self in fact, not merely the ego-self. Nothing short of absolute cessation of self (and/or Self) is capable of coming upon Final Truth and the Ultimate Divine Condition. Those who say otherwise have obviously fallen short somewhere. So the criterion for recognizing one who has completed the path is not the generally expected account of divine bliss; rather, it is the account indicative of a God-Awful experience and a perspective on the human condition that cannot be had from any other dimension of existence.

Now we have only briefly touched upon the major milestones of the completed passage. It would take a number of books to fill in the details and do justice to what has been said here. Books, however, take time, and since we cannot wait for time, we offer these few pages to those presently searching for Final Truth, or searching for those who have realized it and can reveal it to us. If Christ and Buddha went all the way, if their experiences or manifestations were the revelation of Final Truth and the revelation of every man's path, then we need look no further; we need only look deeper. Although other contemplatives, adepts or realizers can lend helpful insights to the journey, they each speak from a different perspective and stage of the journey. When it comes to revealing the entire journey from beginning to end, however, we must look beyond the individual realizer to the path he followed, look to those who revealed the path in the first place. Christ and Buddha reveal and validate the path for all who follow, they alone provide the certitude of the completed journey. Thus we must take our validation directly from them and not from those who follow them – let us beware of following a follower lest we get so far back in the line-up we lose sight of the Revealer.

Conclusion

For those who have adopted Mr. Free John's paradigm as representative of the complete path, and his seventh stage as the final degree of truth a human being can realize, we know in advance all the objections that will be raised by the foregoing presentation. We know how it is possible for some people, whether in good faith or not, to twist and turn other people's experiences to their own persuasion by misinterpreting them in the name of "linguistic differences", or otherwise attempt to equalize all experiences in the name of "different perspectives". By so doing, they can take almost any experience (other people's experience, that is) and fit it into their own criteria or paradigm thereby eliminating that experience. They eliminate it by making it over into something it is not and never was. How this works is very subtle and clever, yet people have been doing it for centuries; there is nothing new here. The problem, however, is that the average reader and follower is not aware of how this works, and thus he is taken in without a blink. But if we can understand how this works we will have discovered the secret of how religious paths gradually become twisted, misinterpreted and watered down until finally, Ultimate Truth is no longer accessible. When that happens, setting the record straight or breaking through centuries of embedded error, ignorance and prejudice becomes an impossible task. About all we can do then is ask for an intelligent, objective, open mind, and call upon the courage of the intrepid seeker to settle for nothing less than Absolute Truth.

For many people it is difficult to face the fact that the reason Buddhism is a separate religion from Hinduism is due to the enormous difference between the cessation of the ego-self and the much further cessation of the Realized True or Divine Self. The truth discovered following these two events, as well as their ensuing conditions and perspectives, is totally different. The problem is that no one can know this difference until he has encountered <u>both</u> events. There is no convincing someone who has come to the first event (cessation of ego) that there is still a long way to go. Indeed, for those in the Vedanta tradition the eventual falling away of the Divine Self or Atman would appear to be a departure from Hindu truth and tradition, which departure, as I see it at least, is precisely where Buddhism begins. The result of trying to reconcile these two different events, however, usually ends with the truth of Buddhism (no Divine Self or Atman, no "God" even) being totally reinterpreted or put down as a mere semantic difference or a difference of perspective. It is a great error to believe that by interpreting the cessation-of-Self as the cessation-of-ego (Jiva, ahankara, little atman or separate self) we have resolved the differences. Once we believe this, then the true Buddhist extinction of Self becomes lost entirely; it is wiped off the map of the journey, explained away, and becomes non-understandable in its own right – its own ultimate Truth.

But if centuries of attempts have been unable to set the record straight, there is little hope of doing so now, more especially in this day and age when we are asked in the name of ecumenical oneness to overlook all differences and point out only our similarities. Indeed, as soon as one illuminates the critical point where similarities must fall away, they are labeled as prejudiced, insufficiently realized, antagonistic, uncharitable and so on. As one writer aptly noted, however, while pointing out similarities may be "interesting", pointing out differences may be "enlightening". Unfortunately few people see it this way. Yet for those who know the difference between no-ego and no-self there is enlightenment.

If there is any hope of distinguishing no-ego from no-self this hope is centered on Western consciousness. Western psychology has already made a vital distinction between the ego and the "true" self (unconscious self), and thus it may be prepared to get hold of the difference between the falling away of the ego and the much later falling away of the true unconscious self and its Realized Condition. If Eastern religions can get this difference straight they will have a truly new beginning in the West; if not, the East will only have translated centuries of errors and disputes to Western territories. We in the West want the truth of the East, but not its errors, illusions and superstitions. The West may not be prepared to accept the truth of the possibility of the final cessation of self, but to even begin to understand it is all we can ask, and perhaps, all that may really be necessary. In this matter, then, my hope is set on the West, not on the East.

Finally, with regard to Mr. Free John, I think he has made an important contribution to our Western understanding of the Eastern Realized Condition. Nowhere in my reading of Hinduism's highest realization (what we have called in these pages the "Realized Condition") did I come upon any mention of the continued arising of the phenomenal self. For the most part Hinduism denies that any phenomenal self-experience remains in their highest Realized Condition – "Satcitananda", as some call it. Carl Jung regarded this Hindu denial as nonsense and argued that the ego – or what he regarded as the ego – was not dissolved after realizing the Self. (For Jung, of course, Self is the unconscious; for the Hindu, Self is Atman.)

Although I do not accept either Jung's or Mr. Free John's definition of "ego", I nevertheless agree that in the Realized Condition (certainly in the Christian Unitive Condition) the phenomenal self-experience remains intact and continues to arise. Since Mr. Free John claims to have realized the highest Hindu state or condition, he therefore verifies what other Westerners have always believed about the Hindu Realization, namely, that the phenomenal self remains and does not disappear or cease. Still, the Hindu pundit will argue to the contrary and quite possibly he has in mind a Condition entirely different than the one envisioned by Carl Jung or articulated by Mr. Free John. This is something to keep in mind because it could be that true Hinduism has yet to come West. So far its Western translation seems to be little more than a kind of theosophical, mythical, Gnostic, new age mish-mash. Once again, we need exacting experiential accounts from those contemplatives thoroughly dedicated, educated, practiced, and steeped in their own tradition. To pick and choose, or to put together our own path is the surest way to a dead end, and no Truth.

/ 3 /

NONDUALITY

NON-DUALITY

Some people have asked if the term "nondual" defined the no-Self condition. The short answer is "No". Beyond Self there is no "one" or "oneness", no "union" or "unity", nothing to label at all. Beyond Self the term "nonduality" has no meaning. Those who understand the true nature of Self or Consciousness and its cessation, would know this and not ask the question.

It seems "nondual" is a Hindu term said to express Hinduism's final realization or enlightenment. Premised on the central Hindu monistic belief that Brahman (or the Absolute) is all that exists, it follows that the ultimate realization of Brahman could not allow for multiplicity or duality – lest the conclusion not verify the premise. Those who do not share this monistic belief, of course, would not be expected to come to this same nondual conclusion.

We will look in vain to find Hinduism's ultimate enlightenment (nonduality) in the monotheistic religions. The monotheist's particular revelation of God is different, it does not share Hinduism's same goal or ultimate realization. Those for whom realizing nonduality is the final goal have obviously adopted the Hindu belief system, thus they seek the same Hindu enlightenment or nonduality. For the monotheist, however, nonduality has no meaning.

Whence the term "nondual"?

Though we may not share the Hindu belief system, we nevertheless question the meaning of "nondual" as the expression of Hinduism's ultimate enlightenment. "Nondual" is a curious term because if it is supposed to mean "one" (the "one" or "oneness" of all that exists, Brahman in other words), it fails to do so. All the term means is "not two". Nondual thus implies the negation of two – but what two? Father Keating said nondual meant "not one, not two", but how could "not one" mean "one"? Actually it means nothing. It might even mean three.

We also question why someone who realized Brahman would not just say so; say he realized Brahman or the Oneness of All – something like that? Why would he say he realized nonduality or "not two-ness"? And even if he realized "nothing", why would he call it "nondual"? In short, I fail to see how the term conveys a piece of enlightenment. If anything, it speaks more of a conceptual overlay, a descriptive after-thought, a term intended to resolve a dispute as to the final state being one or two. Thus it might be asked "who" realized Brahman? Was this Brahman's own realization or was it "you" who realized Brahman? Although both instances involve a duality, the question to be resolved is usually focused on the duality of the realizer and the Realized – "you" and Brahman, that is.

In itself the term "nondual" implies some form of duality, but a duality to be finally negated. If no duality actually existed, there would be no duality to negate – you cannot, after all, negate something that does not exist. So to understand the term it behooves us to find out what, exactly, are the "two" to be negated. Unless we first know the true nature of this duality we cannot hope to understand its negation. So the question is: what is the nature of this duality, and what is the "one" discovered as a result of this negation?

As to how a dispute could have arisen over a "realization" being either dual or nondual, a simple example might be the experience of a divine Presence within ourselves, a divine indwelling "in the cave of the heart", as a Hindu might put it. This experience is obviously dual. For the divine to be **in** us – or in anything – requires someone or something for the divine to be **in**. Just as water in a vase or air in a balloon requires the existence of vase or balloon, so too, an experience of the divine within ourselves requires a self to experience this. Even if the vase and balloon are empty, someone or something is required to experience this "empti-ness".[1] After having described this experience to someone, suppose they

---

[1] Here I am reminded of Buddhism's "emptiness" or Sunyata. Something has to exist in order to be empty, or to experience emptiness. Just as the term "full" is relative to its container, so too is the term "empty". Take away the container and

said to us, "thou art that". Does this mean **you are** the Absolute? Or does it mean **you are your experience** of the Absolute? Because this saying obviously has several interpretations, it warrants a closer look.

Thou art That

It could be said the Upanishad saying ("thou art that") opened a can of worms. Like every identity statement, it is inherently dual. Thus there must be a "thou" to be "that" – no different than saying "this is that" or "they are the same", etc. Without a duality, no identity statement can be made, including "thou art that". Although some people take this to mean you ("thou") are Brahman ("that"), and conclude they are one and the same, yet this may not have been the original meaning. It could just as well be pointing out the error of assuming the **experience** of Brahman **is** Brahman, whereas the truth is: **you** are **your experience of** Brahman. In other words, what thou art **is** "that" experience.

Understood in this sense, the statement is true because 'that' in our self that experiences Brahman (or God) **is** our self or consciousness. Thus we are not only the experiencer, but the experience itself. We are even 'what' we experience in that all experiences are mediated by self or consciousness. Thus the experience, experiencer and experienced are one and the same, they are our self, but they are not Brahman, God, or the divine. In other words, this was not the divine's own experience – the divine did not suddenly realize you! No, it was you who realized the divine. So when "thou art that" is understood to mean you are Brahman (or God, let's say), either the statement is false or we have failed to grasp its true meaning – namely, **you are your experience** of Brahman. Clearly the experience of a divine-indwelling is our own human experience of Brahman or God. Thus any experience of a divine **within** requires a duality of the experiencer and the divine.

Unfortunately, the truth **"you are your experience"** (of Brah-

---

there is nothing to be empty. There's no getting away from the implied duality of "emptiness".

man or God) is such a difficult truth to accept and understand, most people don't. It seems only when there is no "self" – defined anyway you like – this truth can be disclosed. (The disclosure of this truth is actually the big shock of the no-Self event). Until such time, man will always regard his experiences of Brahman or God to **be** Brahman or God, whereas this <u>experience is only our self</u>. While God is truly Present **in** us and the **Cause** of our experience – be it bliss or whatever – yet the experiential **effect** is our own, it is we, ourselves, who experience God. Thus the experience is the **effect**, but not the Cause. As said before, this is not God's experience, indeed, God has no such experiences – no self or consciousness at all. It is because people believe what they experience is God they think God is bliss, love, light, power – whatever the experience may be – whereas the experience is just themselves.

A practical example of this phenomena I have often used is being stuck with a needle. Because you experience the needle does not mean you are the needle. While the needle is the cause of your experience, the experience of the needle is you, certainly it's not the needle's own experience! In truth, everything and anything consciousness or self experiences **is itself**. Were there no self or consciousness there would be no experiences at all. Why? Because first and foremost self or consciousness is **experience itself**. Without it there would be no "experience" of being, life, energy, and so on, much less any experience of an Absolute – Brahman or God.

Atman

If the terms Brahman and Atman mean the same thing or there is no distinction between them, then the terms are interchangeable. Traditionally, however, Atman is defined as a Universal Soul common to everything that exists. Thus there is no ontological distinction between souls – plants, animals and humans are the one same soul. To realize Atman, then, means to realize this universal soul, realize that what gives you life is the same that gives all things life. In this case "thou art that" either means you are Atman, the soul (same soul as the flea and cow), or else you are your experience of soul. Either way you are definitely "that", a soul – call it Atman or universal soul, they mean the same thing. Yet, somehow, realizing one's soul does not strike us as a very profound piece of enlightenment. After all, what is more basic or obvious than one's life force – the soul? To upgrade this realization, however, some have affirmed that Atman is Brahman without distinction. Given this understanding, your soul – which is what you are – is Brahman. In this case "thou art that" would mean your soul (Atman) is Brahman. Now to say Atman is Brahman – or say anything is Brahman – requires a duality. Like every identity statement there has to **be something** to be "this" or "that". While no one would question the statement "Brahman is Brahman", yet to say "Atman is Brahman" poses the question of whether this implies a true distinction or a duality. Even if both are held to be divine but distinct, a way to express this might be "not one and not two" – hence, "nondual". The term is thus a compromising resolution to the quandary of the true relationship not only between Atman **and** Brahman, but between Atman **as** Brahman.

Since the term "nondual" could not have arisen without Atman – or beyond Atman – it had to arise **because** of Atman (Soul), more especially the realization of its oneness either **with** Brahman or **as** Brahman. The question is: which is it?   Is this the Soul's (Atman's) oneness with Brahman, or is Atman (Soul) Brahman itself?   Is this state of oneness dual or non-dual?   If the realized and realizer are **both** Brahman then this would be Brahman's own realization and enlightenment – which doesn't say much for Brahman I'm afraid. As it stands, however, had this realization of oneness not suggested a duality then the term "nondual" would not have arisen.   It is only because a duality is inherent in this realization the term came into play.   So the quandary is whether this state is the oneness of two or a solitary one.[2]   The term "nondual" attempts to satis-

---

[2] We can understand avoiding the term "one" in reference to God, the Absolute or Brahman. The term "one" either evokes a numerical one, like one-among-many, or worse, it suggests a solitary "monad" or self-enclosed entity. Such a view of the Ultimate Mystery (as Fr. Keating calls "It") is unworthy of any of our religions. Even the term "mono-theism" is misleading in this matter.

fy two sides of an equation. It is the acknowledgment of the oneness of two – the oneness of a duality.

Obviously the distinction between Atman and Brahman is critical. If Atman is just another name for Brahman then we can dismiss Atman. It tells us nothing about Brahman we do not already know. It was not for nothing, however, Hinduism made (or saw) a distinction between Atman and Brahman. If Brahman is the One Absolute or sole Being, then what, we ask, is Atman if not the **soul's experience of Brahman?** This truth, however, can only be verified if Atman falls away (all self, that is), beyond which there cannot even be the experience of Brahman – no experience, experiencer or experienced at all. Had Atman been Brahman (Absolute or God) it could not have ceased to exist. So what was Atman, what had it been? Obviously it had been the soul or self's experience of Brahman or God. This affirms more than a mere distinction between Atman and Brahman, this affirms that in the end, there is no Atman at all – no "one", "oneness", and no "nonduality".

It is unfortunate the Sanskrit term for "Atman" was translated by Westerners as "Self ". Because of this, Westerners understand Hinduism's universal soul to **be** self, thus Atman and self have become two terms for the same thing – a Universal Soul, that is. A knowledgeable Indian friend, however, told me the Sanskrit "Atman" had nothing to do with the West's notion of "self ", rather, it referred to the soul (which is **not** self) as Brahman's "manifestation" in man, or man's experience of Brahman. If Hinduism had not made a distinction between Atman as Soul (now the Western Self) and the Absolute or Brahman, we would not have these "dual" terms to deal with.

But as said, the only way to find out if Atman and Brahman are the same – dual or nondual – would be to take away Atman (no-Self); drop it from the equation and see what remains. With no Atman, then Brahman (known and experienced by Atman) is also gone. While (theoretically) Brahman would remain, there would be no one, no Atman (soul or self) to **experience** Brahman. So "who" could tell us what remains or tell us about Brahman? For sure it would never cross one's mind to call this (no-Atman) situation "nondual" or even "one". No matter how Atman is defined – as one's true self, a universal soul, one's experience of Brahman, or a mysterious unknown – Atman is **not** Brahman.

Here I must interject: solely for the sake of discussion and comparison I have equated the Hindu Brahman with the Christian God. To be honest, however, I do not think this can be done. Brahman is understood in the monistic sense as the sole Being that exists, at least all we know exists – or perhaps all we don't know exists. This is not what I know as "God", nor could I equate "Atman" with God. While I can grant Atman to be "that" unknown aspect of soul and psyche that experiences God and to which God alone is privy, yet if Atman is understood as universal soul, God, or self, there is no truth to it. God is not everything that exists, not a universal soul, and not any self – however it is defined. While God is one with all this, yet "this" is not God – "thou art **not** that" – in the end, there is no "thou" to be "that".

I recently heard another definition of Atman. I was told Atman meant God-Immanent (or God within us) and Brahman meant God-Transcendent (or God beyond us). Clearly, however, this is a Christian interpretation of Immanent Holy Spirit and Transcendent Father, which is not, however, the Hindu understanding of these terms.

If Brahman is all that exists, then what is there for Brahman to "transcend"? Nothing! At best it could be said Brahman only transcends mere "appearances". This is not, of course, what monotheists regard as God-Transcendent, or as God existent beyond all that exists – beyond creation that is. But for the moment, to find out what remains beyond mere appearances, let us say we could eliminate all that "appears". Not only would we be gone, there would be nothing and no one left to see, experience or realize anything.

No, the body (matter) is not just something that "appears"; without it, there wouldn't be a soul alive. What "appears" is all part of the mystery and glory of God. So instead of dismissing anything as a mere appearance we have to find out its true nature. To dismiss anything is mere avoidance.

There is another possibility to account for the distinction between Atman and Brahman. In purely Christian terms, this distinction might be between:

God-as-He-is-in-Himself and God-as-He-is-in-ourselves.

Thus we might say Brahman is God-in-Himself and Atman is God-**in-ourselves**. In neither case, however, does this make us God or Brahman. But this distinction would at least define Atman as God **in us** (in our soul) and not merely Atman as **our experience** of God – as noted previously. Though both definitions of Atman would be correct, neither one, however, is Hinduism's view or understanding of Atman as Universal Soul, Brahman, or Self. Then too, if we define Atman as "God-within-ourselves" this requires the existence of an individual person or self for God to be in – an obvious duality. In this case, if one were to come upon Brahman-as-it-is-solely-in-Itself, this would require the negation of **both** Atman (or God "within") as well as the one who experienced Atman – your self, that is. With no self to experience Atman or God within, Atman is no more, simply because there is no one left for Atman to **be in**.

The point is: there has to be "something" or "someone" for Atman to be in, someone who experiences this indwelling. Take away this someone and who or what is left to speak of Atman? No one! This, of course, would be a true instance of a duality ultimately negated – the duality of the individual self and God (Atman). It was negated in order to come upon Brahman (or God) solely as-it-is-in-Itself and no longer as God-(Atman)-is-in-our-self. Because this means going **beyond** Atman (Atman defined as "God in our self") this situation is not to be found in Hinduism. Thus so long as Atman is defined **as** Brahman or the two are equated, there is no possibility of going beyond Atman no matter how it is defined. Indeed, no-Atman or no-Self is foreign to Hinduism.

Since the negation of Atman and all self would be exceedingly problematic for Hinduism, to avoid the problem one need only deny a true distinction or difference between Brahman and Atman. With no difference between Brahman-as-it-is-in-Itself, and Brahman-as-It-is-in-ourselves (Atman) there would be no duality to negate. After negating this distinction, however, there is still more to be negated before one could affirm only Brahman exists. There must also be the negation of individual souls and selves. The idea you are an individual soul and self must be dismissed, regarded as non-existent, nothing more than an error in your thinking. Although conceptually, at least, negating everything but Brahman may be easy to do, these negations fly in the face of the whole human experience. If one honestly believes that Brahman **is** man's true human experience, then it is Brahman who experiences itself as an individual soul and self, so why deny or negate it? If Brahman is the errant thinker and feeler, then what is there to correct – or did Brahman get it wrong?

Negating everything but Brahman poses the question of who or what becomes enlightened; who realizes Brahman? Evidently it can only be Brahman! But if Brahman knows itself as Atman then this self-reflection is as dual as any human self-reflection. It is an anthropomorphic view of Brahman based, no doubt, on man's self-reflecting mind.[3] But how is it Brahman's self-reflection could be regarded as a piece of enlightenment when Brahman has always known itself as Atman? Impossible. No, this can only be a piece of enlightenment to someone who didn't know it, someone who had to learn it, someone who had to tell us Atman is how Brahman knows itself. If no such individual existed then the notion Atman-is-Brahman is but an intellectual belief with no experiential verification possible. Just because someone says "this is that" or "Brahman is Atman" doesn't make it so.

So whether we call "that" in us that experiences God, "Atman", "Self ", "Soul", the "true-Self ", or some other term, it makes no differ-

---

[3] We have a similar problematic idea in Christianity, namely, some theologian' s idea that the Logos (Son) is the Transcendent's (Father's) self-reflection. God spare us these anthropomorphic ideas of God – and Brahman too!

ence (in the end it all goes down anyway), as long as we do not mistake ourselves for God – mistake "thou" for "that". The bottom line is that while we may think our experience of God is truly God, yet the experience itself is only our self. As we have seen, there are two quite different understandings of the Hindu dictum "thou art that". Although Hinduism denies an individual self, yet if this were true, there would be no 'thou' to be 'that'. If the individual self is a mental error or a mere appearance then what 'thou' art is "apparently" an illusion. Art thou really "that"?

Individual Self

I've often wondered why Hinduism and Buddhism deny the existence of an individual soul and self. What could be more obvious than the uniqueness of each human being? This endless variety illustrates the wonder of our One-on-one creation. But now, as best I can make out from the books, Hinduism only denies that the soul is a totally separate entity, a self-existent being separate from the Absolute. But in this they are correct. Christianity also holds this to be true, only without denying the existence of individual souls. All created beings are "contingent", their existence totally dependent on God's Being, and because of this, God is truly one with each of us and all that exists – such is Christian teaching. The fact we are contingent beings, however, does not lead to the conclusion of a universal soul, no individual self, nor that God is everything that exists. The fact of our natural oneness with God neither makes us God nor robs us of a God-given individuality. We are like dependent babes in the womb, dependent yet separate.

To understand the Eastern position regarding an individual self we have to remember Brahman is not a Creator, it never created a thing, but IS everything. To preserve this belief there can be no individuals to suggest any true multiplicity or duality. Thus the great error to be overcome is "thinking" you are an individual soul and self, an error, we might add, said to take thousands of reincarnations to dispel – or so they "think". (Thinking one will be reincarnated is another illusion to dispel). Giving this view our best thought: if it is true no individuals (souls and selves) exist, then it follows no true individual or person has ever realized nonduality! A mere appearance cannot realize this. Evidently this leaves only Brahman to become enlightened – which doesn't say much for Brahman I'm afraid. To explain Brahman's ignorance in this matter I read somewhere that our lives are either a play going on in Brahman's mind or he is just dreaming. (We can imagine how critics would rate Brahman's show!) But who can take this anthropomorphic notion seriously? It sounds like somebody ran out of ideas.

It would seem that to assure us we are not separate from the Absolute, Hinduism goes to the extreme and holds everything to be the Absolute or Brahman. Based on this belief, man cannot possibly be an individual soul and self, he only thinks he is. In reality, he is none other than Brahman itself. Despite the radical difference between God as the **Source** of our being (Christianity) and Brahman as the **sole** Being (Hinduism), the spiritual goals are similar in that both seek an abiding awareness of oneness with God or Brahman. In the Christian journey this abiding awareness is nothing we achieve or realize on our own, but is the result of God's revelation as the abiding Center of our being. Thus having made the descent into the nothingness of our own being – the "nothingness" from which we were created – at bottom we encounter God, the Source of our life and existence, the "Ground of our being" and all being. It would never occur to someone who knew, saw or encountered this divine Center to regard themselves **as** 'that' Center – the Ground and Source of all life. No one who has truly encountered this divine Center could possibly regard It as their self! If anyone said to us, "thou art that", it would be dismissed out of hand as coming from a non-witness. Such a revelation not only bypasses one's belief system, terminology, and individual experience, but as pure gift, having no hand in it, there is also no mistaking It. If we know anything at all, we know we are not "that" which has been revealed, **not** the Source of our own being.

Turning to the Hindu realization, if what is realized as the divine Center is Atman – the universal soul or self – then where, we ask, is Brahman or God? No one speaks of Brahman as this divine Center. Yet if we realize Atman as the center of being, this is but the realization of one's soul, a universal Soul (also called "Self"), which is not, evidently, the realization of Brahman or the Absolute, and certainly not God. What I find curious in Hinduism is that we hear of no love for Brahman, no praying to, or erecting temples to Brahman. It seems Brahman is the ultimate of the impersonal and helpless – doesn't give a fig about man – which explains why one has to "realize" everything on their own. Were something "given", it would be attributed to one of the gods, but never to Brahman.

In Christianity, revelation of the divine Center is not the revelation of soul or self, but of God alone. Although the "experience" itself (like everything we experience) is our self, yet 'what' has been revealed is not our self. This revelation of God's abiding union or oneness with soul and self, neither makes us God, nor God us – "thou art **not** that". From here on, however, there is no I-Thou consciousness, but We-Us.

We can no longer think, "I am", but rather "We are". God is our other half, the fulfillment of soul and self, the completion of our humanity. In the depths of our self, we are a run-on with the divine, which does not make us divine, but rather, like Christ, we are eternally one with God, and as such we live out the human adventure. Here we have encountered the beginnings of Christ's own **dual** nature: fully divine and fully human.

A Nondual Center?

We cannot speak of the "center" (of anything) unless there is a circumference. Something has to exist to have a center, otherwise the term "center" wouldn't exist. Not only does every physical body have a center, but the soul and self as well. By definition a center is a fixed point around which some activity is going on. Although we may search to find this fixed center or still-point in ourselves, even if we think we have found it, it won't last, we can't stay with it.

The marvel of the great Dark Night and, afterward, the Unitive Revelation, is that this whole drama takes place in the depths of our cen-

ter, the very center of our soul and self. When this center is revealed as
God it becomes the divine Center from which we live, move, and have
our being, there being no other way to live.

We can only speak of a divine Center because we ourselves are
its circumference – body, soul and self. If we were not discrete beings or
entities there could be no circumference and, consequently, no center.
Even if we thought of ourselves as ink-blots in the universe, we could still
draw a circle around the blot to find its center. And just as there is no
center without a circumference, so too there is no circumference without
a center. Take away one – be it center or circumference – and both are
gone. The point is that while we might regard the center as singular or
nondual, actually it isn't. For there to be a center there has to **be** a circumference, thus everything that exists is a dual set-up of center and circumference.

With the revelation of the divine as the Center of being – center
of our soul and self – this Center becomes the fixed Still Point from
which we receive our life and being, a center around which we move and
live. But what, we ask, is the true nature of this circumference that lives
from the Center and moves round It? It is our self, our soul, our body, it
is everything we are, **but** the divine Center. Not a speck of self or soul is
that divine Center.

Although we may think of this Center as nondual or standing
alone with no circumference, yet with no circumference there would be
no one to be aware of any center. Even if we counter with the notion the
Center is aware of Itself, we are back to a duality, only this time, a divine
duality, a divine reflexive-mind or self-awareness.

This, of course, is just another anthropomorphic projection onto
the divine. While the Center generates the reflexive-mind, It is not the
mind or reflexive-mechanism. Strictly speaking, the divine does not
know It is the divine, only we know it is the divine. The divine's "knowing" has no resemblance to any form of consciousness. In truth, God is
neither consciousness nor has consciousness.

So who or what is aware of a divine Center, aware of oneness with God? None other than our self. Were there no individual self, there would be no experience of a center – be it the ego, the divine, empty or otherwise. What enables us to be aware of a nondual center is the circumference, that is, consciousness' autonomous reflexive-mind which (in the Unitive State at least) is simultaneously as aware of God (its Center) as it is of itself. Thus the two, God and self, are given in a single reflexion. Without the reflexive-mind no one could even look within themselves, much less be aware of any center. So anyone who is aware of a center, who experiences it, or experiences any interior life, attests to a totally dual state of affairs.

How all this goes down for the Easterner who denies the existence of an individual self and soul (denies the reality of a circumference, that is) I cannot imagine. They speak of a nondual Center yet totally ignore its circumference, ignore the very self that is conscious of its nondual center! Looking East I get the impression – right or wrong – their notion of consciousness is limited to its being only a center, be it the ego-center, an empty-center or a divine-center. They seem to ignore the fact that were it not for the reflexive-mind there would be no awareness of any center at all. They seem to think if you can just stop the reflexive mind, the Center can stand alone without a subject-object consciousness, a state they call "pure consciousness".

It never occurs to them that the whole of consciousness is not just a center, but the center's circumference as well – the reflexive-mind, to be exact. Do away with either one and neither remains. There cannot be a center without the reflexive mind, nor a reflective mind without its center.

In fact, what generates the reflexive mind's action is the center. Take away this fuel and the reflexive mind ceases. Take it away permanently, and out goes the center along with its circumference, leaving no self or consciousness at all. This would definitely be the negation of a duality, the duality of center and circumference.

So as best I can make out, the East points solely to the Center as being consciousness itself – call it Atman, Self, or even Brahman. They ignore the individual self or the Center's circumference – why? Because the reflexive-mind with its subject-object dichotomy is dualistic. They abandon the circumference (conceptually at least) in order to retain only what is nondual or singular – the Center, that is. Thus the focus is solely on the divine Center as all that truly exists, they regard it as consciousness, being, self, Atman, even Brahman – all that matters, at least. (As already noted, however, a center is only relative to its circumference, hence, part and parcel of a dualistic system).

But if the East "conceptually" denies the existence of the individual self or circumference, it is still there – for those who know what to look for, at least. Just the fact one is aware of a divine indwelling or Center, indicates the reflexive subject-object-mind (circumference) is still going and totally present. The circumference thus remains, even though unacknowledged. Were there truly no duality there would be neither Center nor circumference. Should these two be negated there would be no self at all – no phenomenal or individual self – no divine Center, no Self or Atman, no awareness or consciousness, no indwelling, no inner or interior life whatsoever. As for what lies beyond this negation, there is nothing to be known as "one" or "nondual", nothing that could be so designated. On this issue we can understand Buddha's silence. As to what lies beyond Atman or self, nothing can be said of it because it is beyond the mind to grasp or get hold of. Man's human faculties were never intended to grasp the ultimate mystery of God. His faculties were created for an earthly existence, not a heavenly existence where these faculties are of no use.

Apart from the duality of center and circumference, there is the duality of the reflexive mind itself – subject knowing itself as object to itself. From the beginning to the end of the journey, this reflexive-mind remains intact. Thus the true nature of consciousness is a dual-nondual set up: the reflexive mind is dual, the center is nondual. Together these two (center and circumference) make up the **whole** of consciousness, and so it will remain unless God ordains otherwise. If God so ordains, the **whole** disappears in a single swoop (no-Self) and there remains neither center nor circumference, no interiority at all. The point is that at no time can there be a center standing alone without its circumference (or reflexive mind). Take the whole away, and there is no consciousness (center-circumference) remaining.

The Phenomenal Self

If we can legitimately regard the divine Center as our deepest "true self" (because it is the deepest point of self beyond which there is only God) then what are we to call the rest of self – the circumference, that is? Without an ego-consciousness there is no longer an I-Thou relationship to God. Instead there is a "we or us" consciousness, one that can legitimately be called "God-consciousness" in that we are never without the awareness of oneness with God. In this state of affairs we realize that what is eternal in ourselves is only "that" mysterious aspect of soul that is united to God – an aspect of soul known only to God. The rest of self we regard as merely peripheral and non-eternal. We regard this peripheral-self as only meant to deal with earthly life. Somehow we know it will have no part to play in eternal life. Now some people have called this peripheral self the "phenomenal self", but if this means the peripheral-self is nothing more than a mere "appearance", this is unacceptable. But if it means "the only self other people know", that is acceptable. However peripheral it may be, however, this peripheral-self exists as sure as any fact of life. It is not a mere appearance, but absolutely genuine, part and parcel of the "whole self" without fragmentation.

What we may not realize, however, is that this "peripheral-self", while not the center of consciousness, is nevertheless the reflexive-mind generated by the divine Center. Something else not initially known is that this peripheral-self is imperceptibly being diminished as the Center grows larger. This is a phenomenon in itself, a subtlety not easy to detect or articulate – a reality we never hear about in the books. In this I am reminded of John the Baptists' words, "He must increase, I must decrease". Obviously there is nothing casual about this peripheral-self, and if intent on serving the Lord, it goes at it with full force. Although there is a great deal to say about this circumference or peripheral-self, we only want to point it out as part and parcel of consciousness itself, a reflexive, dual, subject-object consciousness. Without it there could be no awareness of any divine Center. There can be no underrating the vast importance of this peripheral-self. Indeed, God will consume it, and transform it all.

Looking to the Eastern religions I find no accounting whatsoever for this circumference, this peripheral or phenomenal-self. It was as if it did not exist. Indeed, in their minds it doesn't – if something doesn't exist there's no need to account for it. As best I can make out, after realizing a divine Center, this is the end of the Eastern journey. All that's left is a physical body. This scenario, however, totally ignores the other half of consciousness, the reflexive mind. Without it, there could be no awareness of any oneness with God or Brahman, no God-Consciousness at all. How could they have missed this fact?

The only way the peripheral-self and its reflexive-mind could cease to exist is for its Central Generator to cease altogether. This can only happen, however, when there is no more fuel for the Generator to consume. With nothing left to consume Its Flame goes out – "it is finished". This is not only the end of the divine Center, but the end of the whole peripheral self as well – the whole circumference, reflexive-mind and all. There is no self left, no duality (circumference) and no nonduality (Center).

"Pure Consciousness"

I have read that "nondual" is said to articulate a state or condition of "pure consciousness". This is a condition whereby one knows, sees, or is aware Brahman is all that exists. Brahman, in fact, is said to be "pure consciousness" or have nondual consciousness. Since only Brahman is privy to this pure consciousness, then the only one who knows this consciousness is Brahman Itself. The true goal, then, is not to attain nonduality, the true goal is to be Brahman, no different than Brahman.

Since no one can say "I" realized Brahman — lest it reveal a duality (himself and Brahman) — one need only affirm to have come upon "pure consciousness" to indicate he is Brahman.

Although most people know the definition of consciousness as self-awareness, what they tend to forget is that the **sole object of consciousness is always itself**, nothing and no one else. Objects in the environment are not objects of consciousness, they are perceptual, sensory objects. It is only because the mind is constantly reflexing on itself we know any "self" (or Self) at all. Were it not for this mechanism man would know nothing of any "self", the very word would never have arisen. This is why or how consciousness and self are (or mean) the same thing. All consciousness — along with its conscious and unconscious levels — is *self-consciousness*.

Take away consciousness and nothing remains that could be called "consciousness" or "self". While it may be comforting to think some type of consciousness remains, in truth, no consciousness remains. Unless we re-define consciousness to include no-self-awareness, the notion of consciousness without a reflexive-mind is a contradiction of terms, literally unthinkable. With no subject-object or nothing to be aware **of**, why call it "consciousness" at all? At best, such a state might be called "pre-conscious". As it stands, however, with no understandable re-definition of "consciousness", there exists no such thing as a subjectless-objectless consciousness, no nondual or pure consciousness at all.

Looking East, "pure consciousness" is thought to be the cessation of the reflexive subject-object-mind. It seems this negation, however, in no way affects the Center or Atman. Thus the Center remains without reflexive-consciousness. Once again, the Center is left standing alone with no circumference or reflexive-mind, and once again I affirm this impossibility. You can't have half a consciousness. Who or what is aware of this divine center if not yourself — the circumference, the reflexive mind? To hold the Center is aware of Itself is merely to impose on It our same anthropomorphic reflexive consciousness.

I can think of several reasons, however, for holding on to the notion of "pure consciousness". First and foremost, if you start with the belief Brahma is pure consciousness, then it behooves you to "realize" the same – if you want to be Brahman. There is also the possibility the term "pure consciousness" was coined to assure people that if they could just stop their reflexive mind they would not pass out or die, but, instead, would discover a different type of knowing, one ineptly named "pure consciousness".

Now there is some truth to this. Only the "knowing" that lies beyond consciousness could never, by any definition, be called consciousness. This "knowing" cannot be grasped by the mind, has no description and cannot be accounted for. It has not a thing in common with consciousness, it is not in or of the mind, not located anywhere, not a function, not experienced, not an awareness or consciousness, not a psychological or spiritual "something", etc. That such a knowing exists, is all that can be said of it.

In truth, there is no such thing as subjectless-objectless consciousness. While God's "knowing" has neither subject nor object, it is also not consciousness. Initially I called this a "cloud of knowing" because it was the opposite of "unknowing ". It is like a "cloud", however, in that it is ungraspable, not available to the mind, cannot even be articulated or put into words. In some way this "knowing" bears a resemblance to what I know and have defined, as "faith" – which is **not** belief (belief is of the mind). The major difference is that whereas faith is typified as dark, this "knowing" can be typified as light. That's about the most that can be said of it.

There is another idea regarding what a nondual consciousness is supposed to be. This is a consciousness where there is no object, but only a subject. The idea of an objectless consciousness, however, is even more impossible than no subject-object at all. You cannot split the reflexive mind in half, it is a **function**. Similar to a muscle it either flexes completely or it doesn't flex at all. There is no such thing as a half-reflex or where subject or object can be isolated. Even if you stopped this mechanism you would not only be out of self-as-object, but equally self-as-subject.

Still, some people think that if they could just get rid of the object half, they could catch the subject in the act. Although this is impossible, let us say someone managed to do this – catch the subject standing alone. Now how, exactly, would he know it was the subject? He wouldn't, there is no way. The sole way we can know ourselves as subject is as object. Once again: no object = no subject. (And needless to say, there is no such thing as two selves, one object and one subject.) Consciousness is a holistic set-up. Without the reflexive mind there could be nothing to call "self" and no center at all.

Keep in mind, self is not a being or entity, it is the major **function** of the soul. As such it is responsible for all man's experiences – all, that is, but his sensory experiences. In Western terms "self" is everything we know as the psyche – defined as consciousness. At any rate, there is no such thing as a "subject" standing alone nor any type of consciousness that is not reflexive.

Having said this, at one time, trying to adjust to the radical new condition beyond self, I thought to call it "pure subjectivity", which did not, however, mean self. I soon dropped the term because it didn't fit the condition or accurately articulate it. At that time the term "witness" might have been better. But after many difficult years of adjusting to such a condition, I knew exactly how it works, which brings me now to say something about "pure sensory perception".

Pure Sensory Perception

One thing that remains beyond self or consciousness is pure sensory perception. The reason for calling it "pure" is because sensory perception is no longer admixed with consciousness or self. The senses are now totally alone, all that's really left. Apart from this being a state of affairs no one would wish on a dog – because initially the senses have no interest in staying awake – yet one thing learned is that sensory "things" are not, and never have been, "objects of consciousness". One thing and one thing only is the object of consciousness – self. Never has anything external been an object of consciousness. We think they are, but they are not.

We do not need consciousness to perceive objects and people in the environment, indeed, even animals do this. We need consciousness to be self-aware; it is self-awareness that makes us human and sets us apart from the animals. Objects (and people) in the environment are not objects to consciousness, rather they are objects to the senses. The proof? Take away consciousness and objects remain as usual. The only difference, we no longer reflect them and they no longer reflect us. Thus we can neither give nor take anything from physical, sensory objects. Actually this is a relief.

It is only without consciousness or self that man can come upon "pure" sensory perception. This is because, as long as consciousness remains, it functions in conjunction with sensory perception, so much so, man can never separate them. Only when there is no consciousness does he know, indeed, must live, with pure sensory perception. Until that time the function of consciousness and the senses are as intermixed as salt in the sea.

The reason for bringing this up is because people mistake sensory *perception* for sensory *awareness*. If "awareness" is the same as "consciousness", then the term "awareness" cannot be applied to any physical sensory data. We "perceive" physical objects, we are not "aware" of objects. This information has been useful to those who ponder how it is that subject and object are said to be the same or no different. Their mistake is thinking physical or sensory objects are objects-to-consciousness, whereas *self alone is the object of consciousness* – hence the subject is the object and vice-versa. Nothing external, physical, or sensory is or can be an object-to-consciousness. So when we ponder the oneness of subject and object this is solely a reference to self, it has nothing to do with environmental objects. As to the identity of subject-object consciousness, you can't even think about it, at least not on its true unconscious level. On a conscious level, however, you are merely thinking *about* yourself, which is rarely useful – or truthful. One can never get their hands on the reflexive-mind, it is not under our control. My point, however, is that I suspect what people may be calling "pure consciousness" is actually "pure sensory perception". If they think there is such a thing as "pure consciousness", they are mistaken, there is no such consciousness.

Conclusion

When all is said and done, "nondual" is a term dug up by the Advaitans who never for a moment considered the possibility of no-Self – no individual self and no divine Self or Atman. They didn't consider this because they denied there was any individual self and consequently denied its true union with God or Atman. Had they considered this or knew it, they would have had to consider the negation of this union leaving neither the individual nor its experience, Atman. What remains following this negation is not a "one"; in fact, the true nature of what remains at the end of the journey can only be revealed. The point is that the Advaitans never for a moment considered no-Self or no-Atman. It was not within their purview.

I have gone over all the definitions of nonduality I know of. Since the term means the negation of two, we have looked over what "two" these might be. Thus we have looked at the duality of:

- "Thou art that" – "not one, not two" – two interpretations of this saying.

- Cause (God) and effect (self).

- Atman and Brahman – the same, distinct or different.

- Atman-immanent and Brahman-transcendent.

- Brahman-in-itself vs. Brahman-in-us.

- The center and circumference (of consciousness), subject-object, duality of the reflexive mind.

- Reality of the individual soul and self vs. mere appearance and mental error.

If all these dualities are negated, how could we possibly end up with "one" – one anything? Negate these dualities and nothing remains to be called "nondual". As said at the beginning, no matter what duality is negated, it can never add up to one, it can only add up to nothing. Let's face it, nondual is a useless term, it means nothing, there is no such condition or realization.

As an Advaitic term, we have looked over Hinduism's basic beliefs to see if there is any state or "realization" that could legitimately be called "nondual". Obviously, I didn't find any. Nondual is a vague term that denotes no experiential reality. It evokes nothing spiritual or defines any state or stage in the journey. The term is pure speculation, an intellectual idea with no truth to back it up.

Having gone over the basic beliefs of Hinduism, we also want to point out why nonduality has no place in Christianity. Briefly, here are Christianity's basic beliefs:

- God is Trinity – three in One essence.

- Creator and created, united and one (which does not mean One is the other).

- The Incarnate Logos or Christ – dual nature (fully human and fully divine) but One Person (of the Trinity).

- Unitive state – God, the Center of soul and self.

- The end or goal – transformation into Christ.

- Beyond self – God-in-Itself and no longer God-in-our-self.

Obviously there is no place here for nonduality. Christianity has never had a problem with duality, multiplicity, or with the One and the many. The Eucharist (Christ with us) is the perfect illustration of the One and the many – the same One in all and all in the same One.

It is unfortunate that those who aspire to a nondual state will never reach it because, in truth, it is just another illusion to be dispelled. With or without self, there is no state in the journey truly "nondual", neither in our earthly journey nor in heaven. So let us beware of this false expectation. From beginning to end or until self or consciousness falls away, its functional and experiential nature remains dual, as well as marvelously whole.

In ending, I still haven't the remotest idea what "nonduality" is supposed to mean. All I know is that the Advaita people dug it up, and, having looked it over, know it should be buried. In my view, the term is a subtle ruse to put people in their place – designate their spiritual status. By telling us only those who know they are Brahman (coined "nonduality") are at the top of the ladder, all others can then be relegated to a lower rung. It's all a ploy of spiritual one-upmanship, nothing else. Though I don't know a thing about Brahman, I do know God, and if there is anything God is not, it is someone who thinks he is God. (Even God doesn't think He is God. The only thing God knows about God is what's on our minds).

Postscript

In all of Hinduism there are relatively few Advaitans or people who adhere to this particular Hindu philosophy. The vast majority of Hindus belong to what is called the "bhakti" tradition of spirituality, which is the way of a personal love of God. There is no place for nonduality in this spirituality. In fact, these people probably wouldn't know what nonduality meant, and if they did, they wouldn't want it anyway.

Some 30 years ago, in a used book shop, I picked up a small thin book about Ramakrishna. As best I remember it was written by a journalist. Unlike books written today about Ramakrishna, this writer was not a follower or devotee, but more an outside observer. He didn't make Ramakrishna out to be some avatar with all its fictitious garnish and nonsense — which Christians also have to endure in accounts of most its Saints. To this writer Ramakrishna was simply interesting, different and totally human. What initially shocked me was Ramakrishna's passionate love for the goddess Kali, a grotesque figure weighed down with dead heads, skulls. But once beyond that, the love he experienced was beyond any image. (And lest we forget, what is the central image of Christianity but a bloody, dead man on a cross? Image- wise, there is not much difference.) Images are meant to remind us of some great mystery or truth of God, and Ramakrishna certainly "got it", got the truth that is.

I regard Ramakrishna as the ultimate model of genuine Hinduism. I even regard him as one of the greatest mystics of all times in all our religions. It seems, however, the Advaita people did their best to discredit him. On one occasion they threw up to him the fact he still had a sense of "I" left, to which Ramakrishna instantly responded, "Then I'll put it to the service of the Lord!" On another occasion he told them, "I'd rather taste sugar than be sugar". Ramakrishna and the Advaitans remind me of Christ and the Pharisees. The Advaitans would rather "think" about the spiritual life than live it, which is the easiest way to make no progress.

The point is: Ramakrishna pooh-poohed nonduality, it was no match for his consuming love of God, had no place in it. Though he never wrote about it, like every genuine lover of God, Ramakrishna went all the way with God. He left far behind the pompous Advaitans who had yet to make a beginning and looked down their noses at the "bhakti's" — the one-upmanship of it all! Compared to Ramakrishna, I have never understood what people see in the likes of a Ramana Maharshi and others who are but mouth-pieces for the Advaita. But let no one be deceived, Ramakrishna is authentic Hinduism at its highest, he is its living truth. But so much for nonduality. The Advaitans invented it, so may they wander through eons of reincarnations chasing down their illusions and wrong thinking.

A footnote: "Realization"

I have a problem with the term "realization" used to indicate anything of importance in the spiritual journey. The term implies something we have mentally figured out, something we had either forgotten or didn't understand at the time and only later "realized". It could also mean the "realization" of one's own expectations or what one had believed all along. It's all a mental exercise, something we actively engage in, desiring to know and the satisfaction of knowing. Just because we "realize" something, however, doesn't make it true. Realization merely attests to our own smarts. The term is solely a reference to a mental life, not a spiritual life.

In the Christian journey the term "realize" is totally foreign. We do not "realize" God, Trinity, heaven, or realize anything. What we know of these mysteries is pure gift, something given to us, not something we got on our own or figured out. Equally foreign is the term "enlightenment". Thanks to the gift of the Holy Spirit we are constantly being enlightened. Were it not for this we'd not make much progress in the journey. As to which piece of enlightenment is most important, they all are. Looking East, I find it curious different people regard their particular piece of enlightenment as definitive or as far as one can go. But this side of the grave, who knows what God can do or what He may reveal? For sure, the sole definitive enlightenment people will ever have is when they are no longer around to tell us about it.

/ 4 /

MYSTICAL THEOLOGY AND NO-SELF

MYSTICAL THEOLOGY AND NO-SELF

The Problem

In every book on the subject of Christian Mysticism, we eventually come upon some statement to the effect that no matter what the mystic or contemplative says or seems to imply, at no time does he ever lose his individuality, his personal identity or sense of self. Not even in the highest estate of heaven does he lose the sense of his own being or particular uniqueness that makes him eternally "other" to God. In the absence of an explanation, the writer – usually a theologian – evidently regards self to be as immortal as the soul, thus all reports of no-self are deemed either a matter of ignorance, a psychological fluke, or in any case, un-Christian. For the contemplative or mystic, however, such a view is inexplicable. Since only God can take away self, how could this divine act possibly be un-Christian, unorthodox, or even un-theological? Without a satisfying theological answer, we are left to doubt the reportage itself. What we do know, however, is that a tension has always existed between the Christian mystics and the academic theologians. It seems that even after two-thousand years not much has changed in this matter.

In the following pages I would like to address the tension between mystic and theologian, more especially as the issues have to do with no-self. Apart from assuring us no-self can never happen, the only reason ever given is that it smacks of some form of pantheism where, as one theologian said, "the 'I' is absorbed in God", or as another theologian put it, "for me, no-self means being dumped into some kind of cosmic soup". Now this kind of theological mentality is beyond me, certainly it has nothing to do with Christianity or what I know as no-self. But if I cannot counter wrong ideas of no-self, I can certainly place it in its Christian context, the only context I know and the only context where no-self can be found. No-self is simply the end of the Way, the "Way" being Christ. The end (no-self) being the culmination of Christ's earthly journey, *the same / or us as it was for Him.*

Beginning at the End

To understand no-self and its place in the spiritual journey we must begin at the end, that is, with an eye to the journey's ultimate goal, the end for which we were created and our final estate in heaven. As the early Fathers put it, "salvation is deification", this is the end for which human nature was created; thus by means of Christ we are to be made divine – deified. By this the Fathers' did not mean we become the Godhead or Trinity, nor Father or Holy Spirit. The sole referent of deification was the Incarnate Christ, the image of God in each soul, who, because his human nature was deified, opened the door to the deification of all human nature. Our journey, then, is to actualize and bring to full life the image (Christ) in which we were created. While the Father's took for granted nothing created could ever become divine, yet the created could be as one with the Uncreated as was the Logos in Its human Incarnation. Thus deification means our transformation into Christ.[1]

While the early Fathers' original term "deification" was later translated in the West as "transformation" these two terms are not equivalent. "Deification" specifically refers to God – becoming God or Godlike – whereas "transformation" makes no reference to God at all, thus it can refer to any kind of change or alteration. So where "transformation" tells us nothing, the term "deification" explicitly states **what** we are to be transformed into – namely, God.

We are all familiar with the early Council's definition of Christ as one divine Person (the Logos) uniting in itself two natures, divine and human. This union (two natures in one Person) was called a "Hypostatic Union" because it was unique and unlike any other form of oneness between God and man.[2] We are also told the Logos did not unite itself to

---

[1] To learn more about deification, its origin and meaning, you can read just about anything by Vladimir Lossky, John Meyendorff, the first two volumes of Jaroslav Pelikan's *The Christian Tradition*, also the works of Maximus the Confessor. The early Fathers derived man's deification directly from scripture, they see it all over the place, sometimes stated explicitly, sometimes implicitly.

[2] Christ's "Hypostatic Union" should not be mistaken for the Christian Unitive

any singular human person, but rather to the whole of human nature or what all humans have in common prior to their distinctiveness as individual persons. This means that in his human nature Christ is Universal man, the Prototype of perfected human nature beyond all accidental or individual differences. Because the divine Person (Logos) superseded any singular human person, Christ was *never a human person,* always Christ remained solely a divine Person. The council also made clear the distinction between the terms "nature" and "person" ("hypostasis" as they called it). "Nature" is what all human beings have in common prior to any singularity or particular person, while "person", on the other hand, is responsible for human differences, distinctions, uniqueness – individuality or what sets one apart from others.

So at the Incarnation what the Logos united to Its divine nature was not any singular human person or individual, but rather the whole of human nature. This fact is important to keep in mind because if our destiny is to be deified, transformed into Christ, at some point there can be no individual person remaining. The early Fathers had the saying: "What was not assumed by Christ cannot be deified", and since Christ did not assume a singular or particular person, it follows that our own singular person or individuality cannot be deified – because Christ never assumed it. Thus the ultimate deification of our human nature means that in the end, the divine Person supersedes our human person, just as it did in Christ.

It is important to have a firm grasp of the Logos' Incarnation to understand who Christ is, otherwise, there is no hope of having a true understanding of the Faith, of ourselves, our life's journey and its ultimate end; and certainly there would be no hope of understanding no-self. To this end, then, let us go over the major points so far:

The term "nature" – human nature in this case – means only

---

state. To be supernaturally united to the divine does not make us a divine Person. If anything, the Unitive State allows us, finally, to be totally human, but not totally divine.

what humans share equally in common. Anything that makes for differences is excluded from the term. What all humans share in common, of course, is a human body and soul, also the fact they were created in the image of God.

According to the Fathers what makes for differences or sets one apart from another is due to the individual expressions of our common human nature, which expressions being totally unique or one of a kind is the "person". The Fathers had an almost mystical notion of person. In itself a person was incommunicable, ungraspable — you couldn't put your finger on it — it was a mystery intelligible only by contemplation of the Trinity. They gave it priority over nature saying it was the person that "contained" nature (body and soul) and also ran-the-show — or at least should run it. They thought letting nature run the show would be a complete disaster — given its potential to sin — thus it was up to the person to manage nature. Furthermore, the Fathers stated it was the "person" that was made in God's image and not human nature — another reason "person" is not easy to grasp. At any rate, there is no underestimating "person", indeed, the Logos itself is divine Person.[3]

From this we can understand why the Logos never united itself to a human person. First of all, the Logos is Itself the "Uncreated" Image of God and had no need to assume Its own "created" image in man. Then too, had the Logos united itself to a human person, Christ would have been two persons — impossible. That the divine Person totally overshadowed and superseded the human person is the only way the Logos

---

[3] For a more social-psychological insight into "person" one might read *The Person of Christ, A Theological Insight*, by Jean Galot, S.J., 1969, (Gregorian University Press, Rome, 1981). In the absence of a philosophical definition of "person" (which was the case at the Council of Chalcedon in 451) the author points out the Council's use of the previously defined Godhead as the "relationship of Three Persons" (Trinity) and affirmed that even on the human level "person" can only be defined as a relationship. The author also believes there can be no "person" without a self, for without a "thou" there can be no "I", and hence, no relationship. Although I am not in total agreement, it is nevertheless a fair book to read on the subject of "person", for which there is no definitive definition.

could become Incarnate – no human person, after all, can supersede a divine Person. And something else, had the Logos united itself to a singular person, Its Incarnation would have been meaningless and ineffective for the rest of us – only that person to whom It was united would have been the beneficiary. It is only because the Logos was united to the human "nature" of everyone that everyone can share in and become beneficiaries of the Incarnation.

To be human means to be a conscious being, literally a self-conscious being. Consciousness is not only something humans share in common, it is what most characterizes what it means to be human. According to the Fathers, consciousness belongs to man's "nature" (and not to "person"), thus in his created human nature, the man Jesus was, like everyone else, a self-conscious human being. The consciousness and self of Jesus, however, was not that of the Logos; consciousness or self belonged solely to Jesus' "human nature", it did not belong to the Logos' divine nature or divine Person. This is why it is important not to confuse the human self of Jesus with the divine Person of the Logos, and why the Fathers insisted on retaining (as dogma) Christ's dual natures. The divine Logos never became a human person, and though it united itself to human nature, It did not become our human nature.[4]

Because of the unique union of divine and human in Christ ("Hypostatic Union"), and because of his single divine Personhood, the Fathers believed Christ's human nature was "deified" or made Godlike. It also seemed reasonable (to the Fathers) that what was possible for one human being was possible for others as well. Thus the fact that Christ's human nature was deified, opens the door for the deification of all hu-

---

[4] Theologically speaking, "self" has never been equated with "person". Though some definitions of person include human nature – and thus include self or consciousness – the two terms are not interchangeable. It is the expression of self that gives rise to person and not the other way around. So while person expresses self, one is not the other. For an expression of self, or self an expression of person, the two are not the same, one is not the other. For the Fathers, person is not identified with body, soul or spirit, but arises from another reality – from a unity that God can transfigure – deify.

man nature. The   Fathers saw this so clearly and without doubt that they believed salvation consisted solely in our deification. For them, there is no salvation without being deified; thus what it means to be saved is to be deified.

Since the deification of Christ's human nature was due to His Hypostatic oneness with the divine Logos, it follows that our deification would be of the same nature – namely, our human nature being one with the divine Logos. With this hypostatic oneness we are truly and totally transformed into Christ. So Christ, then, is not only the goal, the means and the Way, but the very reason for our deification. Christ is the Prototype of man's ultimate destiny, the whole purpose of his existence; for this we were created.

When Christ said he was the "Way", he not only meant he was the "means", but that we were to recapitulate his own human life with God, recapitulate, as it were, his same spiritual journey. Whatever Christ's initial advantage, his desire was that we too have his same advantages; indeed, for this he gave his whole life. Thus we are to know, love and be as one with God as he was, to have his same mind, same body, and ultimately, his same glory. In short, "the way" meant becoming as one with the divine Logos as he was, and through Him, one with Father and Spirit.

As the Prototype of universal man and perfected humanity, it follows that anything possible for Christ is possible for us, and that anything not possible for Christ is not possible for us. Thus whatever Christ experienced or underwent in his human nature, we too can experience or undergo. According to Cyril of Alexandria, the mystery of man's salvation or deification consisted of the self-emptying and abasement of the Son of God – His *kenosis* or self-emptying, in other words. The culmination of this kenosis was His death on the cross. Thus the emptying begun at the Incarnation was only finished on the cross. Now if this complete self-emptying is the way it went for Christ, this is also the way it will go for us, and if Christ ended empty of self, then we too end empty of self. (It would be unthinkable for our individual self to be deified when Christ's human self was not).

If an objection is made that Christ's *kenosis* or self-emptying only referred to his divine nature (at the time of the Incarnation) and not to his human nature (at the time of the crucifixion), there are two points to keep in mind. As said already, His kenosis was only completed with His death on the cross – as witnessed by his cry that the divine had abandoned him (he was empty of the divine) followed by his last words, "It is finished". In light of this emptiness, to think that without the divine the human self is nevertheless deified, makes no sense. In the Unitive state, God is our deepest experience of self – often referred to as our "true self" – thus to take away one (be it self or God) is to take away the other. Just as the two live together as one (God and self), the two die together. This is why, if the divine kenosis was completed on the cross, it took the human self with it.[5]

Secondly, no-self has never referred to the cessation or falling away of the ego ("old self" as Paul put it), nor merely the falling away of the individual self. As said before, we are speaking here of last things, the ending of the journey, not of lesser states. No-self has reference solely to the falling away of the Unitive self ("new self" as Paul put it) in its oneness with Christ. This is the falling away of the whole Unitive state, more especially the Divine Center (God) from whom we take our life and being. Some people call this divine center (which is empty of self) their "True Self" or think of it as a "divine Self" – knowing, of course, this divine center is God and not themselves. The falling away of this Union then, is the falling away of both God and Self, it is the only true death man will ever experience. With this death there is no interior life remaining, none, it is finished. The demise of this oneness (God and self) is not merely a kenosis of our human nature, but a divine kenosis as well.

---

[5] The truth be told, God is never one with consciousness or self, rather, He is one with the soul. Consciousness or self is but a faculty or function of the soul, and as such is the "experiencer" – that which experiences oneness with God and is fully aware of it. Only the cessation of this function (consciousness) can rightly be known as the cessation of self (or no-self), a cessation that leaves behind no experience of anything – life, energy, body, soul, etc. No-self is the death of all experiences.

As to how this went for Christ, we have already said that consciousness belonged to his human nature, not his divine nature (according to the Fathers). As a divine Person, Christ was born with a Unitive consciousness wherein he was as aware of God as he was aware of his human self. The two, God and self, are not the same of course; self is not God and God is not self. I have always thought that in our own spiritual journey we only catch up to Christ when we come to his same Unitive consciousness. Whether this consciousness was the same for Him as it is for us, I do not know – as the Prototype, however, I suspect it was far more powerful and active in Christ than in ourselves. In the final emptying on the cross, it was Christ's whole Unitive consciousness that went out, ceased, was no more. This is the definitive experience of no-self – no self at all, neither divine nor human; the ultimate and final *kenosis*.[6]

Obviously, the whole issue of no-self has first to do with Christ and only secondarily with ourselves. Thus theologians who object to no-self should level their objections at Christ and not at those who have simply gone His Way. Perhaps for the theologian the bottom line to ponder is the question: did the human Jesus ever lose his created human self, or did he retain his human individuality for all eternity?

If he lost it, then it follows we also will lose it; but if he did not lose it, then there is no possibility of any human being losing self – none. In the long run, then, it is useless to ponder if this or that person could lose self when the real focus is on the Prototype of all human nature – Christ. If Christ's divine and human kenosis was not complete, if self was left over when everything else was gone, then no-self could not happen to anyone.

---

[6] Although Christ's kenosis was said to be completed on the cross, one early Father (I can't remember who) insisted this final kenosis referred solely to Christ's humanity, not to his divinity. (I was surprised to learn the Fathers believed what the Logos forfeited to become incarnate was the "glory of the Father" – a view I have long held. This forfeiture of glory, however, was the nature of the divine kenosis, not the human kenosis. The ultimate human kenosis is the forfeiture of self.)

In summary, if we truly recapitulate Christ's same human journey, then our rule of thumb is this: *however it went for Christ is how it will go for us*. This means that whatever can happen to Christ's humanity can happen to our own. Thus if Christ is not a human person, then in the end, neither are we. If in the end he was emptied of his human self, then so are we.

As for the deification of human nature, exactly what this means or where to draw the line between ordinary human nature and its becoming Godlike (or made divine), this has never been made clear. What we know for sure, however, is that whatever became of Christ's human nature is part and parcel of Christ's heavenly estate. So even if we do not know heaven before we get there, the only thing we need to know is that: **however it goes for Christ in heaven, so too it goes for us.**

Questions for the Theologian

Since our salvation is deification or transformation into Christ, the question for the theologian is whether or not this transformation is total or only partial? If it is total, then there can be no individual self remaining – as Paul might have put it, "No longer I, but Christ". If, on the other hand, our transformation is not total, then we are not honestly transformed into Christ and must cease regarding this as the goal of salvation and final estate in heaven. We say transformed "*into*" Christ and not "in" Christ because "in" does not define our end. From the beginning, having been "baptized *into* Christ", we are already in Christ, which does not, however, articulate our end – our being transformed *into* Christ.

Naturally those who deny we are completely transformed into Christ are the same who oppose no-self. The two (no-self and transformation into Christ) go hand in hand. There cannot be one without the other. If, however, we are **not** transformed into Christ, then of course there is no reason for self ever to be transcended or relinquished; in which case, we stay exactly who and what we have been from the beginning – no change or transformation necessary.

It is only if we are transformed into Christ that self must be completely transcended, for after all, Christ is not a composite of myriad of individual selves! The truth be told, Father, Son and Holy Spirit are completely selfless, they have no self and are devoid of anything that could be called "self". Self belongs to human nature alone, indeed, without self we wouldn't be human or have any need to be transformed into the divine image in which we were created. Without question, self is that factor in human nature that keeps man veiled before God.

As to the theological objection to anything that hints of the created being transformed into the uncreated, let us be very clear. It is not human nature that is transformed into divine nature, but rather, human nature united to Christ's divine Uncreated nature (the Logos, that is). In this union our human nature enters into Christ's same Hypostatic oneness.

Thus transformation is more than the transformation of human nature, its deification consists in being one with Christ's divine Uncreated nature. It is not a matter, then, of any aspect of human nature "becoming" divine or "disappearing" into the Uncreated — as some theologians seem to think — but rather, human nature becoming as one with the divine Logos as it is in Christ, no different than Christ.

While most theologians admit to some form of transformation, it has a way of boiling down to mere lip-service. While it is acknowledged we shall participate, partake and share in Christ's divinity — be one body, have his mind, know as he knows, have his same glory — yet theologians tell us we will remain the same soul, same self, same person, same personality, same mind, same substance — same everything. There is an obvious contradiction here, they cannot both be right. Theologically we have been given a static view of human nature, as if it were closed-ended, complete and final from its conception.

So what has actually changed or been transformed? By and large we are told that if God has forgiven our sins and we have determined to sin no more, that's all we need to be saved! To think the Christian end is nothing more than a sinless self or soul is unworthy of the Incarnation. Indeed, Judaism was privy to this long before Christ appeared, and Christ did not come to repeat what Judaism already knew. For the theologian, then, the real question is the extent of our transformation, be it total or only partial. If *not* total, we ask the following questions:

- What part or aspect of our human nature cannot be transformed into Christ? What part must be left out?

- At what point does our transformation stop short of the fullness of Christ?

- How is our human nature different from Christ's human nature, or what was there about His human nature that could be deified while our human nature cannot?

- In short, where, exactly, are we to draw the line between ourselves and Christ?" (Indeed, who dares draw such a line? *Who can separate us from Christ?*)

The transcendence of self is the heart and core of all Mystical Theology. The emphasis has always been the steps and stages of increasingly going out of self to God. From the on-set, putting self aside, overcoming self, going beyond self, this is what the journey is about and how it proceeds – as John the Baptist put it, "He (Christ) must increase, I must decrease". Nothing is more gracious, of course, than God stepping in to remove all impediments of self. In the lore of Mystical Theology we have many such accounts of God stepping in to do just this – remove self. What follows is one such account.

St. Bernard's Question

After giving an account of his experience of no-self, St. Bernard (1090-1153) ponders whether or not this experience could become an abiding state in this world. Though he never doubts the experience belongs to man's final estate in heaven, he does not see how it could be possible while still in this earthly body. Whether or not no-self could become permanent this side of heaven, he asks, *"Let those who have had the experience make a statement. To me, I confess, it seems impossible."* Before responding to St. Bernard, let us first go over the experience he is talking about. In his book, *On Loving God*, speaking of the highest, or 4th degree of love, he says:

"Blessed and holy, I would say, is he to whom it has been given to experience such a thing in this mortal life at rare intervals or even once, and this, suddenly and scarcely for the space of a single moment. To lose yourself as though you were not, to be utterly unconscious of yourself and emptied of yourself; as it were, brought to nothing. This pertains to heavenly intercourse, not to human affection."[7]

Another translation:

"I would say that man is blessed and holy to whom it is given to experience something of this sort, so rare in life, even if it be but once and for the space of a moment. To lose yourself as if you no longer existed, to cease completely to experience yourself; to reduce yourself to nothing is not a human sentiment but a divine experience".[8]

Later he says:

"It is deifying to go through such an experience. As a drop of water seems to disappear in a big quantity of wine, even assuming the wine's taste and color; just as red, molten iron becomes so much like fire it seems to lose its primary state; just as the air on a sunny day seems transformed into sunshine instead of being lit up, so it is necessary for the saints that all human feelings melt in a mysterious way and flow into the will of God. Otherwise, how will God be All in All if something human survives in man?"[9]

Speaking elsewhere of this experience he says:

"I doubt if he (anyone) ever attains the fourth degree during this life, that is, if he ever loves only for God's sake. Let those who have had the experience make a statement; to

---

[7] *On Loving God*, Mission Press.
[8] Cistercian Publications, p.29.
[9] Ibid.

me, I confess, it seems impossible. No doubt this happens when the good and faithful servant is introduced into his Lord's joy, is inebriated by the richness of God's dwelling. In some wondrous way he forgets himself and ceasing to belong to himself, he passes entirely into God and adhering to him, he becomes one with him in spirit."[10]

In response to St. Bernard's question of this becoming an abiding state in this world: "let those who have had the experience make a statement", I would say this to him: With no self remaining, life in this world is indeed possible. The only problem, it's not meant for this world. Still, as you say, "It is in God's hands to give it to whom he wishes It is not obtained by human efforts". But if it's not meant for this world, why would God give it? Whether the experience be fleeting or permanent, its purpose is God informing us – and all who would hear – that in our final estate there is no awareness of any self. It has informed us that in the end there is no eternal self – which is something we could not have known without this graced experience. That other people do not understand this, deny it or don't like it, is not our concern. God gave it, He did it, it is His will.

Something else, while fleeting experiences of no-self are indeed ecstatic foretastes of heaven – which is why we don't see how it would be possible to live this way in the world – yet, should it become a permanent state, the ecstatic experience is gone forever. This is because self – that was suspended in ecstasy – is no more, thus there is nothing left to suspend, no ecstasy possible anymore. Life without self becomes an everyday state with no return to a former state. It takes years of acclimating to no self-awareness, years that are neither ecstatic nor heavenly – in some ways, inhuman. But fortunately there is more to our final estate than noself, more even than your anticipation of the Resurrection, and what is more this, is the Ascension. This Ascension experience, however, is even more unbelievable than no-self.

In two-thousand years of Christian mystical lore, St. Bernard is the sole figure who poses the question: *whether or not there could be a perma-*

---

[10] Ibid.

nent cessation or falling away of self in this life. Though he didn't see how it was possible – nobody knows ahead of time – yet he left the door open, posed the question, a question I have spent almost thirty years answering.

We hardly need ask if other contemplatives or dedicated people have had St. Bernard's experience. The answer is, "absolutely"! I only came upon St. Bernard's experience when reading the life of Blessed Henry Suso, who also knew the experience.

We all know of Meister Eckhart and the stir he created over this issue.[11] And then there is St. John of the Cross who roamed Spanish cloisters four-hundred years before he became known to the public. The list goes on and on. St. Bernard's experience was not unique or rare; it goes on to this day and has always been part and parcel of the Church's lore of Mystical Theology.

Perhaps no one articulated this experience more uniquely than St. Paul. When rapt to the Third Heaven he shifts to the third person, and in this heavenly estate is "someone IN Christ" – people think Paul only said this out of modesty so people won't think too highly of him. Yet he says he has only told the "truth". Paul had no qualms of immodesty about telling us, "It is no longer I who live, but Christ who lives IN me", this too was a truthful statement. Yet note the difference between the two experiences. In his earthly life Paul affirms Christ lives IN him, whereas in heaven there is only "someone" IN Christ, about whom he can say nothing. The difference is between Christ living in us (self) and the final estate of living IN Christ (no-self). If anything could keep man humble it would be a foretaste of heaven – in Christ you are no better than anyone else, in fact, "you" don't count at all.

These experiences were regarded as foretastes or glimpses of a more heavenly estate, an estate wherein there was no self. If, after read-

---

[11] Eckhart's abrupt disappearance from the face of the earth is a mystery. Renowned during his lifetime, a gifted theologian and speaker, a superior of his Order, yet nobody knows when, how or where he died, or was even buried – shame on the Dominicans!

ing these accounts someone tells us there is no such experience as no-self, or that self continues for all eternity, it obviously flies in the face of these accounts – numerous accounts. But what motive would anyone have for denying these first-hand experiences? When St. Bernard says: "To lose yourself as though you no longer existed, to cease completely to experience yourself ", do theologians think he was delusional or that he misunderstood his own experience – as if someone else could know better? All we can say is that throughout the ages reports of no-self have come down to us from numerous saints and others highly revered in the Church. Both Christ and Paul spoke of losing self, even loss of soul – depending on the translation.

Throughout the ages, Christian mystics have spoken of "kenosis" or self-emptying as a state they not only desired on earth, but one they also knew belonged to their heavenly estate.[12] Despite accounts of this experience, however, no one has left an account of no-self becoming an abiding state in this world, which does not mean it did not happen, only that we have no account of it. As to why we have no accounts, let us just say man's ultimate transcendence of self has always been suspect, incomprehensible and problematic for the theologian. The tension between the mystics and theologians is that their encounters with the mysteries of Faith have come from very different sources.

Although Mystical Theology deals with man's experiences of God and the type of knowledge given therein, it has no direct relevance

---

[12] Kenosis was also defined by the Desert Fathers as a state of "apatheia" or freedom from passions, affections, desires, (even suffering), a state of impassability and disinterestedness regarded as necessary for "deification" or complete transformation into Christ. Most accounts of "apatheia" seem to articulate the psychological effects of the egoless Unitive state, a state wherein the affective system is perfectly balanced – and can never be imbalanced. There is much more I could say on this subject. It is interesting to note, however, that reaching a state of "apatheia" was also the goal of the Stoics for whom the ultimate reality was the Logos – the cosmic generating, governing principle and reason imminent and active in all reality. (For Philo, of course, the Logos was an intermediate between divine reality (God) and the sensible world; and for St. John: "In the beginning was the Logos ....").

for other branches of theology.[13]   Where a problem arises is when a non-contemplative or non-mystical theologian goes outside his field to impose his understanding on a piece of mystical literature. With his eye for heresy he takes liberties with his erasure, sometimes changing or adding to original writings. (There is also the problem of the copyist who omits what he cannot grasp, and the translator who can only give his own understanding.) This kind of academic meddling in mystical literature has always been a problem, it has gone on for centuries, a genuine disservice to God and man. But this is one reason, at least, why little has come down to us about a complete and permanent falling away of self. Very little managed to escape the censors.

The primary purpose of my writing, however, was less the subject of no-self than to put into the field of Mystical Theology a whole stage of the spiritual journey presently missing. This is the stage that comes after the Unitive state and continues up to the permanent cessation of self. Traditionally, once one has come to the Unitive state (and acclimated to it), one enters upon what is called an "Apostolic Mission", doing something for God and Church. Thus after going through all the purgative Nights and transforming Union one enters a new life of egoless service. These people are what I call "proficient contemplatives", they've been there, done that – but now what? All we know is they eventually die and go to heaven. Absolutely nothing is said about any further transformation during the interim between Union and heaven.[14] Thus one whole stage of the completed journey has not been covered, is never spoken of, is totally missing from the literature.

Though elsewhere I've said something about this stage, it has yet to be given the more lengthy treatment it requires. The purpose of this

---

[13] My reference to books on Christian Mysticism and Mystical Theology are written either by Catholic lay or religious theologians, which until recently had imprimaturs to guarantee their orthodoxy. Equally important books on the subject have been written by theologians of the Eastern Orthodox Church. (Christian Mysticism, of course, has never been an intrinsic part of Protestantism.)

[14] Although John of the Cross speaks of a further "Beatific transformation", he left no account of it.

present writing, however, is to ferret out objections to no-self that bothers theologians — not mystical theologians, but those of the more academic ilk.

The Theologian's Concern

It is a fact that theology has never tackled the subject of self or consciousness. From earliest writings, self or consciousness has hardly been mentioned. Evidently self was taken as a "given", either as a phenomena that could not be intellectually grasped, or as part of the soul requiring no thought or explanation. In this matter, theologians are like those, who, when referring to their "self", have in mind their entire being, a specific entity, a whole person, body and soul, personality. In short, an eternal identity that can never be lost. Thus words like "soul", "self", "person", "being", "personality", etc. are used as interchangeable terms that mean much the same thing. Given this view of self, it follows that without self, man would be annihilated (non-being), cease to exist, or return to absolute nothingness. This is why, perhaps, theologians think any report of no-self must either be reinterpreted, condemned or eliminated. In the absence of a true understanding of self (and consequently no-self) this, at least, seems to be the theological position. (We wonder, however, if even after knowing the true nature of self this would change a thing, or if no-self would become acceptable. I think not, because as said, the concern is not so much with what is lost, but rather, with "what" is gained).

As it stands, then, the theological understanding of loss of self goes no further than a loss of self-centeredness or selfishness. A loss of what is sometimes referred to as the "false self" (which is neither loss of ego or self). While theology concedes God is the true Center of individual being — a Center that is not self — this Central revelation only entails the loss of an egocentrism that hid God as the true Center of self. Beyond this recognition (God as the Center of being) theology has nothing further to say about any loss of self. It's only when a contemplative or mystical account of no-self does not conform to their usual understanding that no-self becomes suspect.

Simply put, the basis of the theologians' rejection of no-self is the belief that along with the created soul, the individual self is eternal. While self can change, it can never be lost. Without self, there would be no consciousness of any division between man and God, the created and uncreated, no awareness of the "other" – God. Given this theological view, the conclusion seems to be that all knowing depends solely on self-knowing or self-awareness and that without it, no knowing is possible – certainly no knowing God. But how, we ask, do the Persons of the Trinity know one another? Does the nature of God require *three self-consciousnesses?* Are the Divine Persons "other" to one another as we human beings are other to one another?

To claim that God's knowing requires self-consciousness not only denies God's inscrutable knowing, but requires us to make God into our image as a self-conscious being – indeed, I think theology does just that. In heaven, however, there is no need for consciousness or self as a way of knowing; as the Apostle tells us, in heaven we shall know as God knows – have the mind of the heavenly Christ. One does not need self or self-consciousness (or any consciousness) to know God. Indeed, there exists a "knowing" beyond all our human ways of knowing, a knowing beyond self and all its experiences. Thus being wholly transformed into Christ we shall know Father and Spirit as Christ knows Them, and not as we self-conscious beings know Them. When all is said and done, however, the bottom line is that loss of self is solely God's doing and thus it cannot possibly be unorthodox. If God can do this (and has), then either we have to expand our doctrinal perimeters or declare God unorthodox.

I like to think that the theologian's primary concern in all this is neither doctrine nor heresy, but rather, the preservation of Christ's humanity, not only his earthy humanity, but his glorified humanity in heaven. If, say, at the end of his earthly life Christ's human nature had been "absorbed" into his divine nature, what would this say about human nature in general? Apart from making our earthly sojourn relatively meaningless, it does not say much for humanity or its being made in the image of God. So the theologian's concern for keeping divine nature separate from human nature is less a concern for doctrine than for Christ's relevance to all of us. To believe Christ was totally divine and **not** also totally human would rob Him of his relevance because we could not relate to him, recapitulate his life, or even think of our ending as like His own. So we can understand the emphasis on Christ's humanity and the need to preserve it in the face of any mystical experience that might lead us to think otherwise – think that in the end there is only the Logos and no Christ. (Several mystics gave the impression that in the end there wasn't even the Trinity!)

According to the Fathers, in the Incarnation the Logos united human nature to Itself for all eternity, thus Christ's dual nature is eternal. The deification of Christ's human nature, then, did not mean it was transformed into the Uncreated Logos or "became" divine, either on earth or in heaven. So regardless of how Christ's human nature was deified, His human nature remains a "created nature" like our own. This means His human substance underwent no ontological change and that His soul remains eternally non-divine. Neither in his transfiguration or Ascension was there any ontological change in His human nature. Perhaps we could summarize this theological position as follows:

Once created, a creature remains a creature for all eternity. At no time does a creature lose its created nature – essence, substance,[15] etc., or is ever transformed into the divine. Thus, in their nature, essence or substance, Creator and creature are forever "other" and "separate" from one another. Despite terms like "oneness with God", "partaking" and "sharing" God's essence and divinity or becoming "like" Him, this never implies any crossing over from the created to the uncreated, or the created becoming divine. There is no such ontological change or transformation from one to the other. From beginning to end: man is man and God is God.

---

[15] St. Bernard states: "No doubt, the substance remains, though under another form, another glory, another power." (No need for change of substance when Christ's body and soul is the same substance as our own).

Given this theological view, we can understand why, if a mystic says or hints at anything to the contrary, he must be corrected. It is also why religious editors and commentators regard it theologically incorrect to speak of a completely selfless state, or whatever denotes "me, myself and I", lest it imply either that one has become divine or, that only the divine remains. For us to be totally transformed into Christ, however, does not mean our human nature "becomes" the uncreated Logos, rather, it means our human nature is transformed into Christ's deified human nature so to become one with the divine Logos – that is, enter into His same Hypostatic union.

I think the theological fear, however, is less with what is lost (few people actually know what self is) than with what is gained by this loss, namely, complete identity with Christ, no different from Christ. The only problem: without loss of self there is no gaining Christ – our loss, after all, is God's gain. So quite apart from what happens to our earthly human nature, the essence of its deification is being united to Christ's divine nature (Logos) in his same Hypostatic union of two natures.

This means that in the end we are not transformed into the Uncreated, but are as one with the Uncreated Logos as is Christ. And just as the divine Person of the Logos superseded the created person of Jesus, so too the divine Person of the Logos supersedes *our own human person*. The nature of Hypostatic Union, after all, is not a union of two persons – our self and Christ – but rather is solely the one Person of Christ. So while we never "become" God, yet, in the end, there is only God – Christ. This is the way our transformation into Christ works and what no-self is about.

This does not mean "we" (you or I) become Christ or are Christ; without self, there is no "I" to be Christ. So let us be very clear about how this works:

- In the beginning we are not divine.

- We never become divine or are transformed into the divine.

- In the end we are also not divine, because in the end there is no *I* (me, you, we, etc.), any self or human person to *be* divine.

- In the end there is *only* the one Christ.

I find no revelation, doctrine or dogma that conflicts with our complete transformation into Christ or its required loss of self. Those who think there is a conflict are either ignorant of the true nature of self or, possibly, the idea of losing self scares the beegeebees out of them. If nothing else, they have completely underestimated the end God destined for man.

Needless to say, for the mystics, loss of self has never posed a problem; after all, it is God's doing and not their own. That God could do something theologically incorrect would strike them as humorous – though not impossible. We should keep in mind that books about the mystics are written by those whose credentials are academic and not experiential; whose knowledge of the mystical journey is vicarious and not first hand.

That such commentators feel compelled to correct and reinterpret has been the source of some false and misleading notions regarding the spiritual journey and man's ultimate end. While it is always best to read the mystics themselves, unfortunately, few original manuscripts have come down to us that have not been corrected, mistranslated, altered, or otherwise tampered with.

Some Theological Concerns

As regards no-self, as best I can discern, the theologian's concern for orthodoxy is with the following issues: ontological change of substance and the loss of person, individual identity, personality, the "other". We might address each of these concerns separately.

Ontological Change

Although the change of one substance into another or transformation of the created into the Uncreated is a theological no-no, we can think of a major ontological change of substance that lies at the very heart of Christianity – namely, the Eucharist. This is the most radical example of God's affecting a complete ontological change we know of. The Eucharist is created bread and wine changed into the whole Person of Christ, body, soul and divinity.[16] Now if God can transubstantiate bread and wine into Christ, can He not transubstantiate creatures made in His own image? If mere bread can become Christ, why not ourselves? Why would God grant this miracle to bread and deny it to man? Who is to tell us God cannot do this or would never do so? Let those who think this is impossible for God to make a statement; to me, I confess, it is not impossible.

Prior to consecration a drop of water, signifying ourselves, is put into the wine with the Apostle Peter's words, "As Christ deigned to share our humanity, so too may we share His divinity". What is then transubstantiated is not only the wine but the water – ourselves. The water can no more be separated from the wine than we can be separated from Christ. This is not a mere union of two, but an indivisible Oneness – One Christ.

If we ask how God brings about the transformation of the created into the Uncreated, the Eucharist is His silent manifest answer. This transformation is not only what the Eucharist is about, but informs us exactly how God works to transform ourselves. St. Augustine noted that just as the ordinary bread we eat is transformed into our body, similarly, when we eat the Bread of Life we are transformed into Christ's body. Thus God transforms us by consuming us (literally "eats us up"). We are gradually transformed, absorbed and assimilated into Christ's divine being

---

[16] If it be objected that bread and wine is only changed into Christ's body, but not into His soul and divinity, we should keep in mind that without a soul there is no body, and in the unique case of the risen Christ, where there is no body and soul there is also no divinity. (The Eucharist is not the detached body of Christ).

such that we can never be separated out – as Paul said, he wanted to "dissolve" to be with Christ. In experience, this dissolution is also the Living Flame of Love (in the Center of our being), God literally burning us out – consuming us. So whether we are consumed by fire, love, or the Eucharist, it is all the same. In purely philosophical terms, this is a genuine ontological change, a change from what we were not, into what Christ is.

Why anyone would object to the soul's ultimate ontological transformation into Christ I cannot imagine. This transformation was intended from the beginning. It is the direction of our life, our end in God is no different than God. This is the end destined by God's ongoing creative act, an act that is not over until it is over. While we are not transformed into the Father or Holy Spirit, we are, in truth, totally, ontologically transformed into Christ.

Although created bread and wine is not changed into the Uncreated Logos, yet because Christ's incarnate body and soul cannot be separated from the Logos, the Eucharist is the whole divine Person – Christ. So too, in the Eucharist not only is our body and soul transformed into Christ 's body and soul, but in this transformation the divine Person supersedes our individual person just as it does in Christ. Thus to know how our transformation works, the Eucharist is all we need to know. Also, we must not forget that the Eucharist is the heavenly glorified body of Christ, a body obviously not available to the senses – either on earth or in heaven. The Beatific Vision, after all, is not a visual seeing with bodily eyes; heaven is beyond the senses and its particular way of knowing. The Eucharist informs us of all this and so much more. I've always said: the Eucharist is the resolution of all God's mysteries, it is the silent manifestation and summation of them all.

Substance and Person

We can appreciate the early Councils spending much of the time searching for adequate words and terms to express the mysteries of Faith. Several terms especially problematic were "substance" and "hypostasis". It seems the original Greek term "hypostasis" used for the Trinity (three hypostasis in One God) was dropped because its Latin translation was "substance" or "essence", and the Trinity, of course, is not three distinct substances or essences. Tertullian (who later left the Church) came up with the term "Person" to signify a "rational hypostasis", and thereafter the Trinity was defined as "three Persons in one God". Now the term "Person" is unfortunate because the human mind cannot go beyond any notion of "person" other than that of an individual human being – an individual self in fact. Today especially, "person" implies a discrete being, entity or individual, which is why mental images of the Trinity tend to be three individual persons or beings – tritheism, in other words. In Christian icons, for example, the Trinity has often been depicted as: 1) an old man with a beard, 2) a younger man, 3) and a bird.

Even conceptually, the Trinity as three Persons is so difficult to explain or articulate most people avoid it like the plague. (Once I listened to three theologians hemming and hawing trying to explain the Trinity to a Jewish intellectual). Yet the Trinity is the central, pivotal Christian revelation, without it there is no Christ or Christianity.[17] We have to admit, Christian terminology has always been problematic when it comes to expressing the mystery that is God. But since we are stuck with the term "Person", we might use this term to come to a better understanding of no-self. Thus it can be asked: does loss of self mean the loss of person or personhood?

While the Fathers never equated self and person, it stands to reason there can be no human person without self, since self expresses the person. *To be without self, then, is also to be without person.* This would not

---

[17] In all fairness, the Early Fathers' notion of the Greek term "persona" was quite different from the Western notion of "person". For the Fathers, "persona" was understood as the "manifestation" of an otherwise unknowable Godhead, whereas in the West "persona" meant "mask" – an obviously unsuitable term. Rather than philosophical and theological terms, the Trinity might be better articulated in more experiential terms. Thus St. Paul spoke of the "height, breadth, and depth" of God – three distinct dimensions and experiences of God which man can more easily grasp and relate to. Though experience is still not "it", yet it's closer to truth than ideas and concepts.

apply to a divine Person, however, who has no need of a human self to express or manifest Itself.

As already noted, as it pertains to Christ, "Person" denotes the unique union of His divine and human natures – a "hypostatic union" – which is more than the union of body and soul, more even than union with God realized in the Unitive state – or "mystical marriage" as St. Bernard called it.[18] It is because of this hypostatic union the divine Person of the Logos superseded (encompassed or overshadowed) the human person of Jesus, and thus Christ is two natures united by and in One divine Person. And just as the Logos superseded the person of Jesus, so too, in our final transformation into Christ our human person is superseded by Christ's divine Person. Thus when our whole person is transformed into the whole Person of Christ, there is no human person remaining, there is just the one divine Person of Christ. So loss of self is both the loss of person and the gaining of "Person" – partaking in Christ's same hypostatic union. (Once again, this does not mean "you" or "I" are divine or have "become" divine. In the end, there is no "I" to be divine, there is only the divine Person – Christ).

A theological objection might be this: if the Christian goal is complete transformation into Christ, and if those in heaven have reached this goal, this would mean there is nobody in heaven BUT Christ – Christ in the Trinity, that is. It goes without saying that heaven is not peopled by countless different Christs, nor is the heavenly Christ a singular, self-

---

[18] John of the Cross tells us man has many interior centers (or levels of a single center) and thus we have various levels of oneness with God. The three main levels of this oneness are 1). A natural union by which God sustains our existence; 2). A supernatural union by which God is especially present in every soul in the state of grace; 3). A Mystical Union that St. John (following St. Bernard) called "Spiritual Marriage", otherwise known as the Unitive State, which John held to be an irreversible state of grace. Nowhere does John of the Cross – or anyone for that matter – mention the soul's eventual or possible "hypostatic" union with God, a union reserved for Christ alone. The Unitive state has never been regarded as equivalent to Christ's Hypostatic Unity, and rightly so, the two are not the same. In the Unitive state the phenomenal self remains, thus the divine Person has not wholly superseded the human person.

conscious human person; in Christ, there is no self at all. Thus all are transformed into the one Christ, no one is left out and nothing left over. While this reality may fly in the face of our childish notions of heaven – as the ultimate meeting of the clan or where all earthly desires are fulfilled – heaven is "where" God is, that is, beyond all man's images and ideas of it. In heaven, the brilliance and glory of the Beatific Vision blinds all consciousness of self and others. At the same time, the faculties of will and intellect have ceased to function because the reality and truth of heaven is beyond their limits.[19] In heaven there is only God's will; and in place of intellect we shall have "the mind of Christ". So in heaven we have the Father's will, Christ's mind and body, and the Spirit's own life. Nothing is wanting, nothing left out that has not been transformed – nothing but self, that is.

So apart from Father and Spirit, in heaven there is only One Person, One Christ, into which all individual persons are transformed. Otherwise – *"how will God be All in All if something human survives in man?"* Body and soul are transformed into Christ, while self, as a faculty of the earth-bound soul, ceases altogether. It ceases to function because Christ's divine knowing or mind supersedes any earthly need for consciousness or self. Thus, as the Apostle tells us, in heaven, howsoever God knows us – knows anything in fact – is equally how we shall know.

The "Other"

As for the theologian's concern about there being no "other" in heaven, they forget there are two "Others" in heaven beside Christ – we are not, after all, transformed into Father or Holy Spirit. And just as the Trinity is not three *human* Persons, so too, the Trinity is not *humanly* "other" to one another. The Trinity is not three selves or three individual "I

---

[19] In my view, the function or faculties of soul (consciousness, will, intellect) are experiential "created energies" generated by God's non-experiential "Uncreated energy" or power. In the Unitive state there is a certain union of the two energies, but in the end (no-self) Uncreated energy snuffs out (consumes or transforms) created energy, at which point these created faculties or energies of the soul cease to function – cease to be.

am's." In the Trinity, there is no self at all. It should come as no surprise that God's way-of-knowing is not our human, self-conscious way-of-knowing.

A friend once asked, "If we're all to be transformed into Christ, does this mean that in heaven I won't see my parents or loved ones?" My answer: "*However Christ knows them in heaven is how you will know them.*" What few people realize is that the glory of heaven is such that just knowing your loved ones are in this same glory is all you'll ever need to know about them. By its very nature, heaven pales all worldly interests anyway. Having the mind of Christ — the Logos and intelligence of all creation — means we will have his own "knowing". Thus in heaven, "knowing" is not wanting.

But what about those in heaven we regard as "special" friends of God, so special we even pray to them? If only Christ is there, why bother praying to the saints at all? Indeed, are they even "there"? Christ actually gave us the answer when he said in effect, "Those who honor me (or witness to me) on earth, I shall honor (or give witness to) in heaven". This is the why and wherefore of the communion-of-saints. When we pray (or petition) the help of someone in heaven who we know has honored Christ on earth, our prayer goes directly to Christ, who will honor that saint as Christ sees fit. Although every prayer is heard — and answered as God knows best — if Christ wants people on earth to honor those who especially honored Him, this honor may become known on earth by granting the petition or prayer, this is how it works . Christ always honors those who have honored Him, and certainly God has honored no one in heaven more than Mary — in her name, God grants everything! As for our caring for those on earth or those undergoing purgatory — or for that matter, caring for the whole of creation — we shall have Christ's same caring. And who, after all, cares more for us and all creation than the One Who created it?

What Self is Not

Earlier we noted that for most people, theologians included, all references to "self" are understood as references to a whole being or entity, to the total person , a unique individual or personality, and so on. The reason for this is based on their own experience, and indeed, this is the self-experience or what self experiences itself to be. This is also why, when people hear or think of "no-self", there is nothing or nobody left to think about, and thus no-self has a totally negative connotation. While there's no denying the self-experience, we have to be philosophical when it comes to examining the truth of what this experience gives us to believe. Since elsewhere we have already gone over what self is, let us now say what self is not.

Self is Not Our True Identity

Our true identity is not "who" we are within a social structure, but "what" we are in the eyes of the One who created us. Thus when people talk about loss of identity, they can only be speaking about what they thought they were, not what they really are in the eyes of God. (Early in life I realized only God knew me, because only the Creator knew what he had made, knew what I really was – what anything was – thus I left my true identity to God and thought no more about it). So loss of self is not the loss of one's true identity, which one should not presume to know in the first place.

At the same time, no-self does not refer to any loss of one's social identity or life history; nor is it amnesia where one forgets their name and past. (Amnesia is a memory disorder, not the cessation of reflexive-consciousness.)

Here we might recall the apostle's saying: "We do not know what we are now, we only know what we shall be – we shall be like him (Christ)". At that time "we shall have the mind of Christ" and "no longer know ourselves as we do now, but know as God knows us". Thus the Apostle affirms there is an end to our self-knowing (self-awareness or consciousness) when we take on the mind of Christ and His divine way of knowing.

It us noteworthy that the apostle did not say "We do not know *who* we are now", or "*who* we shall be", rather, he said *what* we are now and *what* we shall be. Obviously, our identity both here and in heaven is not "who" we are, but "what" we are and "what" we shall be. The implication is that identity, both human and divine, is not a matter of "who", but of "what". "What" is of the essence, while "who" is accidental – one among many. The Eucharist resolves the mystery of the One and the many. Despite innumerable sensible hosts, their essence or identity is the One same Christ. So too, our ultimate identity is "what" we are (or shall be), not our individuality or "who" we are among the many. Our identity is beyond the multiplicity of individual selves. So loss of self is not the loss of identity, but rather the finding or revelation of our true and final identity – Christ. Needless to say, this identity does not make us God. No one can say: "**I** am Christ" or "**You** are Christ", for in the end, without self, there is no longer "I" or "you" to **be** Christ.

Self is Not Personality

As for no-self being the loss of "personality", it is not that. In my view, personality is man's most superficial and non-eternal feature – in a silent state, for example, there is no personality to speak of. Personality is only as much as other people know of us. As one's individual expression, it is only what appears on the surface, what others see and judge; usually, it's the basis of people's like or dislike of one another. If we cannot love others beyond or despite their personalities, then we will never know the nature of divine love. What is precious to God is the soul made in His own image and likeness, not what sets one human being off from another. Then too, being stuck with a particular personality for all eternity is an impoverished notion of man's final estate. In short, the nature of personality is neither one's true identity nor is it self. Loss of self is not the loss of personality.

Self is Not the Soul

If soul is defined as the "principle of life" or "form of the body" then self is obviously not the soul – because without self life goes right on, and the body as well. With the cessation of self, however, it is no longer possible to make any distinction between body and soul, there is no longer consciousness of either one. Self had been responsible for our whole experiential life, including the dichotomy of body and soul. Having been deprived of this experiential knowledge, however, we are left with no way of knowing the true nature of what remains beyond self. This is why the *true nature of what remains beyond self must be revealed*, there is absolutely no other way of knowing. So let us keep in mind that although self is responsible for the experience of soul and body, self is neither one. (While experience of the bodily senses remains, they're solely concerned with the obvious – material things).

As to the question: "What is the true nature of what remains?", in the absence of consciousness (with its multiple and varied experiences) to provide any answer, this can only be revealed by God – as Christ affirmed, no one knows Christ unless the Father reveals Him. Though we thought we knew Christ all our lives, this revelation is like nothing known before. The ultimate revelation of Christ **IS** the resurrection, this **IS** His identity – as He said, "I am the Resurrection". Thus the revelation of "what" remains beyond the death of self **is** Christ. This is also why, so long as we do not understand the true nature of Jesus' death, we cannot understand the true nature of our own death – the death of self, that is.

The resurrected body, of course, is not what the senses see – just as in the Eucharist, Christ is not what appears to the senses. It is because the resurrected body is not what the senses perceive that its true nature can only be revealed. (Remember, in heaven the senses are also defunct).

What theologians fail to take into account is that self (or consciousness) is only the *medium* of man's knowledge and experience of

God.[20] Self is not "being", but only the experience of being; it is not soul, but the major faculty of the soul. In other words, loss of self does not mean loss of soul or being, but rather the gain of Christ's whole Person.

Speaking of the soul's faculties, in his discussion of "memory", St. Augustine includes the soul's awareness of itself – reflexive consciousness. Whether or not he believed memory was responsible for self-consciousness I cannot say, but we know Aquinas eliminated memory as a separate faculty. Possibly both men regarded the intellect as the seat of self-consciousness, I don't know. But whatever their conclusion, I know that without consciousness (all of which is "self-consciousness") there would be no development of intellect or will. Consciousness, then, is first and foremost **the** major faculty or function of the human soul. (In modern terms, self is also everything we know as the "psyche" and all its experiences). As the primary function of soul, consciousness is responsible for the experience of individuality, "me, myself and I" – expressed by the "person" – but which, when our transformation is complete, ceases to function. Why? Because Christ has no-self, the divine Christ is not an individual separate human self. What is transformed into Christ is not an earthly function or faculty, but the soul created in God's image.

No-Self is Not the Goal or End

The ultimate goal in Christianity is not to get rid of self. God made it, it is what we are, and we are to live it to the fullest extent possible to be what God wants us to be. The idea we can somehow go beyond or transcend a self we never accepted, never lived and never experienced to its fullest, is mere wishful thinking, it won't happen. To live self fully, however, can only be done in oneness with God; there is no other way. Thus our goal is to live with full and continuous consciousness of God, to be as aware of God as we are of ourselves. But no matter how hard

---

[20] We talk about the knowledge of God being either "mediated" or "unmediated" (direct or immediate) and tend to think that an "experience" of God is unmediated, while intellectual knowledge is mediated. This turns out not to be true however. All experience of God is mediated by consciousness or self. Unmediated knowing belongs to God alone.

we strive for this, we can never bring it about by our own efforts. Yet, if we give it our all – only God knows when we've done that – God steps in and makes it happen. In the ensuing Unitive state we are as automatically conscious of God as we are of ourselves – the two (God and self) given autonomously in a single reflexive action. This Unitive state can be called "Christ consciousness" in that we now live with the same unitive awareness of God as did Jesus in his earthly life – in his human nature, that is.

But living this Unitive state was not the end for Jesus, nor is it for us. Few people understand why, on the cross, Jesus cried out that God had abandoned him – what happened? He was uttering his experience of the falling away of the entire Unitive state, his "Christ consciousness" (experience of oneness with God), and thus he gave utterance to the only true death-experience man will ever have. The divine Center, the life-force and cause of consciousness is gone. It is gone because the soul reached a point at which there was nothing left to transform or deify. The soul's created energy is finally consumed and superseded by the Uncreated energy with which it had been united in the union of wills (energies). Transformation (deification) is now complete. It is over, done with – as Jesus said, "It is finished!" This death of self is the end of all experience of life, energy, being, soul; in short, there are no experiences at all. This is literally a state of the walking dead. One thing we do know, however, and know absolutely: this death was a swift, definitive act of God, after which, the sole question that arises is: *what is this that remains? What is the true nature of what remains beyond self?*

As already said, the answer to this can only be revealed, a revelation that is the resurrection. When Christ said, *"I am the Resurrection"* he was making a statement of identity: this is who and what he is. Thus if someone asked, "Who is Christ?" the answer is, "The Resurrection." Christ did not say "I will be resurrected and so will you", rather he said he was "It"- he is what the Resurrection is. Most people, of course, think of resurrection as the body coming back to life, and while this was Christ's way of affirming the Apostles' belief in him ("If Christ had not been resurrected our faith would be in vain"), yet in itself, a bodily reappearance is unnecessary to those who already have Faith – "Blessed are those who believe and do not see." So beyond the death of self, the identity of what remains is Christ. Christ is the Resurrection and the only Resurrection man will ever know. (It's at the Ascension that the body dissolves into its eternal, heavenly and glorious estate). Christ, then, resolves the mystery of the true nature of what remains beyond all self.[21] The Incarnate Christ reveals the mystery that is us, just as his life and journey revealed our own. We not only recapitulate his earthly journey in union with God, but recapitulate his human end and destiny as well. Thus just as Christ gave up his self, so do we. Those who object to no-self need only look to Christ for a true understanding of the ultimate *kenosis* – His and their own.

After the Resurrection, of course, there remains the Ascension, Christ's return (and our entry) into the glory of the Father whence He came. If the truth be known, however, it is only Christ who dies, only Christ who rises, and only Christ ascends. All this is beyond the limits of a mere human being. But who can understand it? Indeed, who can even believe it? The mysteries of Christianity are indeed mystical; yet the way they have been presented and interpreted to the public at large is, I'm afraid, a sad and terrible disservice to Christ and the whole Trinity.

Fear of No-Self

Since no one can know the full extent of self until it is gone, it follows they also cannot know the full extent of what no-self means. By its very nature, the mind is incapable of grasping any kind of life without

---

[21] Should it be objected there has to be someone "other" to whom Christ is revealed (at Resurrection), we need only look to Christ for the answer. In his earthly life Jesus never said, "I am God" or "I am the Logos" because this would have equated his human self (his human nature) with God. Thus if prior to his death the divine Logos was revealed to Jesus, this revelation would not have been to "another person" because Jesus-Logos is the one same Person. If, on the other hand, the Logos was only revealed to Jesus after his death (no-self), then what remained in the absence of his human self-knowing was solely the Logos divine knowing. The point is that in neither case was (or is) the Logos' identity revealed (at Resurrection) to some "other" Person.

its self or self-awareness. (Self cannot even think of such a life, for whatever it thinks such a life to be, it is self's own thinking about it!) This is why, when people think about life without self-awareness they can only think of complete annihilation – body, soul, no one left at all. No wonder they reject no-self. By the same token, however, because the mind cannot intellectually grasp no-self, theology is left with no way to pass judgment on it.

Perhaps nothing is more frightening to the unprepared than a sudden premonition or fleeting experience of no-self – I've heard hundreds of such accounts. There is no underestimating the fear self has of its own demise, a demise always viewed in a negative, ominous light – for some people, just the idea is too frightening to ponder. So it is understandable why, for most people, the prospect of no-self is bleak indeed. This fear of losing self might also be a reason the traditional theologian rejects no-self. Apart from his own fears, he sincerely wants Christ to entice others and not scare them away. At the same time, however, this fear can be a major obstacle to a rational consideration of no-self. It's much easier to dismiss the subject altogether – "Can't happen, not the truth!" – than rationally respond to an argument as to its truth.

Because the average theology student, reader or novice, would only be upset with no-self, we can understand why it would be a useless subject to bring up – why bother with the end when people have hardly made a beginning? While I do not think this is behind the theological objections to no-self, I agree it is a useless subject for beginners. Although there are many fine theologians around, few have delved into mystical theology, and even fewer have contributed anything to it. The bottom line is that for theologians in general, the subject of no-self is not within their purview or range of expertise. Thus the fact they dismiss it out of hand should come as no surprise, on this subject they are out of their element, not in a position to handle it.

I am convinced that those who object to complete transformation into Christ are those who would rather hang on to their self than surrender it to Christ. Whether this choice is out of fear or lack of trust, the fact remains, human nature being what it is, will choose the security of self over the insecurity of an unknown Christ. Until the end of the journey nobody knows the fullness of Christ, thus no one knows ahead of time what they are getting into.

Even though people say they trust Christ and sincerely desire to do so, unknowingly they are only making a choice for what they themselves know of Christ – indeed, who can make a choice for a Christ they do not know? Yet, unless we can someday do this, make a choice for the unknown Christ – unknown to self or beyond all self – we will never know the fullness of Christ or the Truth that is Christ.

Conclusion

As I see it, theology has never penetrated the true nature of Christ's death and resurrection. Perhaps this mystery of Christ can only be known in the reliving of it – our own death and resurrection, that is. No one, of course, can know the fullness of Christ ahead of time, we can only know as much as we have been transformed. Thus, until our transformation is complete, we can never have the full story on Christ or know the fullness of God's mystery – Christ. For sure, the cessation of self is Christ's own kenosis and the only death-experience man will ever know.

When transformation into Christ is complete, self falls away because we have reached Jesus' own death where, in truth, it is not we who die, but Christ who dies for us. This is the ultimate kenosis or "self-emptying".[22] Christianity has always known there is more to the mystery of Christ's death than merely his physical demise. The true mystery of His

---

[22] Elsewhere I have pointed out and explained that "who" dies is not ourselves, but rather, Christ who dies for us. The failure to understand this, however, is a failure to understand the true nature of the Unitive state. The moment self has been totally transformed into Christ, the divine Center goes out because there is nothing left to transform – just as a burning flame goes out when there is no fuel left to consume. This is not just the death of some insignificant little self, but death of the Divine – the Divine that had been transforming or consuming self.

death was the death of his human self (consciousness and its unique energy).

That Jesus also died physically was to manifest and dramatize for all time the importance of this kenosis or no-self event. Christ on the cross is a major symbol of Christianity, a symbol for death of self, a divine doing that opens up a whole new dimension to the mystery of Christ. Both in his death and resurrection Christ manifested, made visible for all to see, a truth we too will come to know and experience.

I will quit this paper with a few words on St. Paul's symbolic use of Baptism as the primary symbol for death and resurrection. Paul likens our baptism to Christ's death and resurrection, thus in baptism we die with Christ, are buried with Christ, and rise in glory with Christ. He says in our Baptism the "old self" dies and a new self or a new person rises. (In modern terms, Paul's "old self" is what, today, we call the "ego", man's original self-center). To think, however, that all we need to get rid of this "old self" (or ego) is to be baptized . . . well, as beautifully symbolic as this may be, it is not, unfortunately, the reality of our actual baptism.

The grace of Baptism is more akin to God's implanting a mustard seed, a seed of faith and grace that must be continually nurtured if it is to grow and mature. So while baptism by water may temporarily purify the old self, it does not do away with it. Doing away with the old self will take a purification by fire, where God burns out the ego-center to make room for Himself – that is, replaces the old self-center with Himself, a new divine Center. With this divine Center we definitely emerge a new self, a new person. So getting rid of the old self is not as easy as being baptized.

Paul's use of Baptism, then, for what in reality entails a whole experiential process of change and transformation, is purely symbolic. At best, baptism only alerts us to the reality of what we have yet to go through.[23] But what I find most problematic about comparing or even

---

[23] I am not aware of any mystic or Saint who has been through this ordeal and

equating baptism with Christ's death is that it can lead people to think that what happened on the cross was merely the death of Christ's "old self" (his ego) and the birth of His "new self" or new person. Nothing, however, could be further from the truth than such a view. Yet I have read books making such a case — that Christ's death was the falling away of his old ego self and the Resurrection, the discovery of His true self as God.

The implication, of course, is that Christ's earthy life and ministry was lived from his ego-center with no abiding consciousness of oneness with God — which means in his earthly life He had not even reached the common contemplative's Unitive state! Preposterous. While I do not believe this was Paul's view of Christ's death — but rather a view of our death — he nevertheless opened the door to such an interpretation when he linked baptism to Christ's death as the death of the old self and rising of a new self.[24] In this, Paul's symbolism was off the mark.

Where Paul was on the mark, however, was equating our death and resurrection (not our baptism) with that of Christ's, only I would take it a step further. We not only die and rise *with* Christ or *like* Christ, rather, Christ dies *for* us — in our stead, that is. I take literally the Christian profession, "Christ died for us" and do not limit its truth to past tense.

While the human Jesus only died once — as all of us will — yet the divine Christ, in like fashion, dies for each one of us in turn. This is why there is no such thing as "death" — Christ dies for us. So the big surprise that awaits everyone is that despite medical pronouncements, life goes right on and doesn't miss a beat! Only now, it is not our life, but Christ's. Thus Christ is not only the mystery of our life, but also the mystery of our death.

---

linked it to Baptism, even symbolically. Although this process is a death of the old self, the old person, and the emergence of a whole new person and new self, yet no one who has been through it regards it as of the same nature as Christ's death and Resurrection — much less their Baptism.

[24] Paul makes our rising with Christ contingent upon our having "grown into union with Him" — Romans 6.5

Postscript

A well-known theologian who has written extensively on the Christians Mystics read the first half of this paper. He said my view of Christ smacked of Nestorianism – an early Church heresy that held Christ was two Persons (one human and one Divine). He also questioned why the tone of my paper was so anti-theologian. (After citing me for heresy, he wonders what I have against theologians?)

Anyway, I'm not anti-theologian. On the contrary, theologians are the only people I know who seriously ponder and question the mysteries of faith. My finding is that most Christians are either totally uneducated – don't know the first thing about Christianity – or are "easy believers". This is why I so appreciate theologians and have a high regard for their contributions, more especially those of the early Church Fathers.

About Nestorianism. Since my theological case for no-self is based on Christ's being a single Divine person, I'm at a loss to understand the Nestorian indictment. I have said repeatedly *Christ was never a human person,* but solely a divine Person. Thus, based on this theology, if one were to be wholly transformed into Christ it stands to reason he would have to transcend his human personhood – cease to be a human person – in order to share Christ's same Divine Personhood. Our transformation into Christ cannot result in two persons – one divine, one human – because such is **not** Christ. That, in a nutshell, is my thesis. It totally depends on Christ's singular Divine Personhood.

Giving it my best thought, the whole problem boils down to theologically equating "self" with "person". In this thinking, if you take away self you take away the person and vice versa.

And not only does theology attribute self to the human person, it attributes self to the divine Persons as well. Thus (it has been said) the Trinity is three Selves, three "I am's", three individuals, three consciousnesses and all this entails. In my view, this amounts to tritheism. But this is why, when theology equates "person" with "self" it follows that my saying the divine Person of Christ is without self, amounts to denying Christ as a divine Person. And so too, when I affirm Christ had a human self, this amounts (theologically) to saying Christ was a human person — and there's the Nestorianism! *What I said, however, was that Christ had a human self, but was a Divine Person. Clearly I nowhere equate self and person.*

But this is why my affirming the divine Person of Christ is without self is viewed by the theologian as wrong — heretical. For the theologian, Christ is equally a divine Person and a divine self. If this were true, however, then Christ had no human self — because as a divine Person he only had a divine self. But who can believe the man Jesus never experienced a human self such as we do? I hold that *in his human nature Christ experienced self just as we do. Christ's divine nature (the Logos), however, from all eternity is absolutely selfless — as is the whole Godhead or Trinity. Self is what distinguishes man, not God. This is my thesis.*

If one really knew what self was, he would never make the mistake of equating self and person — be the person human or divine. Self is a faculty of the soul, the faculty of self-awareness, the faculty of consciousness. The human "person", on the other hand, is traditionally defined as a union of body and soul. So while person includes the soul's faculty of self, person is not a faculty, not a self. Though self is responsible for man's experience of individual personhood, still, self is not the person.

This is also why, without self, there is no longer any experience of individual personhood — nor the experience of any person at all. What is transformed into the whole divine Person of Christ is not a faculty, not a self, but the whole human person — body and soul. The case I have made in this paper is based on this first-hand knowledge of no-self leaving no individual human person.

Obviously, equating person and self is not only at odds with my position, but based on my reading, at odds with the Early Councils that nowhere equates the two. Christ's self (his consciousness) belonged to his human nature, while his Person remained the divine "hypostasis" of the

Logos.   While I doubt anyone has a problem defining a human person, when applied to God, however, the term "Person" is highly problematic, even inapt. God is not a person such as we are, and to expect the human mind to grapple with God as three Persons, well, it amounts to a mental "tritheism" – three separate ideas and images. The bottom line, however, is that few people, including theologians, know what self is. If they knew, they would not equate self and person.

5

A NOTE ON RESURECTION

A NOTE ON RESURRECTION

Given the theological definition of "person" as the union of body and soul, I find the theological belief in their separation at death a contradiction. At death is a person split in two, the soul going one way, the body another? Are the saints in heaven only half-persons? Either "person" denotes the union of body and soul, or the soul alone. We cannot have it both ways at once.

Christian theology dug itself into a hole when it adopted the Greek dualism of body and soul. Initially, because of the Resurrection, Christians upheld the oneness and wholeness of body and soul, yet over time they reverted to the Greek notion of their separation at death. With this split, man's wholeness falls apart, the human person is torn in two, leaving the soul in heaven waiting for its body – at the end of the world no less! That we must wait for the body until everybody else is dead makes no sense.

For each person, his death **is** the end of the world. Since death is a release from time and space, resurrection does not take place in time – whatever time the world is supposed to end. Also, because of this split in the person, people have come to think of body and soul as two discrete entities, which not only perpetuates a faulty understanding of "person", but a faulty understanding of the true nature of death, resurrection, ascension and man's final estate in heaven.

Though we are told that in heaven we have reached our ultimate perfection and glory where nothing is wanting, at the same time we are told no one is completely fulfilled until he is re-united to his body. But if nothing is wanting to those in heaven, what could having an earthly body add to their glory? If it could add something, then we have to redefine heaven as not perfect, and our glory incomplete – until the world is over and our body reappears. If, however, we truly follow Christ, the Prototype of humanity, who revealed both our earthly and heavenly life, resurrection immediately follows death, just as it did for Him. And so too, man's ascension into heaven, into the glory of God, follows resurrection – no waiting for the world to end. *Since this is the way it went for Christ, this is also the way it goes for us.* This means that if the saints in heaven already enjoy eternal glory, they are already privy to the resurrection. (To think the body's resurrection comes **after** the glory of heaven is putting the cart before the horse!)

This whole contradiction, however, only arises for those who espouse the dualistic idea that at death the soul pops out of the body to go its own way. Such a belief is incompatible with resurrection, it flies in the face of what Christ revealed. But then, in heaven Christ's own body is all we need anyway – all of us, one body in Christ's body.[1]

What Christ's resurrection and ascension reveals is that body and soul are eternally inseparable. What experiences a duality of body and soul is self or consciousness, and on this dualistic experience people have based their false beliefs. Beyond self, however, there is no distinction of body and soul, in fact, no consciousness of either one. Indeed, in Paul's heavenly experience he said he did not know if he was in or out of the body, implying: in the final estate there is no awareness of a body – even though the body remains.

Paul also said that when Christ appeared he would rise to meet Him in the air. Now the body's experience of "going into air"(dissolving into air) is indeed the Ascension experience, the *body's* own experience – even though the body does not visually disappear. Such, at least, is the ascended heavenly estate of the body – no end of the world required for its resurrection and ascension.

The true nature of the resurrected and ascended body is not available to the scientific mind or verifiable by the senses, its true nature is a mystery, the mystery of Christ's own glorified body. Because people

---

[1] Thomas Aquinas speculated that in heaven our bodies would be "permeable" – could pass through physical objects. If true, then we can all stand in the one body of Christ – one body, one Person. And no multiple selves.

tend to believe only what they see – and not what they cannot see – Christ had to appear bodily after his resurrection and then bodily disappear at his ascension. But what others saw was not the true nature of his resurrection or Ascension, Christ *manifested* what others will one day only *experience* – know. So while the Apostles truly saw Christ's resurrected body, their eyes were not privy to its true resurrected or ascended nature – much less to its immediate experience. (One should never depend on their senses for ultimate Truth).

As for the timing of resurrection, it seems the apostles and Paul believed their resurrection would take place in their own lifetime. Since the Jews believed the Messiah's coming heralded the end of this world and the beginning of a new kingdom, the early Christians (believing Christ was the Messiah) lived with the expectation their resurrection and the new kingdom was imminent. It never crossed their minds that their resurrection had to wait for some indefinite time down the road.

Indeed, who can imagine Paul, who said he had been "crucified with Christ" still waiting – after 2000 years – "to rise with Christ"? It's not only unimaginable, it's not true. How can anyone honestly look forward to rising thousands of years from now? Certainly Christ didn't, the Apostles and early Christians didn't, and neither should we. Besides, there is something absurd about the scenario of a recreated body re-attaching itself to a glorious soul in heaven. From the beginning, man has never been two discrete entities, so there is no "putting him back together again." Absolutely, this is not the true nature of resurrection.

Despite later Christians pushing resurrection to some futuristic time (theoretically, at least) somehow we have all managed to retain the same immediate expectation of resurrection as did the first Christians. Perhaps nothing so attests to the truth of its immediacy as people's desire and expectation of resurrection following their death – which, as we said, is the end of the world for them. This immediate expectation also explains the constant rash of predictions that the end of the world is at hand – which is all but endemic in Christianity. In my view, this expectation of immediate resurrection is on the mark, it is true and correct, yet it has nothing to do with the end of the world – even Christ had no idea when that would be. So because Christ's resurrection followed immediately on his death, just so it follows immediately on our own.

Though first and foremost, Resurrection is the revelation of Christ – revelation of the true nature of what remains beyond death of self, a revelation that takes place in the body – Christ's Resurrection and Ascension also reveals the indissoluble oneness of body and soul. To make the resurrection nothing more than a reunion of body and soul robs it of its Truth – which is the ultimate revelation of Christ. The body has never kept anyone from Truth, nor can it delay man's final estate in heaven. To attain glory we do not first become disembodied souls.

Christ identified both his true nature and the true nature of resurrection when he said, "I am the resurrection". He did not say "I am the resurrected" (past tense). Rather, he said He was "It" – the Resurrection. Christ and Resurrection are one and the same, and thus our resurrection **is** Christ. Apart from this revelation being in the body, it has nothing to do with the body, nothing to do with being re-united to a soul, and nothing to do with the end of the world.

The whole transformed Person that remains beyond self **is** Christ. As said before, it is not we who die, rise and ascend, but only Christ. But alas, the human mind may never be able to grasp such a marvelous Truth. Sometimes I wonder why God bothered to reveal anything to us at all. How easily it all gets watered down to a childish mentality.

What we have just written may not seem to have anything to do with no-self or the subject we set out to address in this essay. Yet resurrection, ascension, and man's final estate has everything to do with no-self. It is because the full truth of these mysteries is not available to self that there is the tendency is to think they belong only to Christ and not to ourselves. Our end, however, is not simply union with God, but a union followed by death, resurrection and ascension – total transformation into Christ in the Trinity. Nothing else and nothing less can define the end of our journey. The fact that these issues are usually addressed as Christ's mysteries and not our own, means we have missed the whole purpose of the Incarnation, missed what Christ came to reveal – missed the true mystery of our life, our journey, our end.

6

A FALSE UNDERSTANDING OF NO-SELF

A FALSE UNDERSTANDING OF NO-SELF

Buddhism

It has come to my attention that when certain Christians hear that a Christian has written about "the experience of no-self" it is instantly dismissed with, "Oh that's a Buddhist experience!" – meaning, it's not a Christian experience or has no place in Christianity. Whether this is said out of derision or not, it is a completely ignorant statement. What I have written of no-self is nowhere to be found in Buddhism. Search the books, talk to their Masters and intellectuals, and you will not find there what I know as no-self. If one were to find it in Buddhism it would have to be "no-Skandhas", which is unheard of. According to their "an-atman" doctrine, Buddhists do not believe there is any self or soul – ever. So how, then, could something fall away or cease that never existed in the first place? To a Buddhist this would make no sense.

Buddhists neither regard the Skandhas as self, nor believe the Skandhas fall away or cease altogether. I have discussed this at length with an internationally renowned Buddhist teacher who agrees, no-skandhas is not the Buddhist view of no-self. The doctrine of annatta or no-Atman means there has never been any self at all – no ego-self and no divine-self (Atman). Nowhere in the annals of Buddhism will the falling away of the skandhas be found. (This does not mean it may not have happened, it just means it is not in the literature or part of the belief system). So anyone who thinks no-self is a Buddhist experience does not know Buddhism.

While I would not hazard a guess of what, for the Buddhist, their final estate is – enlightenment or nirvana – I think I understand this much: after years of effort to silence their self-experience they discover (or even see) that at bottom – the deepest core of their self-experiences – that this bottom or core is empty of self, no self there at all. Instead there is just emptiness, a void in which there is no self. One Buddhist philosopher calls this bottom or central core the "ground of being" and compares it to the Western view of God as the Ground and Source of all being — God, of course, being without self or no-self. Apart from calling this selfless eternal core "Emptiness" or "Void" (meaning empty and void of self) this may also be what the Buddhists call the eternal "Buddha nature", I'm not sure.[1]

At any rate, this True Center of self — which is empty of self — is very close to the Christian experience of having gone through the dark nights to encounter first, a dark empty center in oneself, yet a center in which God is increasingly revealed as Light, a perpetual Flame of Love at the core of being. The outcome for the Christian is the Unitive state, and for the Buddhist, this might be the state of the Bodhisattva. But nether state (Christian or Buddhist), is no-self. No-self is the extinguishing of the Living Flame — the very core of being — which, for the Buddhist, might be the falling away of the Buddha nature (the Void or Emptiness itself) along with the skandhas. Such an event, however, is nowhere to be found in Buddhism.

In the history of world religions, Christianity is the only one that speaks of loss of self, no other religion has the requirement of transcending all we know and experience as self. That some Christians are surprised to learn Christian mystics and contemplatives have always spoken of no-self, merely attests to the extent that it has been explained away, watered down, or eliminated from the books.

Hinduism

Both the Eastern religions — Hinduism and Buddhism — deny the existence of individual being, deny the multiple, the "other"; deny all ontological differences in fact. Beyond mere appearances, all existence is non-dual. Failure to understand this Eastern belief is to miss the meaning of what no-self means in its unique Western context and belief system.

---

[1] For the Buddhist, self is a bundle of complex and often unknown experiences summarized as the "Five skandhas". Take away the skandhas and man is out of all self-experiences.

It has no counterpart in the East, where there is no individual being. If everything is God anyway, then there can never be a loss of individual being or individual self. This is also why the East does not speak of any ontological transformation or change. "Transformation" and "grace" are rarely found in their literature, they are not central realities as in Christianity. Thus the Buddhist ultimately discovers his true identity (Buddha nature) which, unknowingly, he has been all along; while the Hindu discovers his identity (Atman-Brahman) which he has been from the beginning. There is no radical transformation into something we were not to begin with.

The key premise of the Western religions begin on a totally different foot. Since God is "that" which cannot create Itself, everything God creates is *not* Itself, thus the created universe and man is *not* God. The fact that every created being is unique and one-of-a-kind reflects God's own oneness.

Because man is an individual being, however, does not mean he can stand alone or is ever deprived of God's sustaining presence. God is connected to man not only by reason of his existence, but by the creative act whereby God brings man to his completion and ultimate destiny. Thus our creation is not over until God's creative act has been completed, which completion we know as "heaven".

In the Eastern view, because man (like God) is uncreated, the ultimate goal is to realize who he has been all along. When someone in this tradition speaks of losing his individuality he is not speaking of something that actually exists, but of something that has no true existence, not even "contingent" existence. Since it is impossible to lose something that never existed, the Eastern idea of no-self means losing the illusion of a self or false idea of its existence.

In other words, the Easterner believes that individual being or self is a false belief, a matter of ignorance based on mere appearances. When this ignorance is overcome one has only lost his false sense of individuality or individual being. The loss of this illusion is regarded as "enlightenment" – at least I think it is. (That the East believes it takes thousands of reincarnations to get beyond the illusion of self, however, speaks more of self's truth and reality than its being a mere illusion!)

But this is why, in my research, I have never found in the Eastern literature any experiential event of no-self such as I know it. It is not there. The closest thing to this event would be a permanent and irreversible falling away of the multiple experiences Buddhists' call the "Five Skandhas", or the falling away of the Hindu "Atman" (or Atman-Brahman), a loss that is not reported in their literature.[2]

Instead, enlightenment seems to consist of encountering an Atman or Buddha Nature as one's true identity – the identity of everything that exists. In order to discover this identity, however, one must lose the false notion that one is an individual being, soul, self or person. When this happens, one concludes all existence is nondual.

So where the West regards each human being as a unique ontological being or individual self, the East denies this as a delusional notion or ignorance. For the Westerner, individual being is not an illusion to be overcome, but a reality created by God to be lived and fully experienced.

Thus when the East speaks of a loss of self or individuality, its reference is not that of the Christian for whom this means something real – a whole panoply of experiences – a virtual change in being itself.

So to say there is no difference, or that this loss means the same East and West, has no foundation whatsoever. The East has nothing to offer with regard to what I know as no-self, it fits no Eastern paradigm. Those who think it does simply do not have a true understanding of no-self. What is more, to lift no-self out of its original Christian context and

---

[2] Hinduism believes that beyond reflexive conscious (or self-consciousness) there lies what they call "pure consciousness" or Self ("Atman"). My finding, however, is that without reflexive consciousness or any self-awareness there lies absolutely nothing, no knowledge or experience of anything that could remotely be called "consciousness" or "self". To my knowledge, Hinduism's sole definition of Self or Pure Consciousness is "Brahman", of which I know absolutely nothing.

plunk it down into an alien or Eastern paradigm – which some people have attempted to do – results in obliterating the truth and reality that is no-self.

7

EXPERIENCE VS. THE THING-IN-ITSELF

EXPERIENCE VS. THE THING-IN-ITSELF

The problem with theology – philosophy, psychology, all human knowledge for that matter – is that it never differentiates between man's experience *of* something and what that something actually is "in itself". Here I think of Kant's dichotomy between man's experiential knowledge of something and what that something really is – his "thing in itself". This dichotomy does not belittle human experience and knowledge – after all, God made man the way he is – but it does recognize a higher knowledge, a dimension of knowing that belongs to God and not to man. While human experiential knowledge is of necessary and practical value, it does not yield the true nature or essence of anything that exists.

So while our ordinary knowledge informs us of the existence of things – even the existence of an Uncaused Cause – it cannot inform us of the essence or what they are in themselves. There is a difference, then, between the "thing in itself" (what something really is) and the "thing in our self" – or our experience of it. The two (the experience and the "thing in itself") are not the same. Thus we experience God, but the experience *is us*, it belongs to us (self), it does not belong to God – certainly it is not God's experience! Our experience OF something, then, including God, is quite different from the thing-in-itself.

Our experience of God is not God-as-He-is-in-Himself, but God-as-He-is-in our self, which means: to truly know God-in-Himself is totally non-experiential and beyond all self.

To discover that the "experiencer", the "experience" and the "experienced" are all the one same self, is perhaps, one of the most difficult, hidden and unsuspected truths the mind can ever encounter. Not only is it difficult to grasp, but even more difficult to believe. Thus we are convinced we experience God when, in truth, "what" we experience is only our self. This fact is the deepest mystery of self, its last and final unveiling, a shocking disclosure like no other. This realization is, in fact, the big shock of the no-self event, a truth totally unknown until self is gone.

Up to this point, self is convinced "what" it experienced was God — was sure it was *not* itself.

So the shock of the no-self event is the instant realization that all our experiences of God had, all along, been experiences of our self! (And I'm not referring to one particular experience, but years and years of various, multiple, subtle, even continuous, experiences). This disclosure was followed by a sense of having been duped or cheated all our life. But how could this be? Why would God deliberately dupe us — all of us — in this matter? The answer: God alone is the cause of these experiences, He alone can affect them. Nothing and no one but God can give these particular experiences — and certainly not self. The experiences had been a mysterious aspect of the soul reserved for God alone, an aspect known only to Him, and to which He alone has access or can touch.

This disclosure is actually a remarkable find as regards the human soul. Think of the myriad of descriptions we have of man's experiences of God throughout the ages — in all religions — and then realize these were all descriptions of a mysterious aspect of self or soul! Who can believe it? [1]

---

[1] It turns out the Hindu sage was correct when he said, "Thou art That", meaning, you are your experience, you are "what" you experience. This is why Hinduism believes when you experience the Divine or ultimate Reality, you are it ("thou are that"). And what is "that" you experience? It is your self, your true mysterious self or Atman. In this, Hinduism is absolutely correct. The only problem, while Atman is man's experience of God (or Brahman), Atman is not God-as-He-is-in-Himself, but God-as-He-is-in-our-self, that is, God as self experiences Him. To correct any misunderstanding of "thou art that", or to be sure man has the right view in this matter, Buddhism comes on the scene to tell us that in-itself, ultimate Reality is not Atman, but instead, lies beyond all experiences of Atman or Self. Obviously someone had discovered the Truth beyond self, discovered that the "thing-in-Itself " is beyond our experiences of Atman — the Buddhist "an-atman" doctrine. That this Buddhist finding had little impact on Hinduism tells us how difficult a truth it is to understand, much less accept. Despite this, however, I think the Hindu is in a better position to come upon No-

What this means is that self or consciousness is first and foremost the experiential basis of the human way-of-knowing and the medium of experiencing everything but the sensory body. Because *self* is the limit of human knowing, the sole purpose of *no-self* is to come upon Truth as it lies beyond all self, come upon the "thing-in-itself" – God.

This means that all experiences of God, of life, being and energy are not God, life, being and energy, not as it truly is "in itself". When all these experiences cease or permanently fall away, however, it does not mean there is no God, being, life and energy, rather, it means there is no longer any *experience* of these things. What has ceased is not the thing-in-itself, but the "thing in our self", that is, our experience OF it.

So what, then, is the true nature of these experiences? It is everything man knows as "self", even everything man does not know as himself. So first and foremost *Self is experience*. It is every human experience that is not purely sensory or physical.

Because the existence of something does not depend on our experience of it, some may argue that because self is no longer experienced does not mean it no longer exists. Perhaps they see this as similar to experiencing the absence of God even though God is never absent. There is a big difference, however, between the two. As the Uncreated, God cannot possibly cease to exist, whereas self, but a created function of the soul, can certainly cease to exist. Anything created can be "uncreated" so to speak, whereas the Uncreated cannot be "uncreated". So while God remains beyond all self, all the experiences to which self can give rise are gone forever. Keep in mind, self is not just something we experience now and then. Always it is the experiencer, the experience and, what few realize, even the experienced. How all this works I have gone over elsewhere.

Self than the Buddhist, because as the journey goes – there's no "skipping steps" on the spiritual ladder – one first has to realize Atman before he can go beyond it to realize no-Atman or an-atman. Thus to start out, as does Buddhism, with no Atman at all, is to put the cart before the horse – it won't work.

The point here is that self or the human way of knowing does not inform us of the thing-in-itself or the true nature or essence of anything. Until self is gone we are not even informed of its own true nature (self) or "thing in itself". So while we experience body and soul, spirit and God, self and being, these experiences are not privy to the thing-in-itself. The sole purpose of no-self, then, is to go beyond these limited self experiences in order to know the "thing-in-itself" and no longer the "thing-in-our-self". This way we finally come to know God as He-is-in-Himself and no longer God as He-is-in-our-self.

A Personal Note

From beginning to end the goal of my journey was never to attain any spiritual state, not even the unitive state, it simply never entered my mind. The goal was to love God with every fiber of my being, do His bidding, give my life completely to Him and take whatever came. In making this journey I never heard of "no-self", thus the possibility of living in such a condition never crossed my mind. Like St. Bernard, however, I had passing experiences of ecstasy, but unlike him I never pondered this becoming a permanent state in this world – to walk around in a state of ecstasy? Impossible! Like everyone else, however, I regarded this passing experience as a foretaste of a heavenly estate and thought no more about it. The irony of this is that in my journals I often wrote at length on the importance and greatness of "self" in its oneness with God.

The Unitive state, after all, is man's mature life in this world; without it, no one can live fully or as God intended him to live this life. But this is why my eventual writing about no-self is somewhat ironic, I would never have guessed it. But just as the unitive state is God's doing, so too is no-self, and while a great deal has been written about the journey up to the unitive state, there is nothing written beyond it, much less written about the eventual falling away of the unitive state – no-self. I wrote to give an account of what lies beyond the unitive state because I knew many fellow contemplatives who had come this far, yet would find no account of it in their contemplative literature.

To be able to write on the subject of no-self, God put me in a blessed position in the Church, the position of a total nondescript. Had I belonged to a religious Order or been in a monastery, my writing would never have got past the first superior – who, at best, would have regarded it as "wrong thinking". But as it stands, the Church doesn't know I exist and thus I haven't had to answer to anybody. Because the Church has given me no problems – ever – what I have written here is not a defense, not an answer to complaints or accusations.

If anything, it's the reverse; I would take to task those theologians who object to no-self. The irony of this freedom, however, is that having written solely for proficient contemplatives in the Church, these people will be the last, if ever, to read what I have written. Because I'm not in a religious Order and have no Church affiliations, for my writing to get to the right people will take an act of God. But then, my part has been simply to write what I know and leave the rest to Him. If all the writing disappears, then so be it. Certainly it hasn't done a thing for me – nothing!

One last experience that has to do with the writing of this paper. While writing *The Experience of No-Self* (in 1979) I suddenly realized this event fell outside the usual norm of "orthodoxy" in that it was nowhere in the literature, the mystics had never spoken of such an event. The thought that no-self and what was learned might not be regarded as orthodox stunned me for a moment. In my entire life I'd never given a thought to my being "orthodox" or not. That the idea should arise now, took me by surprise. But how could it be that after spending my whole life living the Catholic Faith to the limits of my ability, God would catapult me outside the Faith? (The falling away of self, after all, is solely God's doing).

Does this mean I am no longer Catholic – or even Christian? I sat there looking at the crucifix opposite me on the wall with not a thought in mind. Then into my head came the clear words: "You are more orthodox than the orthodox". At first this seemed amusing, I didn't know what it meant, yet it stuck. From that moment I never had a second thought about no-self being unorthodox, never. No-self is not unorthodox, it's *more* orthodox – whatever that means. So while it may be more than some orthodox can take, yet as Christ said, "Let those who can take it, take it".

There is no use speculating what my life would have been without the Church. In fact, without the Church I'd never been born. My father was the living personification of "the Church", and without him, of course, I wouldn't be here. I'm probably even more Catholic than Christian. Where "Catholic" means Universal – all over the place and for everyone – the term "Christian" is what sets one religion apart from another. But Christ, as we know, is for everyone.

The ideal for any religion is to be all inclusive, universal, catholic, which does not mean a one-world religion, but that each religion finds a place in itself for the others. By "place" I do not mean re-interpreting another religion to fit into our own – which is what most people do – but rather, understanding and incorporating the Truths of other religions into our own. There is nothing to fear on this score because the Trinity includes all God's revelations to man, all authentic religions, that is. To see and include these truths is to be uniquely Catholic.

8

THE IMAGE AND LIKENESS OF GOD

THE IMAGE AND LIKENESS OF GOD

For a moment let is recall the often quoted notion that man was made in the image and likeness of God, and then ask ourselves:

- Does God really have an image and likeness?

- When God looks at man does He see Himself?

- Or when man looks at God, does he see himself?

- Who is really looking at who?

If God sees us as His image and likeness, then he must be horrified. But if we see God as our image and likeness, then we are glorified. I am afraid this is the way it goes: God horrified, man glorified. To say man is made in God's image and likeness is a small step from making the reciprocal mirrored statement, namely, that God is made in man's image and likeness. If there is no mutual reflection, then neither can be said to reflect the other.

We know it is forbidden to make a graven image of God – as if it were even possible! – yet what about the images of God we carry about in our minds? While no one believes in a graven image, people do, in fact, believe their mental images of God, that is, believe their own reflections on God. By "image" here, we do not mean an imaginary mental picture – like a piece of art work we may have seen – but rather a self-reflected image by which we know ourselves and thus also believe we know God. An example might be this: When a father says his son is his image and likeness, the first image in the father's mind is the image of himself.

His first image is not another person or thing, but himself. All "other" images will thus be compared (or likened) to the first one he knows – himself, that is. Thus all images are filtered through this primary image. So how we see ourselves has everything to do with how we see other people, and also how we see the divine. This also holds true for ideas and concepts: how we "know ourselves" is the filter through which we know everything not ourselves, the divine included.

It is only after seeing and knowing ourselves we can know someone else. This is due to the reflexive nature of consciousness. Unlike purely visual or sensory objects, all the images of the human mind are stamped with a subject-self. Thus everything and everyone we see or know bears this subjective stamp. The primary image of this subjective stamp, of course, is ourselves. It is simply the nature of self-awareness. So the fact we are "aware" of anything attests first and foremost to our self, and only secondarily to what we are aware of. We can also be aware of our awareness of others, or we can be aware of ourselves as the object of someone else's awareness. Awareness can become very complex, it has many levels, yet all awareness or consciousness hinges on the reflexive mechanism of the mind – that it reflects us. This is our human way of knowing and experiencing and is unique to man alone.

Now then...

Since the first image in our minds is a self-image, it is the first thing we unconsciously see when we see or know anything. Thus when we think of knowing God, seeing or experiencing God, the very mode of this appearance, or experience, will be according to our human uniqueness – consciousness or self. This is why God always manages to come across in some anthropomorphic fashion as somehow similar to, or like, ourselves.

Thus the divine may be an image, a concept, an archetypal energy, our notion of beauty, of love, goodness and so on. The ultimate of all anthropomorphic notions, however, is that God IS self or consciousness. This is really getting down to the bare roots of human uniqueness; indeed, it is the ultimate definition of "man"! What this means is that the Divine or Absolute IS our human mode of knowing and experiencing! This is all anthropomorphic, of course, it is all consciousness making

God into its own human image and likeness. Consciousness cannot help but do this. Indeed, this is the way man was made to be. So there is no use apologizing for it, we need only to admit it.

So...

Because the first thing we see when looking into ourselves is our self, just so, when we see God within, we naturally see him in our own image and likeness – as our being, our life, our true self.

If we had no self-image, then of course God would also have no image, in which case we could not speak of being made in the image and likeness of God. Thus if the mind was incapable of self-images, it would never have occurred to the mind that it was made in the image of God.

I think the point is obvious. We only believe we were made in the image of God because we have made God in our own image. Thus the notion of being made in God's image could never have occurred to the mind if we had not first made God into our image.

Furthermore, the notion of being made in God's image assumes that God has an image-making mind like our own – meaning, God has reflexive consciousness and, consequently, a self. (It is a curious thing that the lower down we bring God, the higher up we go).

By this time we should be ready to face the truth of God and ourselves. This truth is simply this: because God is an image in our minds, we conclude that we are an image in God's mind. To arrive at this conclusion actually takes a very small step; one no bigger than reversing the mirrors of our mind. If there is any difficulty with this truth it would not be its obvious psychological reality, but rather its more theological implications. It could just upset some people's apple-carts.

Now, if at first this is a shocking truth, it also leads to a marvelous truth. The divine designed consciousness, it was meant to work the way it does, there is no mistake or chance involved. Consciousness is not only our mode of knowing and experiencing human existence, but also our mode of knowing and experiencing the divine. God does not communicate himself to the vegetative body, the external senses, or even to the intellect, rather God communicates himself to consciousness, which in turn affects the body, the senses and the intellect. This is why working our way through consciousness is the essence of our spiritual-psychological journey.

As the great designer, God knew from the moment of our creation how consciousness would work, knew that man would make God into his own human image and likeness. Thus from the beginning Christ's incarnation was in the plan. Christ was to be the fulfillment of consciousness, literally, God in our own image and likeness. Christ was to satisfy and justify human consciousness by giving man his longed for human God. So, finally, in Christ we have true God in our own image and likeness; and because of Christ, we can truly say we were made in God's image.

Christ the Fulfillment of Consciousness

God's image

But Christ was not only to fulfill and satisfy consciousness, but also to show us the way to God beyond all image and likeness – beyond consciousness or self.

Not only did Christ reveal our passage through consciousness and man's ultimate destiny, but in doing so revealed man to himself. I have always thought that Christ's first revelation was not the revelation of God (after all, God had already revealed himself to the Jews and others around the world), rather, Christ is first and foremost the revelation of man himself.

Christ is the revelation of our self, our humanity, our relationship to God, our Way and ultimate end. Thus when consciousness has realized its oneness with the divine, it can be said that Christ is, indeed, our 'true' self. With this oneness we are truly the image of Christ's own oneness with God.

This is why I say that Christ was less a reconciliation of God with man than a reconciliation of man with himself. No one can fully accept themselves and their human lives until they have realized their oneness with the divine. With this realization we are free to be human, free to fulfill our humanity in the true image of Christ. Thus Christ reconciles us to our humanity because in him we see the oneness of the human and the divine.

We know our humanity is not separate or apart from God, thus we now live without fear, guilt and unknowing. We no longer have to apologize for our humanity and our image making machine, we no longer have to strive for deification or desire to be what we are not. Because of Christ, we know we are on target, we are as we should be – or as we were made to be – and thus all is well with man.

Christ 's incarnation was the forfeiture of his divine (Logos) condition, and the taking on of consciousness. To be human is to be a conscious being. Thus Christ traversed the great void between consciousness and the divine condition in the opposite direction than the one we traverse in our ascension to the divine.

When in our journey we have fully realized our oneness with the divine, we meet up with Christ who began his human journey in this same condition of oneness. At this juncture we enter his same consciousness, we are "other Christs" and know the oneness he experienced and spoke of.

But this is not the end of the journey. We must keep going. Like Christ, we too must know death, resurrection and ascension; his path is our path, and how it went for him is how it will go for us. Any misreading of Christ's path to the Father is a misreading of our own path and own ultimate destiny. In fact, any misreading of Christ is a misreading of ourselves.

While consciousness was the essence of Christ's human nature, it was ultimately deified, totally transformed. The consciousness that dissolved at his death was not merely the consciousness of a single individual, not even the consciousness of oneness with God, but rather it was the consciousness of all men, those past and those to come. How this works, however, is unbelievable.

It turns out, only Christ dies, rises, and ascends to the Father. Only Christ traverses the void between consciousness and the divine condition. Whenever consciousness reaches the identical transparency as that of Christ, there is an explosion of sorts. Consciousness dissolves, dies, ceases, falls away, however we care to think of it. "That" which then makes the journey beyond consciousness, crosses the great void and ascends to the Father, "that" is Christ. It could not be our self because there is no self anymore.

This then, is the mystery of Christ. It may sound very mystical and transcendent, but in reality it is a great Truth. God is an easy Truth, Christ, however, is a difficult Truth. Once beyond the image, Christ is beyond the limitations of the mind, which is why His ultimate Truth is so unbelievable.

I am skeptical of those who say they know the ultimate truth of Christ. From what they say, I think they have not gone far enough. But I can understand those who do not believe in Christ or those who affirm they do not understand him. Until one is completely transformed into Christ it is not possible to know or understand Him fully. We only know as much of Christ up to that point in the journey that we have been transformed into. Thus the fullness of Christ is a gradual revelation, it cannot be otherwise. Thus the way we knew Christ as a beginner is not the way we know Christ as the Ender.

In sticking with our simple faith and images, however, we cannot go wrong. When the time comes for us to move beyond the possibility of images and concepts, there will be no fear because it is not we who traverse the void; but rather it is Christ who makes this journey for us.

Christ alone returns to the Father, thus Christ is all of us.

Since ultimately God has no image, then ultimately, neither should we. Only when we have no self-image can it be said we are truly made in the image of God, who also has no image. By self- image, however, I do not mean how we think about ourselves (self-knowledge), nor any mental picture, but rather autonomous reflective-consciousness ever bending on itself to know itself. Without this reflexive action man would never have coined the term "self" – would not even be aware of himself.

Unfortunately, the commandment forbidding images of God has been misconstrued to mean solely material images – which are basically innocuous and totally after the fact – whereas it really forbade mental images of God. In this matter, everyone has sinned because everybody has some mental image of God – because this is the way the human mind works. While we may not have a material shape in mind, we imagine God as a discrete being or entity who may be angry, loving, and all the rest of it. But God forbad images – why? Because God has no image!

So...

If God has no image, then how can it be said man was made in the image of God? The answer: Man becomes the image of God when he too, has no image.

/ 9 /

APATHEIA

APATHEIA

My first encounter with the Greek term "apatheia" was many years ago when reading the lives of the early Christian ascetics, sometimes called "The Fathers of the Desert". That the goal they sought was a state of "apatheia" struck me as curious. Curious, because the term denotes a psychological, rather than a spiritual state of being. In other words, it did not address any Christian goal at all. When I first went in search of a more thorough account of the term, apart from a few brief definitions here and there, I found nothing satisfying. Instinctively, however, I knew there was more to the term than was warranted by casual mention, knew the term articulated a profound experiential state. And indeed, the more I researched the term, the better I understood its place in the spiritual journey. As a state of being, not only does the term denote an egoless condition, but carried to its extreme, the term even defines a totally selfless condition. It is this possibility that sparked my interest and why I think there is more to be said about "apatheia" then is generally found in the books.

Definitions of "apatheia" are so varied and numerous we had best start with the simplest synonym – "dispassion". The term not only means freedom from irrational passions, but implies an inner equanimity and calm enabling one to live rationally or in accord with right-thinking. According to the Stoics, who basically coined the term, apatheia was the state of the wise man, whereas living by one's emotions or passions was the state of the fool. Thus life was not to be governed by man's lower nature or how he feels that day, but governed by his higher nature in tune with the Logos, the immanent Intelligence or Reason governing all things to the good of all.

Perhaps the most extreme definition of apatheia is "impassibility", an unchanging, immovable state of stillness with no reaction one way or the other to any event in life. Obviously, between "dispassion" and "impassibility" is a wide berth, one I find intriguing in that the former can lead to the latter. As a fairly open-ended and unrestricted term, however, how one might define or understand "apatheia" will no doubt depend on the degree to which he can experientially identify with the term.

As originally used, at least in its Christian context, the state of apatheia, if properly understood, articulates the psychological benefit or outcome of having come to the Unitive State. I would even say that no one can permanently achieve apatheia who has not come to the Unitive State. Of ourselves, however, and regardless of our practices, we can never achieve a permanent state of apatheia – why? Because it is solely the result of the Unitive state, an automatic, psychological by-product of it. Thus the abiding Unitive State is equally an abiding state of apatheia. Although solely in themselves Union and apatheia are not the same thing, yet it would be impossible to have one without the other.[1]   Later I will explain why this is so, but first we need to give some background.

Achieving a state of apatheia was originally the goal of the ancient Stoics. The Stoic School of philosophy had been around some 300 years prior to Christianity and from what I gather, it was a popular philosophy at the time of Christ. Many of the early Christians were converts from Stoicism. One convert highly influenced by this philosophy was Clement of Alexandria (150-212) who wrote rather extensively on the subject of apatheia. Whether he was the first Christian to write about apatheia is inconsequential because, as a practice, it was already well known. It is said that over the door of the school where Clement taught were the opening words of St. John's Gospel: In the beginning was the Logos, and the Logos was with God, and the Logos was God. "Logos", of course, is another Stoic term.   Though as a doctrine originated by Heraclitus around 500 B.C., "Logos" only became fully developed by the Stoics, and later, of course, even more developed by the Christians.

The Stoics philosophy was centered around the Logos, without

---

[1] I have no understanding of how apatheia could be a "practice". Apart from sheer avoidance (if it is not too late already), how does one "practice" getting rid of their passions?   I don't have the slightest notion, the idea never crossed my path.

It, the Stoics would never have discovered or adopted the path of apatheia. Apatheia is the path to the Logos, or better put, apatheia aligns one with the Logos to live accordingly. Thus apatheia and Logos go hand in hand as means-end. Without question, the Stoics had more impact on the future of the Christian contemplative and mystical tradition than any other Greek philosophy. While Plato (and later, Aristotle) may have served the more theologically minded Christian, it was the Stoics who best served and inspired the early Christian contemplatives.

To understand apatheia then, you first have to understand the Stoic view of the Logos. First and foremost the Logos is **the** cosmic principle, It is the rational ordering of the universe that pervades all reality. As such it is both the generating and governing principle immanent in all things, more especially, immanent in, and governing, man himself. For Philo of Alexandria (a Jewish mystic-philosopher, 30 B.C.- 50 A.D.), the Logos was the immaterial instrument, even the personal agency, through which a transcendent God not only created all things, but continues to act in all things. For the Christian, of course, the Logos is "that" of the Godhead or Trinity that became incarnate in Christ. That the Latins translated St. John's "Logos" as "Word" can only be regarded as a sin.[2] A better choice, at least, would have been the Stoics' transcendent "reason" or "intelligence". Actually, the Latins should never have translated the term at all.

According to the Stoics, the highest pursuit in life was to live as perfectly in accord with the Logos as possible. This meant leading a well-ordered, rational life, a highly virtuous life. To do this one could not be subject to ever fluctuating feelings, moods, desires, and above all, those irrational passions, which were to be avoided like the plague. Something else unique to the Stoics, they are the only people in all Greek Philosophy who consistently stressed overcoming "self", ever putting the good of all before themselves. This is because they regarded the Logos as governing

---

[2] Today in Church they hold up the Bible and say, "This is the Word of God" – lo and behold, a paper God no less! It's idolatrous. Nobody would hold up that book and say, "This is the Logos".

the universe for the good of all, not merely for the good of individuals. Their reasoning and judgment was thus based on what was in the best interest of all, of others, never just themselves. The discipline of apatheia required constant self- control and the overcoming of self.

Although some writers have labeled the Stoics as Pantheists – indeed, they were accused of this in their own day – yet the Stoics stoutly denied this. The Logos was the unseen, unknown aspect of matter, It was nothing that could been seen, nothing man could ever intellectually or scientifically know about matter itself. Basically, the Stoic notion of the Logos was a form of monism, the Logos was the Whole of Reality, not the sum of parts, "not this or that". Although the Stoics were certainly not materialists – quite the contrary, in fact – they nevertheless did not believe in the existence of what we might call "pure spirit".

The Logos was not some disembodied spirit, but the unknown of matter itself. (When I think of St. Paul addressing the "Unknown" God of the Greeks, I think of his addressing the Stoics' Logos, who, as Paul says, has now become "Known" – in the incarnate Logos, Christ.) But just as the Stoics did not believe in a disembodied Logos, so too, they never believed in an immaterial soul. In fact, they used to challenge others to try and "think" about such a "thing", think about the existence of something – anything – totally immaterial.

Strictly speaking it cannot be done. Anything that enters the mind is always attached to some sensory medium. So while one can certainly believe in an immaterial soul or spirit, one can never so much as think about it, imagine or conceive of it without some attached material aspect. At any rate, since the Logos was the law governing all for the good of all, the highest life of man was to be governed by the "Logos" same law of reason and intelligence. To do this is where the discipline and goal of "apatheia" comes in.

Now we all know how the passions can so blunt one's reasoning as to make clear thinking and judgment impossible. Run-away emotions not only swamp the mind, blind the intellect, but can even disable common sense. Then too, because passions are irrational in themselves, they can only lead to irrational behaviors – indeed, heinous crimes. In the heat of passion people are literally out of control. People do and say irrational things all the time when they are led-on by feelings instead of by reason. Indeed, the biggest ruse of all is to rationalize one's feelings, justify them, all of course, to the end of exonerating one's self. There is no greater ego-ic ruse than this. But the Stoics' goal was not to overcome good or positive emotions; rather, vigilance was focused on that irascible aspect of soul or self that could get caught up in over-emotionalism – the passions. Nothing so guarantees a disorderly, disastrous, unhappy and unthinking life than the passions. The passions are even the main cause of suffering.[3]

This not only runs contrary to the Logos, but contrary to the good of one's self and everyone else. The goal to reach, however, was not just control of the passions, but ultimately, to get beyond them, get to the point of their not arising at all. This state of non-arising passions was call "apatheia". In this state one was: freed to live a well ordered, rational life, a life of good judgment, balance and equanimity, a state, we might add, in which one is of best service to their neighbor. (Stoicism was the most altruistic and civic minded of all Greek philosophies) . Above all, this state enabled one to live according to the Logos, the soul's true immanent Intelligence. This alone made for a virtuous and happy life.

So as a practice, the goal of apatheia was to attain a passionless state. This state has nothing in common with the modern day notion of "apathy" – a totally disinterested, uncaring, unfeeling indifference. (I tend to think of apathy as a condition of energy-less ennui). It is unfortunate

---

[3] It is generally held that the state of apatheia is a state of no-suffering, and no-desires as well. As to suffering, I doubt everyone agrees on just what it is. As long as the senses are intact there will always be physical pain – which some people regard as suffering. For the most part, I regard suffering as psychological in nature. Thus pain can be accompanied by fear and foreboding, anxiety, impatience, anger – who knows? There is also a spiritual suffering that seems not to touch the psyche at all or produce any of its responses. Even beyond the psyche, there are certain "voids" for which any kind of suffering would be preferable.

that some of the ancient slurs against the Stoics have endured to this day.

Thus even the word "stoic" is regarded as negative – meaning some dead-pan tin-man. But if the Stoics' goal was right on target, it is somewhat sad that despite all their vigilant practices and efforts, they generally held it was not possible, ever, to achieve a permanent state of apatheia. All they could do was aim for it – and no doubt make great progress toward it.

It seems that even after apatheia entered the Christian domain, this negative view came with it – that apatheia could never become a permanent state. Thus Clement of Alexandria held that only Christ lived in such a state (apatheia) and "maybe" some of his disciples. Clement said that if any of the rest of us could come to such a state, it could only be toward the end of life or on one's deathbed. Unfortunately, this perspective has endured to this day. (How is it that perspectives, misconceptions and prejudices can so tenaciously endure down the centuries? With no possibility of setting old records straight – about anything – man is getting nowhere!)

Unfortunately, the term "apatheia" did not last very long after it filtered down to the Christian rank and file. For one thing, St. Jerome could not stand the term and condemned the whole idea. For him apatheia implied a sinless state – akin to Christ's own state of apatheia – which he deemed impossible for the rest of us. What is interesting about this condemnation, however , is that to this day, the debate goes on as to whether or not the Unitive State "confirms one in a state of grace" – meaning, in this state one could no longer sin. (John of the Cross says yes, one is so confirmed, but Teresa of Avila, however, says no.) Obviously, merely doing away with the term "apatheia" didn't resolve a thing in this matter.

Then there was the monk, John Cassian, (5th century) who not only eliminated the term apatheia, but basically changed its meaning to "purity of heart". In a thousand years it would not have occurred to me to equate apatheia with "purity of heart", not even remotely do they mean or imply the same thing. In the stretch it takes to link these terms (apatheia and purity-of-heart) so much is lost it's not worth the verbal effort. At any rate, after Cassian, the term disappeared from the Western or Latin front. It was not, however, lost to the Eastern front or the Eastern Orthodox Tradition. This is because most of the Early Fathers, including the Desert Fathers, ascetics and early monastics, were "Middle-Easterners" (as we call that part of the world today) and not Europeans or Latins.

As said, with John Cassian (a Latin), "apatheia" disappeared from Western spirituality. Today the monk's goal is said to be "purity of heart" – which is nebulous at best. Apatheia, on the other hand, is very specific and practical with no soft or embellished beating around the bush.

So far we have only given the briefest background of the term "apatheia". We have made no mention of the Christian monk, Evagrius Ponticus, (Cassian's mentor), who had more to say about apatheia than anyone else. I believe his first book, *Praktikos*, is devoted to this subject and its practice. Before moving on, however, it is important to emphasize that whereas for the Stoics apatheia was the goal itself, for the Christians, it was never regarded at the goal.

As said before, the term has nothing to do with Christianity; it does not articulate its goal. At best it was regarded as a practice that led toward the Christian goal – toward an abiding Union with God. In fact, someplace I read that no one was ever fully transformed (in this Union) who had not first come to apatheia, was rooted in it, or had accomplished its goal. I'm not sure I understand this – it's putting the cart before the horse. For me the term only has relevance after the fact, or after one has come to the Unitive state. Here the term apatheia most accurately articulates the psychological result of the abiding state of Union. In fact, just the experience of apatheia is one of the surprising phenomena of this state, truly a wonder to experience. As to how it works, this is what I have intended to speak about from the beginning. In a way, it will be my extended contribution to the importance of the ancient term "apatheia".

How It Works

Many people think of "heart" as the center of their being, but it's not. While linguistically or sentimentally "heart" can also mean "core", yet, in actual experience the center of being – if experienced at all – is just below the navel or thereabouts. In this matter Carl Jung was correct in equating the center of ourselves (psyche and soul) as the body's center of gravity – literally the same gravity that keeps us earth-bound. This center is not only the ego, but underlying it is the deepest point of our being. This center is also where God can breakthrough and be experienced. Should anyone doubt this ego-center, just let him be rubbed the wrong way, denied, hurt, or whatever, and there arises a gut-level pain, agitation, tantrum, or burst of passionate anger perhaps.

No question, the ego is the seat of all passions, desires and suffering, especially experienced when we don't get our own way. This is the true ego, the original center of self, the center from which the whole affective system arises – passions, emotions, all sorts of subtle feelings. We don't experience any of this in our heads, we experience these in the pit of ourselves, the center of our being, the ego.

Having mentioned only the ego's negative effects, there is also its opposite effects. Thus we can experience all kinds of good things, joy, bliss, sympathy and so on. As long as no over-emotion swamps right-thinking and good judgment, there is no problem with these experiences. The sole problem with the ego is not only that it can go either way – positive or negative – but its potential for giving rise to inordinate passions (positive or negative) can literally nullify the rational faculties. To live intelligently, man cannot be governed by his feelings, much less his irrational passions.

Most people, of course, would like to get rid of the ego's negative experiences. While I do not see this desire as sufficient reason for embracing a spiritual life – this being more self-serving than God-serving – yet, for the sake of going forward with this account, we have to presume a genuine love of God and a sincere determination to dedicate our whole life and being to God. The onset of this new life is a stage of "refor-mation", the effort to center our whole life around God and no longer around our self.

Thus having God as the sole center of our life is the task at hand, and any practice that will help us do this is always welcome – some prac-tices work for some people, some work for others. No one actually knows when they have done all they can in this matter or know when every aspect of their life has been given over to God.

Only God is privy to this knowledge since only God truly knows us, knows what He has created here. We can assume, however, that it is only after we have done all we can – and this by the grace of God – that God steps in and takes over.

When this happens we know it is God's doing because it is noth-ing we could have brought about ourselves, indeed, we never even knew it was coming. I am referring here to the onset of the terrible Dark Night of the Spirit. This is going to break and remake us.

The first step is a shrouding of the mind like a veil over the head. The second step is the appearance of a black hole in the center of our being. Because this center had been our encounter with God (God's Presence within us) it seems as if God had suddenly disappeared and left a black hole in His wake. On seeing this we are thrown through a loop. The irony of this situation, however, is that in the dark, we are actually seeing God face to face, whereas before, we unknowingly had seen God though the veil of the ego – our own self-center that is. Now, however, that ego-center is gone and, seemingly, taken God with it. We will never have the ego's experience of God again. We are literally on new Ground here.

How we cope with this situation is another story. Let us just say we gradually acclimate, find peace of soul, and recognize God in this darkness. The only thing that can possibly go wrong in this situation is running about trying to find something (or someone) to fill in the empty hole in ourselves. Once the ego is gone, however, there is no putting it back together again, this is an irreversible state of affairs. Even if we spend the rest of our life trying to escape this hole — fill it with people, things or whatever — it won't work. All we are doing is prolonging the journey we must make to the blackest, bottom-most level of that hole, and then stay there.

But let us say we have done this and have come to know this new Center as God's dwelling place. Now the center is no longer dark. At some point, when all has been integrated around this new center, God grants what can only be called the "Unitive revelation". This is a quiet but decisive turning point in the overall journey. It is both a seeing and knowing God as the abiding Center of our being — or better put, our deepest being is God. There can be no underestimating this piece of "Gnosis" or knowing. Instantly there is a sense of being a "whole" new person and the recognition the "old person" is gone forever, will never be experienced again. There is also a sense of tremendous freedom, as if some burden had been lifted. In short, we know this is the onset a whole new life with God as part and parcel of our very being. This is actually more than the union of two, because there is only one true Being in this union. Whatever our being may be — God only knows — it is hidden in God. Though our being rises directly from divine Being, yet the phenomenal self rises from our "true self" hidden, as St. Paul put it, "With Christ in God." This is not, then, the joining of two separate beings, but rather our new life rising from the single Being of God.

No one can possibly know ahead of time what life in this state will be like until he has actually lived it. And not only lived it thoroughly, but even lived it to its dire end. At this Unitive point, however, we see no end other than heaven itself. But just as there is the sense of a new beginning, there is also a sense of ending. Where to this point it had been an inward journey, from here on it will be an outward journey — can't go deeper than the Deepest. And here, finally, this brings us to the point where we can talk about apatheia, the psychological by-product of this Unitive state. Obviously, there has been a radical change of consciousness. God has literally replaced the ego-center, thus there is no longer mere self-awareness, but rather a "we" or "us" awareness. Now we are as aware of God as we are aware of ourselves – no split possible.

As the true Center of our being, God is silent, immovable, unchanging, untouchable, impassable, imperturbable and so on – this fact alone, explains this being a state of fearlessness. Instead of that flappable, vulnerable ego-center, there is God as solid as a rock. So without the ego-center, let us give a few examples of how this state of apatheia works. Let's say we were deliberately kicked and slapped. Initially our feelings are hurt, but as this hurt sinks down to the Center, at some point or threshold, it dissolves, goes no further, comes to naught. How could it be otherwise when this divine Center is immovable, untouchable? Instead of hurt or anger there is peace and equanimity, even a genuine sense of compassion for the perpetrator who seems to endure such terrible feelings, passions or emotions. Again let us say we have been confronted with something joyous and delightful. As we initially experience this joy, it too sinks down and dissolves in an even greater joy – an unfelt knowledge – the joy of God surpassing all joys of this life. This is the way it goes with every emotion in every circumstance in life. The reason the affective system is incapable of experiencing any passion is because the irascible aspect of psyche and soul, the ego, is not there anymore!

Instead, it is totally empty of self and full of God. While we could go on and on with such examples, if one has not grasped how or why this works, then giving more examples would be futile. Something else peculiar about this state, emotions do not arise from the Center, but rather from outside circumstances. So this is not a totally emotionless state, though it is, in truth, a passionless state, an abiding state of apatheia. Absolutely.

But let us move on. Because we are without fear, we take on all kinds of challenges we would not have dared prior to coming to this state. One reason we go out of our way to seek challenges is that with the arising of any feeling, be it success or failure, we experience its dissolving in God. I think it was Teresa of Avila who said of this experience, it all worked to remind her the more of God. Her reference was not to memory, but to the experience of all dissolving in God. This is why the Saints even sought suffering the better to experience their oneness with God, which is ever its own kind of joy. (Just like the "peace of God" is not like anything we normally experience as peace, so too, the "joy" of God is not like anything we normally experience as joy. They are as different as apples and oranges.) How all this works is a marvel. Initially it struck me as a kind of miracle. But then, one gets used to it.

Over time, in the full and fearless living the Unitive state – many years in fact – the Center imperceptibly enlarges, the Living Flame of Love is virtually consuming us. Thus there comes a point where anything incoming sinks to no depths at all, but almost immediately dissolves. Finally, there comes a time when anything that so much as touches us, is like water on a duck's back, it doesn't get in at all. And we are not referring here to small trials, but to those that stretch the human limits. There has to come a point when no matter what we are faced with, there will not be a single movement. It is not a matter of mental indifference, but a matter of knowledge and absolute perfect trust in God. Perhaps no one spells out this situation better than John of the Cross. Just as he initially tackled the problem of the passions, so too, he later goes over, passion by passion, what it is like to live without them in the Unitive state. Perhaps his best exposition of how this works can be found in Stanzas 20 & 21 of the *Spiritual Canticle*.[4]

As said elsewhere, living the Unitive life is the experiential reality of that saying: "I must decrease, He must increase". This is how it goes. Imperceptibly the Center is taking over, consuming us. From here, it is just a final step before there is nothing left to decrease, nothing left to consume, no circumference left at all – no-self, that is. What no one could suspect ahead of time, however, is that with no circumference remaining, there is also no Center! The final step is just that – no Center.

---

[4] Although John mentions this phenomena in the later verses as well – which deal with other new experiences of the Unitive life – yet, as said, what was initially a new phenomenon soon becomes par-for-the-course.

This is the ultimate disappearance of the entire psyche, all consciousness, awareness, all but the senses that is.

Now then, we have gone from a simple abiding state of apatheia to a condition of such radical, total apatheia, that strictly speaking, the term no longer applies. While no-self includes the most radical understanding of apatheia, the term does not articulate its true condition, much less define what it actually is. So once again we are faced with a spiritual or supernatural reality being totally distinct from any psychological counterpart. Just as apatheia did not define the Unitive state, so too, it does not define no-self (or no Unitive state). But having said this, apatheia remains a useful, meaningful term throughout the journey, it expresses, even illustrates, the purely psychological side of it. If transforming grace had not brought about a change in our psyches, consciousness or self, there would be no change to speak of, and no apatheia possible.

Conclusion

In this day and age many people have mistaken the spiritual journey for a psychological journey. But be assured of one thing: nobody can ever bring about any permanent transformation of consciousness or psyche by any efforts of their own. Only God can bring this about. Spend your whole life trying, even make some progress, but in a split second it can all unravel and you are back where you started. Even Jung said he never met anyone who had gone through transformation who was not also a religious person. Psychology is not the path, the practice or the goal.

Although the psyche is obviously effected throughout the spiritual journey, yet, in the end, the whole psyche – consciousness or self – gives way, disappears. What matters in this journey is not the psyche, but the soul. What is really being transformed and deified is not the psyche, but the soul. The psyche is merely the experiential faculty of the soul, it is not, however, the soul itself. So let us not confuse psyche and soul. A psychological journey nets us nothing, a spiritual journey nets us All.

There is much more to be said about the path of both the Stoics and the early Christians not covered in this paper. There is much that is beautiful and insightful, and those interested can read it for themselves. My purpose has not been to do other people's research for them, but to expand on something already known, "apatheia", which has been around for several thousand years. Someone who knows both apatheia and the Unitive state will recognize the point I wished to make here: namely, that apatheia articulates the psychological effects of the Unitive state. I have tried to show how it works in the living out of the Unitive state.

Note:

If one would like to know more about "apatheia" I highly recommend a research report (50 pgs.) written by Rick R. Milas, entitled "*The Correspondences of Clement of Alexandria's view of Apatheia to that of the Stoic Philosophers*". It was written in 1978 as partial fulfillment for a Master of Divinity Degree at Concordia Theological Seminary. It is excellent. (Maybe one could get it off the internet).

If one is interested in how John Cassian derived "purity of heart" from his mentor, Evagrius Ponticus (the Christian writer on apatheia), one might read the article, "Apatheia and Purity of Heart in Evagrius Ponticus", by Jeremy Driscoll, O.S.B, found in *Purity of Heart in Early Ascetic and Monastic Literature*, published by The Liturgical Press, 1999.

Needless to say, one should read Evagrius and the Stoics for themselves. I think Evagrius can be found in the Classics of Western Spirituality – Ancient Writers. As for what the Stoics have to say on "apatheia", this is somewhat piecemeal – or so I found some years ago when I went looking for it. While Stoicism is covered in numerous philosophy books, the issue of apatheia gets little print. This is why I recommend Rick Milas' report. He does a better job of bringing it all together than anything I've read on the subject. Above all, don't bother to read the work by Marcus Aurelius, it's dull reading – probably because he never practiced what he preached. He's a case of a Stoic in name only.

MEANS – END

MEANS – END

What is the relationship of religion to mystical experience? Is mystical experience an end in itself, or is religion a means-end regardless of mystical experience? Put another way, is there some type of common mystical experience that transcends all religions, an experience with no essential connection to religion? Although I have discussed this issue in my retreats, "The Essence of Christian Mysticism", it is important to expand on the subject because the notion that mystical experience transcends religion has become all but the accepted norm today. This belief seems to be based on the notion there exists a common pool of experiences, the same experiences for everyone, quite apart from religion – any religion. As such, religion is regarded as no more than an interpretive tool for understanding and validating one's experience, a tool many people find objectionable. The following quote from Jacques De Marquette's book, *Introduction to Comparative Mysticism*, reflects this popular view.

It is increasingly admitted that in their interpretation of their experiences, mystics are readily influenced by the images and ideas of their particular religion which led them to force the aspects of their new experiences in the old molds of their religious tenets. The study of the psychological conditions of illusion has showed us how easy it is to read expected traits and characters in an experience, which is not of the utmost clarity and definition. The mystics have an almost irresistible tendency to organize their strange and subtle experiences along patterns provided by their religious education. Thus while the intrinsic quality of their contact with the transcendent reality is in no way impaired, because it takes place above the world of forms and formulations, the informative value of their accounts risks to be sterilized from the start. Of course, this does not disturb the type of minds which attach an exclusive importance to the literal aspect of religion. They would have any use for mysticism or anything else, only in the measure in which it can serve to confirm their own interpretations of the sacred texts.

. . . It is obvious that in the present stalemate of religious efficacy in the Western World, a mere confirmation of the presently impotent formulas would not lead us much further than the extant achievements of organized religion. The study of the mystics of the different denominations, in the literature of these denominations, runs the risk of

being exposed to the sterility which has been ascribed to logic as a means of discovery, and which comes from the fact that it can only give in its conclusion that which has already been introduced in the premises. On the contrary, the method of a comparative study of mysticism enables us to begin to make a distinction between those aspects of religious experience which have been colored by traditional group-representations and those which their similarity in the mystics of different faiths authorize us to believe to be based more on real experience than on the dictum of ingrained and perhaps arbitrary pre formations.[1]

The author's view is not unique, it is typical of most writers on mysticism – Evelyn Underhill to name but one. Needless to say, I take issue with this view and consistently address it in my talks. The present author merely provides fodder to further articulate my objections. Before beginning, however, I must acknowledge that despite his criticism of the mystics, the author goes on to treat their various religions with equal fairness and respect.

Also to his credit, he disallows paranormal experiences as authentic mysticism and basically sticks to its religious value. He does not, however, accomplish his goal of separating the mystic and his experience from their respective religions. On the contrary, he falls into the same rut he criticizes when he articulates mystical experiences in the same language, terms and religious tenants as the various mystics. Actually he has no choice in the matter, mysticism has no language outside its religious origins.

Directly or indirectly the author raises the following issues:

1. Of itself mystical experience has no immediate connection to religion. Thus religion is not a valid interpretation of the experience – even though the mystic thinks it is.

2. All we know about mystical experience is purely the mystic's interpretation of it. The very nature of mystical experience requires

---

[1] At the end of this essay is a letter I received from someone who shares this same view – the finger pointed directly at me.

interpretation, without it, the mystic wouldn't know what he experienced.

3. There exists a common pool of mystical experiences and thus everyone has the same experiences. All that varies is the individual's take on the experience – usually interpreted according to his religion or belief system.

4. Mystical experience is an end in itself. Religious practices are only a means to this end.

5. Since mystical experience is "contact with the transcendent" anything else that can be said of it is purely the mystic imposing or "forcing" his view on it.

6. The mystic always ends up reiterating the same truths he began with.

I think these six issues pretty much summarize the author's perspective, his concerns and criticisms. Because I do not agree with any of it, what follows is my take on his perspective. Because the issues overlap, however, it may not be possible to address them on a strictly individual bases.

1. The author could have avoided many a misconception had he started out by defining what he meant by "religion". As it is, he nowhere gives us his definition. Based on what he says, however, we are left with the impression he regards religion as so much mythical lore devoid of any ultimate Truth. Based on this notion of religion, it follows that interpreting a mystical experience in terms of some myth or other would never give one the truth of anything. If, on the other hand, you defined religion as the revelation of ultimate Truth (which I do) then basing your interpretation on religion would not be wrong, it would be the truth. Obviously one's objection to religion depends on how one defines it. Given the author's view of religion, I too reject mythical inter-

pretations of experiences. One can only wonder what sterile view of religion underlies the author's perspective.

2. Another obstacle to understanding an authentic mystical experience, is the author's belief in its purely interpretative nature. This means that "what" you experience is whatever you "think" it is. (Little does the author realize that nothing so shrouds the thinking mind as authentic mystical experience. But for the moment, let us go along with the author). In his view the mystic is always interpreting his experience in light of his religion or belief system. But what, we ask, are the mystic's choices in this matter? If he has no religion, what would be the basis of his interpretation, where would he get it from – the birds? To interpret an experience there has to be something in your head, something you've already heard of. And given all the possible variables from which to pick and choose, how would you know if you picked the right interpretation? How would you know if there was any truth to it at all? I fully agree with the author's criticism of "interpretation", in truth, any experience that has to be "interpreted" is not, in my books, an authentic mystical experience. Any "thinking" about the experience is totally after the fact. But like the author's view of religion, so too his belief that all mystical experience is interpretative, is equally off base. It won't work. What he wants is only the mystic's non-interpretive experience, yet never tells us what that could be – lest it bring him back to religion, no doubt. The author has simply been caught in his own circle.

3. But let us say we could clear away all interpretations; are we to assume everyone has the same experiences? Are we to believe that underlying all possible interpretations, mystical experiences are the same across the board? What possible proof could be provided for this view? There is absolutely none. There is no way to prove any two experiences are the same. Even for a single individual no two experiences are the same, much less across the panoply of possible experiences. The belief that everyone has the

same mystical experiences doesn't have a leg to stand on. Such a belief is too naive for words .

4. There is always the problem, of course, of defining just what a "mystical experience" is. The author refers to it as "contact with the transcendent", so let us go with that definition. Actually, people are in contact with the transcendent all the time whether they know it or not. What a mystical experience is, is simply "knowing that", having that contact. There is nothing actually new or spectacular about this, it is simply knowing something already in place, a truth that has always been the case. Only now we know It. In a nutshell, this knowing is all a mystical experience is about. In early Christianity this experiential knowing was simply called "Gnosis". There is nothing to interpret here, either there has been "contact" or there hasn't. But as to how this contact and the "transcendent" is communicated to others is bound to vary according to one's knowledge , language, religion, culture, etc.- how could it be otherwise? We would not expect an ancient Incan, for example, to express his experience in Buddhists terms, nor a Hindu in Jewish terms. Besides, they probably didn't have the same experience anyway – that's something we will never know. Of course you can always say nothing and keep it to yourself. One of the reasons these experiences are called "mystical" is because words cannot convey "that" which has been contacted, we simply do the best we can with the terms at hand.

5. Another problem regards the "transcendent" itself. Just what is It? The word "transcendent" could mean anything. Indeed, it means a lot of different things to a lot of different people, there's no consensus. If you have the slightest idea "what" It is, then, according to the author, you must be checked off the list of acceptable mystics. While the term "transcendent" may satisfy a beginner, it couldn't last. Once contacted, we want to know more about It than Its merely "transcending" us. We long to know it ever better, ever more intimately, know all we can about it; even,

have an abiding, permanent, contact with It. No one is satisfied with an arbitrary, passing experience. By definition, however, a mystical experience is just that, a passing experience. No one can count on it or make it happen — keep in mind, it is never we who contact the transcendent, but the transcendent who contacts us. But what could be less fulfilling than a passing experience? How could this satisfy anyone? It doesn't. While the term "transcendent" may be sufficient for some people, it would never satisfy the mystic who wants to penetrate that transcendent and know it from the inside out.

6.   The author notes — actually laments — that mystics always end up reiterating the same truths they began with. What is ironic about this complaint is that he does the same thing. What he starts out believing about religion and mystical experience he ends up believing, his conclusions are no different than his premises. Should one's premises be wrong or false, of course, then his conclusions could never be right — it would be logically impossible. So everything depends on the premises you start with because it dictates what you will, or can, end up with. The point is this: whether or not there is prior "knowledge" of a transcendent in no way changes the mystical experience of It. While the religious person has ready terms to express the experience to those who might understand it, the non-religious will either coin his own terms — which nobody may understand — or go looking through the religious books for terms he thinks best conveys his experience. In neither case does this lessen the truth imparted. The advantage of religion is not only providing a plethora of terms, but the companionship of those who may even share the same.

So if the Muslim expresses his contact with the transcendent as "Allah", and the Hindu as "Brahman", what's the matter with that? Why is it unacceptable to make contact with the truth one may have pursued from childhood? Instead of criticizing them for ending up with the same truth they began with, we should thank God they did. It would be a different matter, of course, if one started with no truth at all, or worse, be-lieved something true that wasn't. His contact with the transcendent would only leave him scrambling and his paradigm in tatters. Only pride would prevent him from acknowledging the truth of religion – which he may have thought he had "transcended". The bottom line: if you don't end up with the same truth you started with, then you never started with the truth in the first place.

In conclusion, the author sees a disconnect between religion and mystical experience. For him the end goal is some kind of mystical experience beyond religion. As he sees it, religion (the means) is not proportionate to the end (mystical experience) and thus religion is inadequate to get you to the end, not, at least, the end he envisions.

Is the Goal Some Particular Experience?

Pivotal to the issue is what one accepts as the means and as the end. Only if we understand religion as a means to some kind of mystical experience lying beyond religion, would it be reasonable to believe mystical experience is literally the end of religion (meaning no religion). If, on the other hand, we do not accept mystical experience as an end in itself, then it would not be reasonable to regard any mystical experience as the end-goal of religion, nor religion as merely the means to some mystical experience. So the question is whether or not we can define religion as nothing more than a means, and whether or not we can define man's ultimate end as a particular kind of experience? My answer, of course, is negative. Mystical experience cannot define the end because its purely subjective nature precludes its being an objective truth for everyone. As to the end itself, this can only be ultimate Truth because it is the only unchanging, objective Absolute there is. If religion is not first and foremost the revelation of ultimate Truth, then of course it would be inadequate to lead us to Truth. In other words, if the means (religion) is not proportionate to the end (Truth), or if the means did not already contain the goal or end to be realized, then religion cannot get us to the end and would be valueless as a means.

I have no problem with religion as a means, but I reject any kind of experience as the end-goal or final estate of man. Since mystical experience is only as good or desirable as what is learned from it, experience itself is a means, but not an end. Thus what is experientially learned, "that" is the true end – ultimate Truth, that is. Obviously this is a switch. Where people regard knowledge as a means and experience as an end, I regard experience as a means and knowledge as the end. All the bliss in heaven would not satisfy without knowing Truth. It is just not possible to have a true understanding of the mystic without first accounting for the interconnection between his religion and his experiences. Only where we can prove no direct connection can we regard his religion as merely a means to some mystical experience beyond his religion. As we know, however, this disconnect cannot be done. We know of no mystic without his religion – none.

The reason I have never been able to grasp the end articulated by the Eastern Religions, is because they seem to depend on having – or reaching – a particular type of experience . While I would not venture to guess what "nirvana" is, in Hinduism the end seems to be a state of uninterrupted bliss. The problem with this is that every "experience", mystical or not, is by its very nature, relative and passing. Should some experience become one's sole uninterrupted condition then it would no longer be an "experience", instead, it would be so every day as not to be noticeable at all. When there is no other experience to which it can be compared, or to which it would be relative, there is no "experience" to speak of. This is why the idea of some unchanging "experience" is a contradiction of terms. It is also why no experience can possibly mark the end or goal.

This is why I say those who talk about experiences of bliss are not there yet. The moment bliss is permanent is the moment bliss disappears and will never be experienced again. With nothing comparable to it there would be no way of knowing if we were in a blissful state or not. In what I call my "circle tour", I illustrate and explain how this works. While we may have blissful glimpses of what lies ahead, yet when we actually get there it is not a blissful experience at all. Instead, it is only our

new "everyday" condition of being and not what we had previously experienced – why? Because that aspect of self that had experienced bliss is
gone. And because it is gone we will never have that experience again. We
might add that while this new state is not as we may have expected it to
be (a state of continuous bliss) it is actually a thousand times better. No
question: the less self, the better the life.

It is important to understand why there is no such thing as a
permanent or eternal "experience". All experience is relative, impermanent and only known by comparison to some other experience, or to no
experience at all. Even the experience of stillness, silence and so on, are
all relative experiences that will someday disappear. Because nothing is
worse than experience-dependency, no type of experience can mark the
end of the journey or be the end in itself. Here I think of Origen, an early
Christian, who believed that souls pre-existed in heaven before they "fell"
into an earthly body. When asked why these souls fell, he said because
they got "bored with bliss". Evidently one man's bliss is another's poi-
son. So let us hope there is more to heaven than bliss.

Another problem regarding the end as a particular experiential
state is: "who says so?" Who sets the norm or defines it? Given the variety of blissful experiences, how are we to know which is the last – or if it
will last? Among the mystics there is no consensus regarding a final abiding experience, in fact, they would be the last to offer any. What is indescribable is just that – indescribable. The point is not to denigrate anyone's bliss, but to point up the insufficiency of mystical experience as an
end in itself. Surely the end is more than a blissful mystical experience. In
this matter people have been totally hood-winked. People who set out on
the spiritual journey with this false expectation will never last.

Is Religion the Means?

If I reject mystical experience as an end, I totally accept religion
as a means. People have asked if it was possible to attain the end – some
ultimate state or condition – without religion. My answer is a question:
"have you ever heard of it?, who do you know who has done it?", and,

"what other means is there?" I know of none. We hear all the time, however, of people interested in the spiritual journey who claim they espouse no religion – and want none. Yet when they speak of their means-end it is no different than what is espoused by a particular religion – usually Hinduism or Buddhism. If you know something about these religions (or philosophies) it is not difficult to detect these people's basic beliefs and what influences them. They have obviously adopted one or other of these religious perspectives, studied them, use their terminology, attend their talks, perhaps sat Zen or practiced Yoga – you name it. These people use religion but avoid commitment. They take from religion but give nothing back to it. They don't even acknowledge its influence in their lives. This refusal to credit their indebtedness to religion is just so much pride and prejudice.

Some people have pointed to the late Krishnamurti – renowned for debunking all religions – as someone who found his means-end outside religion. This, however, is not the case. With his indoctrination into the Theosophical Society – a concocted stew of various religions – he was indeed influenced by the tenants and goals of religion. In eventually debunking the Theosophical Society he simply threw out the baby with the bath water, virtually cut off the rungs of his ladder and burnt his bridges so no one can follow. The advantage of religion is that its well-worn path, accessible for thousands of years, remains intact and accessible to all who would take it. When all people 's mystical experiences have long passed, our religions will still be around. As they say, "truth endures".

If we believe religion is, at best, only a path to Truth, but that Truth (some mystical experience or other) lies beyond the path, then between the path and Truth exists a gap or void. Now if religion only gets us as far as a void, then as a means this religion is not proportionate (or sufficient) to the end – sufficient to span the void, that is. If a path is not the truth itself, then it can never get you the truth, and any path insufficient to Truth cannot itself be true. We might state it this way:

- If the path (religion) does not contain, include or encompass the Truth.

- The path is not the Truth.

- Because it is not the Truth, it cannot be a means to Truth.

- If the end (Truth) lies beyond all means of getting there, then no means exist to get there.

All this is saying is that if the mystic's religion is not the truth itself, then merely as a means it cannot get him the truth. He can only get there if his religion is both the means and the end itself. This, at least, is how it goes in Christianity. We will come back to this later.

Life On The Other Shore

We are probably familiar with the Buddhists saying that once you have crossed to the other shore you no longer need the vehicle that got you there. I take this to mean that once you have attained the goal or end of the journey, you no longer have use for the means that got you there. Like crossing the river in a boat or ferry, once on the other shore, you don't need the vehicle anymore.

Considering religion as the means or vehicle, does this mean it (religion) is discarded once the end (other shore) is attained? The saying seems to imply as much. It also seems to imply that the goal was neither inherent, nor in the religion or means itself. Had the means been equally the end, the means could never be left behind.

I think what this saying means is that those particular religious practices that moved us along the path no longer move us at all — because there is no further to go. What it is not saying is that the religion or vehicle is discarded once the goal is attained. Not only is the vehicle preserved to hand on to others, but gratitude alone obliges keeping it in good repair, teaching others how to use it, and above all, acknowledging our indebtedness and extolling its beneficence.

So once on the other shore, does this mean no practice at all? The answer depends on what is meant by "practice". A good example of practice is the Buddhist eight-fold path. Once on the other shore does one cease "right living", "right mindfulness" and so on? How could he? The only difference is that what before had been a "practice" is now his whole life, he wouldn't know how to live otherwise. It works much the same way for the Christian. Having dedicated his whole life and practice toward an abiding oneness with God, having come to the Unitive state he could not live otherwise.

It is important to understand that long before getting to the other shore the devotional and ascetic trappings of beginners already had been left behind along with all the inner work. Thus by the time we get to the end there is not much left to drop away – maybe a hair. What is never left behind, of course, is helping others or good works. Life on the other shore is not that of an isolated, inaccessible hermit sitting on a throne. In one form or another community life goes right on, and with it, community practice – which was never private in the first place. Here, for the first time, one can practice without there being anything in it for himself! Finally, he is free of all the self-seeking that underlies "practice". He gets nothing out of it, takes nothing from it, expects nothing – this is perfect practice. So practice goes right on, only no longer as a means, but as the life of the goal itself.

In the course of our journey the only thing we really leave behind is ourselves. First we leave all our childish, adolescent and immature selves with their particular perspectives regarding religion, truth, and the journey. We may let go or switch devotional practices that no longer inspire, sustain, or move us along. What we can never leave behind, however, is Truth. To give but one example: Catholics believe the Eucharist is Christ, no different than Christ. Receiving the Eucharist we have always been assured of our union and oneness with Christ. So the Eucharist has never been a means to anything, but the end Itself. Strictly speaking the Eucharist – and other Sacraments – is not a "practice" per se, but rather the ultimate goal itself. As said before, the journey is realizing the Truth already with us and then allowing it to transform us.

So those who reach the other shore are always grateful for the vehicle that brought them there. That one no longer needs it for himself makes no difference, having realized its benefits he now envisions the same for others. What, in heaven's name, would prompt anyone to denounce, hack up, and throw the vehicle away? What anger or hatred is this? Such behavior is not indicative of one who has arrived on the other shore. As it stands, we know of no one who reached the other shore untouched or uninfluenced by religion. No one. This is why those who arrive, whatever their sympathy for other paths, invariably promote the path they know. They could not, after all, promote a path they never lived.

It has been my finding that those who try to straddle several paths at once (so-called "eclectic approach") make little or no progress. It takes all we have to thoroughly live a single path, a single-minded, undivided commitment of our whole being. Flitting between different paths so dissipates one's forces he ends up on no path at all. Though I know people who think they live several paths at once, my finding is they don't. Because different paths (religions) do not operate on the same premises (ultimate Truths) they have different goals and practices. Nothing so confuses than trying to straddle two paths at once. People who do this have their own religion and live neither one.

Interpretation

The idea the mystic always interprets his experiences according to his particular religion is a subject I have gone over before. I will only say that any experience that has to be interpreted is not an authentic mystical experience. When God reveals himself, communicates to us or teaches us, the idea of His relying on us to "get it right" is simply absurd. Where revelation or Truth is concerned , God does not depend on us — level of education, mentality, biases — much less abide by our understanding. Such willy-nilly subjective interpretation is pure guess work. It would be a waste of God's grace to depend on man for the Truth. As said before, experience is only as good as the knowledge it conveys, which is to inform us of what, otherwise, we could never know first-hand. Having said this, however, people will go right on believing Truth is just some mystic's private interpretation. Somehow this seems to serve their own biases.

But if I deny the "what" of mystical experience can be interpreted, I readily admit to a retrospective interpretation of what certain experiences mean in the context of the overall journey. It often happens that an experience is only fully understood in retrospect when it fits into place like the piece of a puzzle. While this never alters the content, the initial perspective or understanding may well be subject to change. Thus what may have seemed important at one time is later diminished, and what initially seemed un-noteworthy may turn out to have been a definitive turning point. It seems only in retrospect we can understand the ordering and unfolding of our path. Indeed, we can never see the whole of it until it is finished – over and done with.

The Mystic's Language

Although the author cites the mystics for using their religion's language, he suggests nothing to take its place. But, we ask, what other language (and religion) can they use except the one they know and live? Is the Eastern Orthodox expected to express his transcendent experience in the terms of a Zen Master or some American Indian? This would be so contrived and inauthentic as to be unbelievable. It makes no sense to expect mystics to express their experiential truths in any other than their own religion, more especially when none of them have ever done otherwise. The only reason he goes on about this is because he desperately wants to separate mystical experience from any tinge of religion. He wants religion out of the way.

To communicate the transcendent to others, one does not need to invent a language no one understands, on the contrary, the same terms, concepts and images are employed as before, only no longer as hearsay, but as a living experiential reality – and that is the sole difference. One can always, of course, say nothing. But if anyone has ever remained silent we have never heard of them – how could we?

What bothers the author the most, however, is that the mystics always end up articulating the same truths they began with. In his view, they "force" (deliberately force) their experiences into "old molds". He accuses them of being too "readily influenced by the images and ideas of their particular religion", or they have read religion into their experiences and "patterned them according to their religious education". This is the next thing to calling the mystics liars. (One does not get the sense he has a very good impression of mystics). If the author was a mystic, however, he would know that authentic mysticism is always linked to religion as the experiential counterpart of its more intellectual component.

Thus the mystic is not concerned with experience for its own sake, but rather with "that" which he experienced, literally the Cause of his experience. If we regard "that" which is experienced as content, then we cannot separate it from its experience, one without the other is impossible. Thus if we stub our toe the content and experience are one and the same, the toe is not a later interpretation of the pain experienced. So too, whatever the experience of God, neither God (as content) nor the experience can be separated. (Strictly speaking, God in Himself is not an experience; it is God in our self that is the experience.)

Now it is one thing to intellectually know something, and another to know it experientially. These are two different dimensions of knowing that are not, however, mutually exclusive. For the mystic, these two dimensions (intellectual and experiential) exist in the same person at the same time. We have to get over the stereotypical image of the mystic as a dim-wit ever at odds with intellectual and theological knowledge. We need to let go the image of someone utterly absorbed in their transcendent experiences. By the same token, we must get over the stereotypical image of the intellectual or theologian as anti-mystical, concerned only with his books, authorities, and rational knowledge. Without question these stereotypical images of the religious mystic and intellectual (or theologian) have a way of being etched in cement.

Something to ponder. The only thing anyone knows about "mystical experience" is what the experiencer has to say about it. Regardless of the terms used, a listener has no choice but to understand it in some intellectual form – as an idea, concept, image – it can't be otherwise. Thus the listener's understanding of mystical experience can only be intellectual or conceptual – and there's the rub. After taking everything in, the listener (author) then denounces all these ideas and concepts as purely an intellectual rendition of the experience! He accuses the mystic of labeling his experience, using religious terms, forcing ideas, and so on. The listener's criticism, of course, is totally misplaced. What he is criticizing is not what the mystic knows, but rather what he knows – knows of the experience. What he is denouncing is his own limited, un- mystical, understanding of what he learned. Unknowingly he has created his own vicious circle. The only way out is for him to move to a different field of study.

Grace and Personal Effort

A major difference between Christianity and other religions is that in Christianity, grace is the primary means to the end whereas in the other religions, personal effort is the primary means to the end. While grace and personal effort are not mutually exclusive, grace is as central to Christianity as keeping the law is central to other religions. Thus in Judaism and Islam the end depends on one's keeping the law as laid down in the Torah and Koran respectively. In Buddhism and Hinduism the end depends on working out the Law of Karma governing one's life. In Christianity, however, grace is the sole means.

What exactly is grace? In essence, Grace is God. It is because we cannot "get" God by our own efforts that Grace can only be a gift. Although Grace is indeed a "Presence" in us, it is also a working Transformer, Deifier and Sanctifier. If our humanity were full of Grace we would indeed be a different Person. Formally, then, Grace is a participation in God's very essence, God's divine life. It is because our end (transformation into Christ) is such a feat and miracle, that only God can bring this about. By ourselves we cannot do this – we wouldn't even know how. Whatever we can do ourselves goes no further than ourselves, but whatever God does, goes beyond ourselves. Thus the goal, transformation in Christ, is far beyond our doing. The only sufficient mean to this end is Grace, God's own life and doing.

For grace to be efficacious, however, or for it to accomplish its total effect in us, much depends on our cooperation, our own doing and effort. Like the parable of the talents, if we do not work with what is given, we will lose what has already been given. Thus just as grace is an unmerited given, so too it can be squandered and lost. A traditional dispute between Protestant and Catholic is just this: what God gives, God can take away. While both recognize salvation is a grace, the Protestant holds that once given, this grace can never be lost or taken away, whereas the Catholic holds that unless we cooperate with this grace (via our own efforts) it can be lost – which is what happened in the parable of the talents.

The point is that without grace we underestimate God's end for man and overestimate ourselves, our own doing, that is. At the same time, without human effort and cooperation, like the mustard seed that falls on dead soil, we go no place and simply stagnate. So even though grace is a gift, if we do not work with it, it will not work for us. Grace (God's work) and effort (our work) are two sides of the same coin.

The issue of grace never comes up in the Eastern Religions, instead, the only way to achieve salvation (or enlightenment) is by one's efforts and merits – as Buddha said, "Work diligently toward your salvation". Though a Christian might see grace at work in the East, the Easterner does not recognize it as such. Thus when someone becomes enlightened, it is believed to be due to the accumulative efforts and merits of his past lives – good karma, in other words. So enlightenment (or salvation) is something he or she achieves by their own efforts, attains through their own merits, it is not a gift from the Absolute. In fact, the Absolute never helps at all, it's not even on the scene. Such as least is the Eastern view.

The reason for bringing this up is to point out a major difference between Christianity and the Eastern religions as regards means-end. Where grace is the central and sole means for the Christian, for the Eastern religions, the central means is personal effort and merit. As I see it, the difference boils down to a matter of proportionality, i.e. whether or not the means are proportionate to the end. If the end is God, then only grace is the proportionate or sufficient means. But if the end is some kind of "experience", then perhaps personal effort is sufficient means. Obviously, the goal totally governs the means. Thus should the goal be to transcend our self, certainly self can't do it, only "that" which transcends self can do it – God, that is.

Conclusion

All that mysticism is, is the experiential side of a revealed religion. Thus we have Jewish mysticism, Islamic mysticism, Christian and Buddhist mysticism and so on. The author, however, having determined mysticism is a transcendent experience apart from religion, is upset when the mystic reiterates the truth of his revealed religion. What he fails to understand is that all the mystic has experienced is, in fact, the revealed Truth of his religion, the same, unique, ancient revelation on which it was founded. The mystic has not experienced anything new, on the contrary, something so old there is no date for the original. The author's problem is solely of his own making in that he has espoused a wrong view and understanding of authentic religion. For him religion is so much speculation, myth, and organization – he never bothers to define it. When we start out with a wrong premise or wrong view, we can never reach a right conclusion, much less a right understanding. This author, however, is not alone with his wrong views. As said at the outset, most books on mysticism share his same limited and incorrect premises.

Needless to say, the popular notion that mystical experience and religion are separate entities is totally foreign to me. Christ's revelation, "I am the Way and the Truth" allows no separation between the Way (means) and its end (Truth). Our end being transformation into Christ, when the Christian comes to the end of his journey there is the same truth he began with, only now unveiled in all its reality and marvel. The journey is one of gradual transformation, ever seeing and living more profoundly the Truth already with us. Truth was never somewhere beyond or down the road, it is always here and now, the means (Christ) being the end Itself.

If one really had to go beyond their path to attain truth, then the path neither contains the truth nor is the truth. Only if a path points or leads to truth beyond itself, would this explain the notion that the path or religion is left behind when the end is attained. But since this is not the way it works in Christianity, the views expressed by this and other authors regarding the relationship of mystical experience to religion, do not hold true and cannot be applied to Christian mysticism and its mystics. If given a choice either to base my life on the truths of a religion or on the hope of having some kind of mystical experience, I'd go with religion any day. Quite apart from the passing, fleeting nature of mystical experience, every "contact with the transcendent" has self in it. The only thing around that has no self in it, is simple Faith, it alone transcends all self. It even transcends all belief.

A Footnote

I constantly meet and hear from people who share Mr. Marquette's perspective. What follows is part of a long letter I received several years ago. It seems some people are upset to find I am still a Christian – even worse, a Catholic – because they think I should be beyond all religion. This letter was written by a Japanese gentleman (affiliated, I believe, with a Zen Center in Canada), so we can excuse some of his English phrasing.

"*Overall, I have noticed your inclination for the emotional comfort rather than logical integrity. You told me that you were born to argue, but that is not true. You were born to believe, ready to accept any answer, which would shut up your emotion. All your life, you   have thought only to fit the reality of not-so-distorted experience into Christian schema without asking why using this frame of reference rather than the other one like science, atheist, other religion, independent position. You have been brain washed into Christian way of thinking and never put enough doubt toward that.[2] You have deeply fixed unconscious valuing habit shared by many Christians, namely "God is good," "Christian is good", "Christ is good", "church is good", "believing is good", and so on, and you got this while you were not even aware yet, and never really argued this. With all these inclinations, your search was hampered from the beginning. Your urge, or I would rather call it as a disease, of putting labels on things, and classify experience of something mysterious, and continues till this day most probably. Instead of leaving it as something unknown, unclassified, you tried hard to put one label or other and fix the position of the position-less things. As you know, if you peg down something, you are pegged with it, whether experience, idea, word, insight, god, Christ, anything, unless your pegging appear and disappears in a same moment."*

After this he goes on to list my other mistakes. His perspective is no different than the previous author. Stated in one form or another it represents the conviction of many people, at least those interested in a spiritual life. Expressed in a different way, a gentleman once said to me in all seriousness, that considering my completed journey and the knowledge gained, I was now in a position to become the "founder of a religion". He also took for granted I had fallen outside any known religion and had discovered something new. But as said before, in the context of religion I never came upon anything new or previously unknown. There is nothing I learned that cannot be found in our existing religions taken singly or collectively. What I did discover, however, was the true nature of self or consciousness. But so far I have never found a single person seriously interested in the true nature of self or consciousness.

Also interesting, if I tell people I am a woman, a mother, an American, no one bats an eye. But if l tell them I am a Catholic, there is always a reaction – one never really positive. (Pretty much I grew up with this kind of prejudice so it's nothing new or surprising). It seems people expect me to be either a Hindu, Buddhist or have no religion at all. They object to my references to God, Christ, the Trinity, the Eucharist and so

---

[2] If a Buddhist believes he will enlightened by espousing Buddha's doctrine and keeping the Eight Fold Path, could we call him "brain-washed"? Of course not, only Christians are brain-washed!

on. In their eyes it's all theory, labels, interpretation, doctrine – anything but the Truth. Out of hand they reject these revelations being the truth of one's experiences – can't possibly be! Instead, it is all a matter of semantics or just sheer ignorance on my part.

That people are turned off because I am Catholic, however, is actually a good thing. It automatically weeds out those I could never help anyway. People into the Eastern religions should consult their own masters and gurus because I never practiced or lived their religions. With no first-hand experiential knowledge of other religions or practices, I cannot address their goals, means or concerns. I only know the path I took and lived. Actually, this is the way it goes for everyone who is honest about it. Those who inform us of a religion they never lived are speaking out of turn; they are incapable of getting it right. In this matter there comes to mind many well-known people – Ken Wilber, to name but one. Always beware of these people's "version" of Christianity!

/ 11 /

AN INTERVIEW

AN INTERVIEW

Bernadette Roberts is the author of two extraordinary books on the Christian contemplative journey, The Experience of No-Self (Shambhala, 1982) and The Path to No-Self (Shambhala, 1985). A cloistered nun for nine years, Roberts reports that she returned to the world after experiencing the "unitive state", the state of oneness with God, in order to share what she had learned and to take on the problems and experience of others. In the years that followed she completed a graduate degree in education, married, raised four children, and taught at the preschool, high school, and junior college levels; at the same time she continued her contemplative practice. Then, quite unexpectedly, some 20 years after leaving the convent, Roberts reportedly experienced the dropping away of the unitive state itself and came upon what she calls "the experience of no-self" – an experience for which the Christian literature, she says, gave her no clear road maps or guideposts. Her books, which combine fascinating chronicles of her own experiences with detailed maps of the contemplative terrain, are her attempt to provide such guideposts for those who might follow after her.

Now 55, and once again living in Los Angeles, where she was born and raised, Roberts characterizes herself as a "bag lady" whose sister and brother in law are "keeping her off the streets." "I came into this world with nothing," she writes, "and I leave with nothing. But in between I lived fully – had all the experiences, stretched the limits, and took one too many chances."

When I approached her for an interview, Roberts was reluctant at first, protesting that others who had tried had distorted her meaning, and that nothing had come of it in the end. Instead of a live interview, she suggested, why not send her a list of questions to which she would respond in writing, thereby eliminating all possibility for misunderstanding. As a result, I never got to meet Bernadette Roberts face to face — but her answers to my questions, which are as carefully crafted and as deeply considered as her books, are a remarkable testament to the power of contemplation.

Stephan: Could you talk briefly about the first three stages of the Christian contemplative life as you experienced them — in particular, what you (and others) have called the unitive state?

Bernadette: Strictly speaking, the terms "purgative", "illuminative", and "unitive" (often used of the contemplative path) do not refer to discrete stages, but to a way of travel where "letting go", "insight", and "union", define the major experiences of the journey. To illustrate the continuum, authors come up with various stages, depending on the criteria they are using. St. Teresa, for example, divided the path into seven stages or "mansions". But I don't think we should get locked into any stage theory: it is always someone else's retrospective view of his or her own journey, which may not include our own experiences or insights. Our obligation is to be true to our own insights, our own inner light. My view of what some authors call the "unitive stage" is that it begins with the Dark Night of the Spirit, or the onset of the transformational process — when the larva enters the cocoon, so to speak.

Up to this point, we are actively reforming ourselves, doing what we can to bring about an abiding union with the divine. But at a certain point, when we have done all we can, the divine steps in and takes over. The transforming process is a divine undoing and redoing that culminates in what is called the state of "transforming union" or "mystical marriage", considered to be the definitive state for the Christian contemplative.

Inexperience, the onset of this process is the descent of the cloud of unknowing, which, because his former light had gone out and left him in darkness, the contemplative initially interprets as the divine gone into hiding. In modern terms, the descent of the cloud is actually the falling away of the ego-center, which leaves us looking into a dark hole, a void or empty space in ourselves. Without the veil of the ego-center, we do not recognize the divine; it is not as we thought it should be. Seeing the divine, eye to eye is a reality that shatters our expectations of light and bliss. From here on we must feel our way in the dark, and the special eye that allows us to see in the dark opens up at this time.

So here begins our journey to the true center, the bottom-most, innermost "point" in ourselves where our life and being runs into divine life and being – the point at which all existence comes together. This center can be compared to a coin: on the near side is our self, on the far side is the divine. One side is not the other side, yet we cannot separate the two sides. If we tried to do so, we would either end up with another side, or the whole coin would collapse, leaving no center at all – no self and no divine. We call this a state of oneness or union because the single center has two sides, without which there would be nothing to be one, united, or non-dual. Such, at least, is the experiential reality of the state of trans-forming union, the state of oneness.

Stephan: How did you discover the further stage, which you call the experience of no-self?

Bernadette: That occurred unexpectedly some 25 years after the transforming process. The divine center – the coin, or "true self" – suddenly disappeared, and without center or circumference there is no self, and no divine. Our subjective life of experience is over – the passage is finished. I had never heard of such a possibility or happening. Obviously there is far more to the elusive experience we call self than just the ego. The paradox of our passage is that we really do not know what self or consciousness is, so long as we are living it, or are it. The true nature of self can only be fully disclosed when it is gone, when there is no self.

One outcome, then, of the no-self experience is the disclosure of the true nature of self or consciousness. As it turns out, self is the entire system of consciousness, from the unconscious to God-consciousness, the entire dimension of human knowledge and feeling-experience. Because the terms "self" and "consciousness" express the same experiences (nothing can be said of one that cannot be said of the other), they are only definable in the terms of "experience". Every other definition is conjecture and speculation. No-self, then, means no-consciousness. If this is shocking to some people, it is only because they do not know the true nature of consciousness. Sometimes we get so caught up in the content of consciousness, we forget that consciousness is also a somatic function of the physical body, and, like every such function, it is not eternal. Perhaps we would do better searching for the divine in our bodies than amid the content and experience of consciousness.

Stephan: How does one move from "transforming union" to the experience of no-self? What is the path like?

Bernadette: We can only see a path in retrospect. Once we come to the state of oneness, we can go no further with the inward journey. The divine center is the innermost "point", beyond which we cannot go at this time. Having reached this point, the movement of our journey turns around and begins to move outward – the center is expanding outward. To see how this works, imagine self, or consciousness, as a circular piece of paper. The initial center is the ego, the particular energy we call "will" or volitional faculty, which can either be turned outward, toward itself, or inward, toward the divine ground, which underlies the center of the paper.

When, from our side of consciousness, we can do no more to reach this ground, the divine takes the initiative and breaks through the center, shattering the ego like an arrow shot through the center of being. The result is a dark hole in ourselves and the feeling of terrible void and emptiness. This breakthrough demands a restructuring or change of consciousness, and this change is the true nature of the transforming process. Although this transformation culminates in true human maturity, it is not man's final state. The whole purpose of oneness is to move us on to a more final state.

To understand what happens next, we have to keep cutting larger holes in the paper, expanding the center until only the barest rim or circumference remains. One more expansion of the divine center, and the boundaries of consciousness or self fall away. From this illustration we can see how the ultimate fulfillment of consciousness, or self, is no-consciousness, or no-self. The path from oneness to no-oneness is an egoless one and is therefore devoid of ego-satisfaction. Despite the unchanging center of peace and joy, the events of life may not be peaceful or joyful at all. With no ego-gratification at the center and no divine joy on the surface, this part of the journey is not easy. Heroic acts of selflessness are required to come to the end of self, acts comparable to cutting ever-larger holes in the paper — acts, that is, that bring no return to the self whatsoever.

The major temptation to be overcome in this period is the temptation to fall for one of the subtle but powerful archetypes of the collective consciousness. As I see it, in the transforming process we only come to terms with the archetypes of the personal unconscious; the archetypes of the collective consciousness are reserved for individuals in the state of oneness, because those archetypes are powers or energies of that state. Jung felt that these archetypes were unlimited; but in fact, there is only one true archetype, and that archetype is self. What is unlimited are the various masks or roles self is tempted to play in the state of oneness — savior, prophet, healer, martyr, Mother Earth, you name it. They are all temptations to seize power for ourselves, to think ourselves to be whatever the mask or role may be.

In the state of oneness, both Christ and Buddha were tempted in this manner, but they held to the "ground" that they knew to be devoid of all such energies. This ground is a "stillpoint", not a moving energy-point. Unmasking these energies, seeing them as ruses of the self, is the particular task to be accomplished or hurdle to be overcome in the state of oneness. We cannot come to the ending of self until we have finally seen through these archetypes and can no longer be moved by any of them.

So the path from oneness to no-oneness is a life that is choicelessly devoid of ego-satisfaction; a life of unmasking the energies of self and all the divine roles it is tempted to play. It is hard to call this life a "path", yet it is the only way to get to the end of our journey.

Stephan: In The Experience of No-Self you talk at great length about your experience of the dropping away or loss of self. Could you briefly describe this experience and the events that led up to it? I was particularly struck by your statement "I realized I no longer had a 'within' at all." For so many of us, the spiritual life is experienced as an "inner life" – yet the great saints and sages have talked about going beyond any sense of inwardness.

Bernadette: Your observation strikes me as particularly astute; most people miss the point. You have actually put your finger on the key factor that distinguishes between the state of oneness and the state of no-oneness, between self and no-self. So long as self remains, there will always be a "center". Few people realize that not only is the center responsible for their interior experiences of energy, emotion, and feeling, but also, underlying these, the center is our continuous, mysterious experience of "life" and "being". Because this experience is more pervasive than our other experiences, we may not think of "life" and "being" as an interior experience. Even in the state of oneness, we tend to forget that our experience of "being" originates in the divine center, where it is one with divine life and being. We have become so used to living from this center that we feel no need to remember it, to mentally focus on it, look within, or even think about it. Despite this fact, however, the center remains; it is the epicenter of our experience of life and being, which gives rise to our experiential energies and various feelings.

If this center suddenly dissolves and disappears, the experiences of life, being, energy, feeling and so on come to an end, because there is no "within" any more. And without a "within", there is no subjective, psychological, or spiritual life remaining – no experience of life at all. Our subjective life is over and done with. But now, without center and circumference, where is the divine? To get hold of this situation, imagine consciousness as a balloon filled with, and suspended in divine air. The balloon experiences the divine as immanent, "in" itself, as well as transcendent, beyond or outside itself. This is the experience of the divine in ourselves and ourselves in the divine; in the state of oneness, Christ is often seen as the balloon (ourselves), completing this Trinitarian experience. But what makes this whole experience possible – the divine as both immanent and transcendent – is obviously the balloon, i.e. consciousness or self. Consciousness sets up the divisions of within and without, spirit and matter, body and soul, immanent and transcendent; in fact, consciousness is responsible for every division we know of. But what if we pop the balloon – or better, cause it to vanish like a bubble that leaves no residue. All that remains is divine air. There is no divine in anything, there is no divine transcendent or beyond anything, nor is the divine anything.

We cannot point to anything or anyone and say, "This or that is divine". So the divine is all – all but consciousness or self, which created the division in the first place. As long as consciousness remains however, it does not hide the divine, nor is it ever separated from it. In Christian terms, the divine known to consciousness and experienced by it as immanent and transcendent is called God; the divine as it exists prior to consciousness and after consciousness is gone is called Godhead. Obviously, what accounts for the difference between God and Godhead is the balloon or bubble – self or consciousness. As long as any subjective self remains, a center remains; and so, too, does the sense of interiority.

Stephan: You mention that, with the loss of the personal self, the personal God drops away as well. Is the personal God, then, a transitional figure in our search for ultimate loss of self?

Bernadette: Sometimes we forget that we cannot put our finger on anything or any experience that is not transitional. Since consciousness, self, or subject is the human faculty for experiencing the divine, every such experience is personally subjective; thus in my view, "personal God" is any subjective experience of the divine. Without a personal, subjective self, we could not even speak of an impersonal, non-subjective God; one is just relative to the other. Before consciousness or self existed, however, the divine was neither personal nor impersonal, subjective nor non-subjective – and so the divine remains when self or consciousness has dropped away. Consciousness by its very nature tends to make the divine into its own image and likeness; the only problem is, the divine has no image or likeness. Hence consciousness, of itself, cannot truly apprehend the divine.

Christians (Catholics especially) are often blamed for being the great image makers, yet their images are so obviously naive and easy to see through, we often miss the more subtle, formless images by which consciousness fashions the divine. For example, because the divine is a subjective experience, we think the divine is a subject; because we experience the divine through the faculties of consciousness, will, and intellect, we think the divine is equally consciousness, will and intellect; because we experience ourselves as a being or entity, we experience the divine as a being or entity; because we judge others, we think the divine judges others; and so on. Carrying a holy card in our pockets is tame compared to the formless notions we carry around in our minds; it is easy to let go of an image, but almost impossible to uproot our intellectual convictions based on the experiences of consciousness.

Still, if we actually knew the unbridgeable chasm that lies between the true nature of consciousness or self and the true nature of the divine, we would despair of ever making the journey. So consciousness is the marvelous divine invention by which human beings make the journey in subjective companionship with the divine; and, like every divine invention, it works. Consciousness both hides the chasm and bridges it – and when we have crossed over, of course, we do not need the bridge any more.

So it doesn't matter that we start out on our journey with our holy cards, gongs and bells, sacred books and religious feelings. All of it should lead to growth and transformation, the ultimate surrender of our images and concepts, and a life of selfless giving. When there is nothing left to surrender, nothing left to give, only then can we come to the end of the passage – the ending of consciousness and its personally subjective God. One glimpse of the Godhead, and no one would want God back.

Stephan: How does the path to no-self in the Christian contemplative tradition differ from the path as laid out in the Hindu and Buddhist traditions?

Bernadette: I think it may be too late for me to ever have a good understanding of how other religions make this passage. If you are not surrendering your whole being, your very consciousness, to a loved and trusted personal God, then what are you surrendering it to? Or why surrender it at all? Loss of ego, loss of self, is just a by-product of this surrender; it is not the true goal, not an end in itself. Perhaps this is also the view of Mahayana Buddhism, where the goal is to save all sentient beings from suffering, and where loss of ego, loss of self, is seen as a means to a greater end. This view is very much in keeping with the Christian desire to save all souls. As I see it, without a personal God, the Buddhist must have a much stronger faith in the "unconditioned and unbegotten" than is required of the Christian contemplative, who experiences the passage as a divine doing, and in no way a self-doing.

Actually, I met up with Buddhism only at the end of my journey, after the no-self experience. Since I knew that this experience was not articulated in our contemplative literature, I went to the library to see if it could be found in the Eastern Religions. It did not take me long to realize that I would not find it in the Hindu tradition, where, as I see it, the final state is equivalent to the Christian experience of oneness or transforming union. If a Hindu had what I call the no-self experience, it would be the sudden, unexpected disappearance of the Atman – Brahman, the divine Self in the "cave of the heart", and the disappearance of the cave as well. It would be the ending of God-consciousness, or transcendental consciousness – that seemingly bottomless experience of "being", "consciousness", and "bliss" that articulates the state of oneness. To regard this ending as the falling away of the ego is a grave error; ego must fall away before the state of oneness can be realized. The no-self experience is the falling away of this previously realized transcendent state.

Initially, when I looked into Buddhism, I did not find the experience of no-self there either; yet I intuited that it had to be there. The falling away of the ego is common to both Hinduism and Buddhism. Therefore, it would not account for the fact that Buddhism became a separate religion, nor would it account for the Buddhist's insistence on no eternal Self – be it divine, individual or the two in one. I felt that the key difference between these two religions was the no-self experience, the falling away of the true Self, Atman-Brahman. Unfortunately, what most Buddhist authors define as the no-self experience is actually the no-ego experience. The cessation of clinging, craving, desire, the passions, etc., and the ensuing state of imperturbable peace and joy articulates the egoless state of oneness; it does not, however, articulate the no-self experience or the dimension beyond. Unless we clearly distinguish between these two very different experiences, we only confuse them, with the inevitable result that the true no-self experience becomes lost. If we think the falling away of the ego, with its ensuing transformation and oneness, is the no-self experience, then what shall we call the much further experience when this egoless oneness falls away? In actual experience there is only one thing to call it, the "no-self experience"; it lends itself to no other possible articulation.

Initially, I gave up looking for this experience in the Buddhist literature. Four years later, however, I came across two lines attributed to Buddha describing his enlightenment experience. Referring to self as a house, he said, "All thy rafters are broken now, the ridgepole is destroyed." And there it was – the disappearance of the center, the ridgepole; without it, there can be no house, no self. When I read these lines, it was as if an arrow launched at the beginning of time had suddenly hit a bulls-eye. It was a remarkable find. These lines are not a piece of philosophy, but an experiential account, and without the experiential account we really have nothing to go on. In the same verse he says, "Again a house thou shall not build," clearly distinguishing this experience from the falling away of the ego-center, after which a new, transformed self is built around a "true center," a sturdy, balanced ridgepole.

As a Christian, I saw the no-self experience as the true nature of Christ's death; the movement beyond even his oneness with the divine, the movement from God to Godhead. Though not articulated in contemplative literature, Christ dramatized this experience on the cross for all ages to see and ponder. Where Buddha described the experience, Christ manifested it without words; yet they both make the same statement and reveal the same truth – that ultimately, eternal life is beyond self or consciousness. After one has seen it manifested or heard it said, the only thing left is to experience it.

Stephan: You mention in The Path to No-Self that the unitive state is the "true state in which God intended every person to live his mature years." Yet so few of us ever achieve this unitive state. What is it about the way we live right now that prevents us from doing so? Do you think it is our preoccupation with material success, technology, and personal accomplishment?

Bernadette: First of all, I think there are more people in the state of oneness than we realize. For everyone we hear about there are thousands we will never hear about. Believing this state to be a rare achievement can be an impediment in itself. Unfortunately, those who write about it have a way of making it sound more extraordinary and blissful that it commonly is, and so false expectations are another impediment – we keep waiting and looking for an experience or state that never comes. But if I had to put my finger on the primary obstacle, I would say it is having wrong views of the journey.

Paradoxical though it may seem, the passage through consciousness or self moves contrary to self, rubs it the wrong way – and in the end, will even rub it out. Because this passage goes against the grain of self, it is, therefore, a path of suffering. Both Christ and Buddha saw the passage as one of suffering, and basically found identical ways out. What they discovered and revealed to us was that each of us has within himself or herself a "stillpoint" – comparable, perhaps to the eye of a cyclone, a spot or center of calm, imperturbability, and non-movement. Buddha articulated this central eye in negative terms as "emptiness" or "void", a refuge from the swirling cyclone of endless suffering. Christ articulated the eye in more positive terms as the "Kingdom of God" or the "Spirit within", a place of refuge and salvation from a suffering self.

For both of them, the easy out was first to find that stillpoint and then, by attaching ourselves to it, by becoming one with it, to find a stabilizing, balanced anchor in our lives. After that, the cyclone is gradually drawn into the eye, and the suffering self comes to an end. And when there is no longer a cyclone, there is also no longer an eye. So the storms, crises, and sufferings of life are a way of finding the eye. When everything is going our way , we do not see the eye, and we feel no need to find it. But when everything is going against us, then we find the eye. So the avoidance of suffering and the desire to have everything go our own way runs contrary to the whole movement of our journey; it is all a wrong view. With the right view, however, one should be able to come to the state of oneness in six or seven years — years not merely of suffering, but years of enlightenment, for right suffering is the essence of enlightenment. Because self is everyone's experience underlying all culture. I do not regard cultural wrong views as an excuse for not searching out right views. After all, each person's passage is his or her own; there is no such thing as a collective passage.

12

THE TEN OXHERDING PICTURES

THE TEN OXHERDING PICTURES

In 2009, Jeff Shore, an international Zen teacher from the Hanazono University in Kyoto, wrote a commentary on the Oxherding Pictures which was published in *Zengaku Kenkyu/Journal of Zen Studies*. He asked Bernadette if she would contribute her Christian understanding of these pictures to that article. Years ago, wanting to know something about Buddhism, I picked up a book with a set of pictures. These pictures obviously depicted a spiritual journey. The idea of graphically depicting the journey struck me as unique and delightful. I decided, however, before reading the Buddhist interpretation, I'd looked them over to see if (or how) they might be understood in terms of my own Christian journey. What follows is how I understood them.

I

Looking for the Ox

God is looking for us. He wants us. We may not know it, but we belong to Him. He even hunts us down to be sure we know it. Though we may hear His voice calling, even see Him from afar, we keep going our own way. Still, He follows relentlessly – and we know we are being tailed. He must want something from us, but what could that be? What can anyone possibly give God?

II

Noticing the Footprints

Seeing our footprints going in the wrong direction, God no longer bides his time. Like the Hound-of-Heaven He begins to chase us down. So what are our options now? Should we run faster, try to hide, or, as a true bull, daringly turn and face Him, boldly ask Him what He wants of us?

III

Catching Sight of the Ox

Since He is now too close to escape there is no choice but to turn, look Him in the face, and bluntly put our question to Him. What we never planned on, however, was the nature of this face-to-Face encounter. Just seeing God face-to-Face is all it takes to turn anyone's life around – forever! For a moment we even lose sight of our self. God, however, never loses sight of us. He alone knows what He has created, knows his plan for our eternal destiny, knows the "Way" and can bring us there.

But what, we ask, could God possibly get out of all this? Now no man can fathom God's love for all He has created, yet all He asks is that we love Him back. This is all He wants, all He has ever asked of us. And what is our reply?

IV

Getting Hold of the Ox

Having seen God, we are so overjoyed at being caught that we rue all the time we wasted without God on our tail. Quickly we become friends with much exchange of affection and delightful treats. The only blip in this scenario is when God suddenly goes off, disappears on us and we grow anxious, miss Him terribly. Now we must forage for ourselves and spend lonely nights. In time, however, we learn to patiently wait out these absences; our trust is becoming unshakable, and too, we are learning to see him on ever deeper levels – even, see him in the dark! And with every sudden return, his light and love become ever more exalted – totally worth the wait! But who can understand the demands of exchange in such a great love as this? Love, after all, demands equality – no happiness in an unequal exchange. To be given everything and return nothing is the anathema of love – better not to love at all. Yet all we can give God is what is ours, what we ourselves have made, which is a nothing compared to everything God has given us. All we have to give God is what he has made – ourselves, our whole being. He can take it, exchange it, recreate or transform it, even to the point of no return. It is this supernatural re-fashioning that becomes the make-or-break of the journey, this is the or-deal of becoming God-proven – if we can put it that way. This is the or-deal of ordeals.

V

Taming the Ox

The Ox is no meek lamb, and the Herdsmen, no good shepherd. Only a tough herdsmen can deal with a strong-willed bull. God knows just what will happen when he brands the bull with the Seal of His Image, yet only this can seal the Ox to Him forever as his own possession. This seal, of course, will burn the bull to the depths of his being, burn a Center right through him, and it will be painful. At the onset of this ordeal, however, a film-like veil is put over his mind, a veil through which, in time,

God can be seen everywhere, a depth of vision that never leaves – though initially it all but blinds the Ox. Following this, the moment he looks inward to his familiar center, instead of light, there is a bottomless black hole, the sight of which begins the painful burning through to the depths of his existence. Now there is a fire in the belly and the bolt goes wild. First on his agenda is never to look "within" again – but how can this be avoided? Finally, screwing up his courage he decides to "face it", to deliberately look down into this dark pit even if it kills him – it might be better to be dead anyway. But lo and behold, looking down, there is God's Big Eye looking back at him! What a shock! But now he knows the direction: go down into that pit where, at the bottom, God is. So he makes this journey through a revolting self to his bottommost existence – a point where one can go no further and where one eventually finds a peace that surpasses definition. This sacred space, the peace of God, becomes a refuge from a self still storming wildly about and above us. We hang on to this peace for dear life until, finally, the storm gradually subsides and the Center becomes bright, rises to the top and is ever available. Where we thought God was out to break our spirit, it turns out God gives us His Spirit instead, this is the way it goes. Then comes the certifying revelation of an abiding, permanent oneness of the two, and with that, a whole new person (Ox) appears.

VI

Riding Home

Who goes home is a "branded" new Ox – the old one is dead. And here begins a whole new life, a life "I" no longer live, but "We" live. The Ox can no more be aware of himself than he is of his other half – God. The two are one in knowing and willing. With a fearless freedom and a divine center of imperturbable peace and joy, they set out and return to the marketplace from whence they came. The marketplace, however, is but a testing ground, a challenge to the imperturbable Center into which everything that touches self (the Ox) ultimately disappears. Making their way through the market place, the divine Center imperceptibly expands as every aspect of self that can arise disappears into It, never to be experienced again. Thus the divine Center expands in proportion and as self (Ox) disappears – "He must increase, I must decrease," the saying goes. The Rider does not lead the Ox – no rein is needed – because the Ox comes to know the Rider's mind so well he can anticipate Its will and direction – usually the hardest. And so the two, the Ox and Herdsmen, bull their way through the ups and downs of life, always landing on their feet. Then there comes a time when nothing can touch the Ox at all, there being nothing left to touch – self has been lived through completely, there is nothing left to experience. Now this has all been a good and adventurous life, a great life that God intends everyone to live in oneness with Him. Here nothing is wanting, nothing left to be achieved, no further to go in this life. From here on we can only head for our eternal, heavenly home.

VII

Ox Vanishes, Herdsmen Remains

In the silence of ecstasy self is gone, this time, forever. Initially we do not know this, but wait for its usual return (after ecstasy). When this does not happen, all we know is that "something" is missing. It takes a while to realize self will never return, but with this certitude there is joy, a burden lifted, a lightsomeness, now we can fly! But alas, the moment we try to look inward to the Rider, to our divine Center, Oh No ...!

VIII

Ox and Herdsmen Vanished

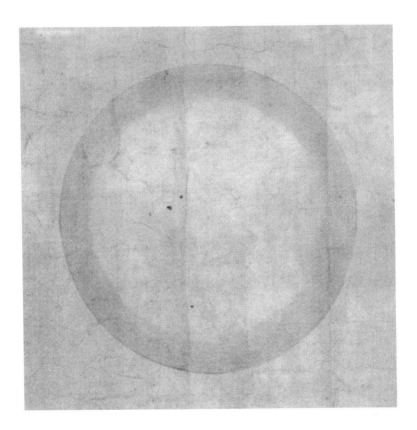

In one fell swoop of the Divine Center leaves whole body! God is gone too! The one who dies is not self (it merely slipped away unnoticed, and who cares about it anyway?), rather, it is God who dies. But who can believe such a thing? Unheard of! Considered rationally, of course, it all makes sense: Since Ox and Rider were indissolubly One, there cannot be one without the Other. Just as they lived as one, so they die as one.

IX

Returning to the Source

Beyond this death there is only a Void of Voids – Meister Eck-hart's "breakthrough" into the unknowable Essence of the Godhead, the Source, which is God-as-He-is-in-Himself and no longer God-as-He-is-in-our-self. This is the Meister Eckhardt's "barren desert," the "waste land," the "abyss" of the Godhead. The Essence of the Godhead, howev-er, is not fit for a human being, in fact, there is nothing worse in human history than this Void of Voids. Sensory perception remains, the mind is

Void, all form is Void — no God in nature, all creation is an absolute Void. With no experience of life or being, of body or soul, of mind or thought, the only question that can arise is: "What is the true nature of 'this' that remains?" Obviously something remains, but the mind has not a single idea. The answer can only be revealed — and so, eventually, it is.

X

Return to the Marketplace

Lo and behold! Who is this who has risen from the dead? It is Universal Man, the sum of all creation – Christ! Now Who, besides Almighty God, could have 'thunk' of such a thing, much less make it happen?

"On account of his infinite love He became what we are, in order that He might make us what He Himself is."- St. Irenaeus (125 – 202 AD)

EPILOGUE

In the Christian tradition "Return to the Marketplace" only comes after the egoless Unitive Condition (Ox and Rider as one) but never after the No-Self event – there being no one to return anywhere. It's all over for this world.[1] As for Christ showing up, well, just remember, neither "I" nor any human person is Christ. It would seem, however, the Oxherding Pictures were made just for Christ – after all, "I am with you always" is the Truth! What initially struck me about these pictures was the two-step depiction of loss-of-self – a fact most people miss. First, self (Ox) is gone, then shortly after, God (Herdsmen) is gone. This is exactly how the experience of no self goes, and why I found these pictures so remarkable.

---

[1] Following the Unitive state, traditionally one is given some "Apostolic mission" to go out and do some work for the lord – go to the missions, found an order, or whatever. What I discovered, however, is that what people need most in life is God's interior grace, and I could not give it. Apart from praying this grace for others, the market place was a complete failure for me. The fact I could do nothing for God was the bane of my existence. It is a hard lesson to learn, but in time I saw, knew, that for us, God does indeed give his grace to others – I have seen miracles! In truth, no prayer in is in vain.

13

THE EUCHARIST – A CHRISTIAN PATH

THE EUCHARIST – A CHRISTIAN PATH[1]

Usually our discussion of the spiritual-psychological journey is in terms of consciousness and its developmental milestones: transcendence of the ego, transformation, realization of the true self, and so on. This approach is largely ecumenical because these stages of consciousness are common to everyone regardless of their religious tradition, culture or background. Within each tradition, however, there is a distinctive way of travel not generally shared by others, and thus, for the Catholic, the distinctive path of revelation is the Eucharist. Not only is the Eucharist central to the belief and practice of the Church, but the fountainhead of its mystical contemplative dimension, the alpha and omega of the ultimate revelation of Christ. Our view of the historical Christ (Jesus) cannot exceed his historical limitations, however the Eucharist embraces all dimensions of Christ and offers a dimension of his Godhead not accessible from a purely historical perspective. Then too, the Eucharistic Christ offers a profound dimension of contemplative experience and insight wherein the unfolding revelation of Christ is equally an unfolding of ourselves, our own human mystery and destiny.

What follows is the account of how I, for one, discovered the Eucharist as the path, the teacher and very life of the spiritual journey. While this journey may not be typical of other Catholics, it is the only one I know first-hand. I am not an authority on other people 's experiences, nor are my experiences an authority for anyone else's, and where I might speak objectively of consciousness and its developmental milestones, it would be impossible to speak of the Eucharist in a similar manner. Alt-

---

[1] The following article, "The Eucharist, A Christian Path", was written many years ago for a small Catholic magazine, whose name I do not recall. Its focus was on Catholic practices that promote the spiritual life. Every issue featured someone's account of the spiritual benefits found in a particular Catholic practice. I was asked to contribute and did. (The periodical may no longer be in publication).

hough we may never know the exact nature of how the divine works directly on consciousness to bring about our ultimate destiny, from our side, we know the experiences, the effects and changes, and of this, at least, we can give some account.

Discovering the Path

Although raised in a devout Catholic home, my early experiences of God had nothing to do with Christ. They evoked no image or thought of him, and were not linked to any religious practice. When, at the age of eleven or so, I became aware of the disconnectedness between my experience of God and the historical Christ, many questions came to mind, questions about the true nature of my experiences and about the true nature of Christ – whether or not he was, in fact, the One True God, and whether or not I had the faith to believe it. On the one hand I knew that without this belief I could not be Christian, but on the other hand, how could I not be Christian when this was the only faith I had ever known and practiced? Based on the externals there could be no doubt, but deep within, there was no such certitude.

Since those around me evinced no problem in this matter, my conclusion was that I had not been blessed with their gift of faith, or that "my Baptism didn't take"- which is how I put it to my father. Although my father seemed incapable of believing this – which is why I felt he never honestly understood the problem – he nevertheless went to great lengths to discuss all matters of faith with me. Though I blamed God for this dilemma – that is, giving me experiences that had nothing to do with Christ – I was also sure God could resolve this dilemma. To this end I continued to question my father and chase down his answers.

Initially, some of our discussions ended on a bad note. When I would ask, for example, "Who said so?" or "How do we know?" he would reply, "The Church said so," as if that was the end of the subject. For me, however, this was no final answer at all. Because someone else "said so", would never constitute final Truth for me. I did not see how anybody could base their entire life, heart and soul, on the vote of a majority of conciliatory men, no matter how smart or holy they were. That human beings could decide ultimate Truth by vote, discussion, or any other means, struck me as incredible.

Realizing that his proof was not working, my father changed his tactic. When we would get down to the final "How do we know?" he would throw up his hands and say, "This is as far as the intellect can go," – meaning, of course, that the ultimate Truths of our faith were a mystery beyond the range and limitations of even a God-given intellect. And meaning too, that where the intellect came to an end, only faith could keep going. This conclusion was more acceptable to me, because God, as an intellectual mystery, was so easy to understand, I needed no faith in the matter. With this conclusion, I could at least hold out for Christ as the totally unknowable, unfathomable mystery of God, and thereby make some claim to be Christian.

Eventually, however, this solution proved insufficient. However true it may be – Christ as the unknowable mystery of God – I felt that if this truth made no difference in my life, then it was meaningless – I could just as well live my life with God and forget about Christ. But how to forget about Christ? It was because this had proved impossible, I was seeking a resolution. My father did all he could to convey to me the mystery of the Trinity, yet it too left questions in my mind – to name one, the nature of Christ before his Incarnation.

My problem was not with Jesus as the Son of God, there was no problem with his life or the beliefs based on it. What I could not see was how Jesus of Nazareth, walking on earth, could be at the same time Everywhere, the creator and sustainer of the universe, the One God. Then too, if Jesus was the God of my experiences, why could I not see that? Between the Infinite and the historical Christ there was an unfathomable gap in my mind. What was equally mysterious, was the faith to bridge this gap. In myself I could find it nowhere.

By age thirteen this dilemma reached a critical point. It was imperative to know once and for all if I was a Christian or not. It had become impossible to get on with life when I did not know its true direction. The continuous search for answers was getting nowhere, and because of this, I had the peculiar feeling that my life had come to a complete standstill, that I had been stone-walled or that the spirit in me had come to a complete halt. It was not a happy predicament.

Finally, I decided to put the whole dilemma together in a nutshell, formulate it in a single question and put it to my father for a single, definitive answer. On the one hand I had toward the question as truthfully as possible, but on the other, I had to word it as subtly as possible, for my father was as theological and dogmatic as the Pope himself and I didn't want to hit a wrong nerve. If there was any advantage in asking my father, however, it was that he at least knew my background, our years of discussion, and our daily attendance at Mass together. More importantly, perhaps, I regarded him as the most informed and devout religious individual I knew.

So one evening at dinner, I put it to him. "Let us say", I began, "just for the moment – hypothetically, of course – that someone could believe some of the truths the Church teaches, but could not believe certain other truths, would this mean he could not be a Christian?" Instantly he replied, "The Church does not say you have to understand the mystery of God or the Truths of faith in order to be Christian. What it is saying is that if there is any hope of ever understanding these truths, then you have to practice your faith. Without practice you cannot expect to understand because understanding can only come through practice. If you wait until all the understanding is in before you practice, then you will never understand, never practice, and will have wasted your life waiting and searching for what never comes. So all the Church is saying, all it is asking of you, is that you practice, practice, practice!" The last words were pounded on the table. After this he went back to eating his dinner. The silence that followed, was golden.

Like a flash his words struck me as a great truth, words that would remain with me all my life. I was aware his reply was not the typical all-or-none response I would have received from an official representative of the Church or clergy – which is why I never bothered to ask them. But this made my father's response all the more startling and insightful, so much so, I felt God had inspired him against himself. Then too, I knew that somehow, in some way, he would not want any of his children to lose "the faith."

With his words the dilemma dissolved and in its place came a great joy. Now I saw that to be a Christian was the ultimate goal, the end of a life of practice, and in no way its beginning. Thus it would be sufficient to spend my life in the process of becoming a Christian, a process of striving to see and understand Christ, that eventually I might believe that which was, for now, only a mystery. Thus becoming a Christian would be the practice, and being a Christian, the ultimate goal.

The Practice

As someone born into a practicing family, no one had to tell me how to go about it. Because reception of the Eucharist was the central practice of my faith, it now became central to my journey, so central in fact, that without the Eucharist I could never have become a Christian. Although receiving the Eucharist is not exclusive of other religious and virtuous practices, for me, it would become the heart and soul, the key to all other practices. As mystical as it is, the Eucharist is actually very earthy – Christ's humanity, body and soul, melding with our own and infiltrating every cell of our body. Thus what is ultimately revealed is not only Christ's transcendent Godhead, but the true nature of his physical body as well – the true nature of all matter, in fact – for I eventually saw how these two could never be separated.

Without my consciously realizing it, reception of the Eucharist automatically focused my mind inward, to God within and my immediate oneness with Him. One of the first things I became aware of was that for some time after communion there was a difference, some difference had been made. As the day wore on, however, this difference imperceptibly wore off or faded away. Initially it was impossible to put my finger on this subtle change or explain it in any way, but through sheer repetition of the experience, one day I discovered the true nature of the difference, it was as simple as silence.

Before receiving communion my mind was moving about from one thought to another; but after communion this content, virtually my whole life, gradually faded away, became superficial, insignificant – as if it counted for nothing. Although this silencing was so subtle it seemed like the most natural thing in the world, at other times, the silence was so enforced it was impossible to move my mind against it, which did not strike me as so natural. One way or the other, this silence informed me that this was It, this was the one important thing in my life, this was home where I belonged, and where I must stay. Somehow I knew I must learn to live in this silence, live with and from it and never be without it – because this was It.

My interpretation of this silencing was that the Eucharist was imperceptibly drawing me into its own silent state. I realized that the living Christ was wordless, formless, motionless – silence itself, and that it was asking me to make the match, to become as silent as it was silent. Thus the silence seemed to be two things at once: on the one side it was the Divine itself, and on the other it was myself, myself increasingly being silenced. This experiential phenomena of the Eucharist – silence – became the singular consistent phenomena of my journey. Through all wind and weather it was the sole unfailing anchor. Though I went right on wondering if the historical Christ would ever turn out to be the ultimate Godhead, I never questioned the Eucharistic Christ because for me it was working. I had found my direction, the stone-wall was gone, and a new dimension of life opened up.

Early on, I decided that since God already knew my thoughts, desires, problems and aspirations, then there was no need to inform him of any of this. To do so would be little better than talking to myself. It was sufficient just to be in His presence, be with Him and say nothing. I figured that if in total silence He knew what I knew, then in this same silence, I might know something of what He knew, and there was a great deal I needed to know. What I learned is that silence itself is a way of knowing, for in this silence I eventually learned everything I ever needed to know. I also learned that it was not always easy to remain in silence, or do so for any length of time. But this was the challenge – the practice. The goal of course, was to make a perfect match between myself and the Divine, and though I knew I could never match the silence the Divine could bring about, yet from my side, I could be ready and waiting. In time I learned to ignore my roving mind and focus instead on the silent will, which, by contrast to the mind, was steadfast, non-moving, silent, glued to the Divine as to the stillpoint of being. It was obvious that my true oneness with God was not mental, not dependent upon whether or not I could think of Him. Rather, it was my will that was the silent energy center of my being that, like an umbilical cord, was somehow attached to the Divine.

As the journey got under way I became increasingly aware of the great disparity between the divine silence and my lack of it. I was aware of the continuous movements of my mind, feelings, desires and expectations – in a word, aware of the lack of unity within myself. Effortlessly and in simple silence, however, the Eucharist could bring these scattered faculties to a standstill and in doing so, revealed the disparity between us, kind of like before-and-after. Gradually it dawned on me this journey was not only a gradual revelation of God, but equally a revelation of myself, of aspects of myself I never knew I had prior to the divine silence. Like two sides of a single coin, the Eucharist was revealing two things at once: on one side, myself, on the other side, Itself.

So too the silence was two things at once: the positive Divine and the negative of self. Thus the ever deepening path of the Eucharist was a path of self-knowledge and Divine-knowledge rolled into one. Initially I had not planned on this; somehow I had the notion that the self would be quietly phased out, whereas what I learned is that the depth of the Divine is only revealed in proportion to the depths self revealed. Thus throughout the journey the true nature of self is revealed along with the true nature of the Divine. Even at the definitive end of the journey, what is ultimately revealed is the true nature of the Divine as well as the true nature of self. One is not the other. Indeed, discovering the true nature of self is the shocking and unbelievable end of the journey.

Several years after I had begun to practice in earnest, an insight came that resolved the question of why my experiences of God had nothing to do with the historical Christ. Quite simply, I realized that the God Christ had experienced within himself – the "Father" as he called Him – was not Christ, was not himself. So too, the God I experienced within myself was not Christ; what I experienced was the same God Christ had experienced. In other words, Christ did not experience merely himself, or tell us he was one with himself, rather, he spoke of his oneness with God, his Father, which is the same experience of oneness he wished for all of us. With this understanding it dawned on me what it really meant to "follow" Christ. It meant to follow his most profound experiences of God, his own spiritual journey, and not merely the externals of his life, limited as they are to historical circumstances and mentality. Thus everything he said and did came out of his interior experiential life with God, this was the source of his external public life, his words, insights and behaviors.

What he wished for us was that we too discover the inner Source, and from this same Source work out our own historical lives, manifest this Source in whatever circumstances we might find ourselves. There could be no premature manifestation, however, we could not put on Christ like a coat or work from the outside in. First we had to realize Christ's same permanent, abiding state of oneness with the Divine before we could live out of that oneness or hope to manifest It in our own lives. It is one thing to believe and at times see or experience oneness with the Divine, but it is quite another to experientially abide in that oneness such that it would be impossible to live any other way or to have any other choice. So this is how the contemplative practice of oneness gradually becomes the whole of our life. Practice eventually brings us to a turning point, after which, life itself is the practice, is the manifestation. Even when I saw how this worked, however, I was still a long way off. Yet I knew the immediate goal: to come to Christ's same abiding oneness with

God and live out this oneness in my own daily life.

Another insight, but one that was most premature, was that "that" in me which experienced God, "that" was Christ – true Christ. Since I had taken for granted it was "I" who experienced God, this insight was a fleeting prospect of no-self, that all but bordered on a sense of fear – so much good news and bad news rolled into one. (Later on I realized that the element of fear is always present when some truth or insight is beyond our present spiritual level of development, hence the tendency to back off, deny, or explain it away). Although I saw how this would work, namely, "I" being transformed into Christ, yet it was impossible to grasp such a reality ahead of time.

Thus I had no idea this transformation would be an ordeal to stretch the human limits, or that it would mean a radical change of consciousness. No, there is no way to understand or discover the "true self" ahead of time, much less know its revelation as the Christ- self. (By the Christ-self, of course, I do not mean the unique phenomenal personality or individuality of the historical Jesus. Jesus' true self was "that" in him which was one with the Father – "that" being the same in us that is one with the Father. "That" of course, is self or consciousness, which, although it has realized its oneness with God (Christ-consciousness) is nevertheless distinguished from God. With Christ's death, however, there was no consciousness or self remaining to make this distinction, thus nothing to be one with the Father. What this means is that we must first be transformed into Christ before we can die and rise with him).

Naturally I could not have understood any of this ahead of time. It seems no matter how wonderful or true our insights and knowledge, it is as nothing compared to its immediate reality. The reality of a particular revelation can only be realized after our human limits have been stretched to their furthest potential, not before. This is why the furthest dimensions of Christ can only be revealed to the degree that the furthest dimensions of our selves have been realized. Thus a new level or dimension of Christ is only revealed after we have experienced a similar level or dimension in ourselves.

This, then, was the unusual phenomena I noticed in taking this journey, namely, that Christ seemed to follow me, and not I, him. Where I had expected Christ to show me where next to put my foot, that was not the way it worked. Instead, it was only after I had put both feet in, taken the risks, accepted the challenges, and been through the dark nights, that a wholly new dimension of Christ would suddenly be revealed. Thus Christ cannot be revealed ahead of our time or ahead of our own level or stage of spiritual transformation – this is what I mean by saying he comes after us and not before. Incoming after, Christ sheds light on our experiences, states or milestones, thereby verifying and validating our new dimension, giving us the necessary certitude this is the way the path goes, this is its truth. Nothing and no one else can do this for us. In fact, if the truth be known, it is this validation by Christ that makes it a distinctively Christian path.

Thus Buddha, Krishna, Moses and Mohammed never verified a thing for me, nor can I imagine Christ verifying anything for those of other traditions – but then, who knows? What is being validated is not only an ancient path or a particular way of life, but more importantly, a great Truth of the Divine, a Truth unique to the Christian revelation and tradition. That we see similarities in our traditions is all very well, but when we get down to the bottom line, it is our differences that are truly enlightening.

It would be impossible and even irrelevant to detail this journey any further. Suffice it to say it was an experiential, insightful, life-time journey wherein the Eucharist was absolutely central, so central that without it, there would have been no journey. Recently several people asked me what particular techniques I used and how I managed to travel without a teacher. The question drew a blank, I could find no way to give them a satisfying answer. If I told them my Teacher not only taught without a single word or technique, but did it all as well, this would make the journey sound so totally passive it would only have discouraged them.

Just how much we do on this journey, and how much we do not do, seems to be a problem for many people. To illustrate the way it goes I have often compared our journey through human existence to a moving sidewalk (such as we find in airports) whereon we are all going in the same direction, toward the same end, whether we care to go with it or not. Our choice is either to tune-in to the movement and go with it, or to spend our whole lives walking backwards on the sidewalk, going contrary to the forward movement.

As easy as it sounds, nothing could be more difficult than to go with this movement, to be passive to it, because nine times out of ten, it means going contrary to ourselves, the way we think we should go or would like to go. It is only when we come to the point of perfect passivity or oneness with this Divine movement that we come upon the undauntable, fearless courage to live fully, to push the human limits and fulfill every aspect of our human potential.

Thus perfect passivity would also be perfect living. Prior to coming to this point, however, the active-passive dichotomy or struggle going on within ourselves is symptomatic of our own disunity. In the unitive state this struggle is resolved. As one of the characteristics of this state, St. Teresa notes the perfect coming together of Martha and Mary — the active and passive tendencies in ourselves. From here on, while living an active life, there is nothing that can possibly move us from our Divine center. Any discussion of an active-passive life (either-or debate) is wholly premature. Once we have it all together — as in the unitive state — this discussion becomes meaningless.

But if I cannot address the subject of teachers and techniques, I can say this journey was not without help and inspiration from others. At fifteen my mother became so concerned about my ascetic, contemplative practices — school and social affairs had fallen by the wayside — that she, along with a few others, decided I should be sent to a priest, one who had both feet on the ground, to have my head straightened out. I went with all defenses up, I knew the way I had to go and what I had to do, nobody was going to change any of that. Fortunately for me, though not for my mother, this priest was a Discalced Carmelite, one who became an instant ally. On one of my visits to him, I complained there was nobody in the

Church for me, nobody going my way. I had read the lives and treatises of the great saints, but could not identify with their lives or paths. He replied, "I know someone for you", and left the room. When he returned, he handed me *The Spiritual Doctrine of Elizabeth of the Trinity* by M.M. Philipon, O.P. Not only was Elizabeth's path of interior silence going my way, but equally significant, was the theological context through which the author viewed her particular journey. This context was totally in keeping with everything I learned from my father in our years of discussion, and how it all came together in this book, struck me as remarkable. This would be one of two books – later, the other was John of the Cross' Spiritual Canticle – that placed my journey within the much larger context of a very old contemplative tradition.

Although Elizabeth of the Trinity and John of the Cross cannot give light, they nevertheless articulated the light they were given, thereby bequeathing their insights to those who would come after. Both contemplatives drew from sources that had gone before them, and thus the Christian's contemplative path is handed down from generation to generation. We share the same Teacher, the same Eucharist, the path is well worn, and we are never really alone or one of a kind. The marvel of the Eucharist is that Its path is not exclusive, it was not meant just for monk or nun, clergy or a few privileged souls. Rather, the Eucharist is a dynamic phenomenon ever present and ever waiting to lead all who come to It into the depth and mystery of Christ.

In ending, I would like to mention there was a certain irony in the conclusion of my particular odyssey. When it was over, and I finally saw how it worked, or in what way the historical Christ was the divine Logos, the thought came to mind, "Now, at last, after 35 years of searching, finally I am a Christian". But just as suddenly, the thought dissolved; there was no truth in it. The one who had made the journey and sought to be a Christian was gone, and there was no one remaining to make such a claim. But then that followed Christ, who never thought of himself as a Christian and made no claim to be one. In truth, Christ was not a Christian, and thus his ultimate reality belongs to no religious system. If there is a moral to this story it is that those who go all the way with Christ will, like Christ, ultimately go off the map of all comprehensible religious and psychological paradigms. To say that in the end there is no "one" remaining, is a great truth, yet who can understand this or see how it works? The only clue I know that might convey this mystery is the Eucharist itself. Multiplied the world over, we can say there is no "one" Eucharist, for the Eucharist is the All and Everywhere of Christ.

14

WHAT IS SELF? – A RESEARCH PAPER

WHAT IS SELF? – A RESEARCH PAPER

This paper was written at the request of Dr. Nini Praetorius, Docent Professor, University of Copenhagen. It was written as a contribution to her research project entitled *"A new approach to the studies of Self, its development, function, and relation to consciousness"*. The questions posed are *"whether or not self has any real existence, i.e., is there something of substance being referred to by the notions of "self", "I", and "me", or is the self a mere narrative construction, a cognitive representation, or is self a linguistic artifact, or a neurological induced illusion?"*

Since I have already written and spoken rather extensively on the true nature of self, the focus of this paper will be on *"Self as the cause of individuation"*. What I can contribute to this subject, however, is not academic, but arises solely from my experiences as a Christian contemplative - i.e., a life centered on God. Apart from this particular context, I find the subject of "self" of no particular interest. While this background may narrow the scope of this paper, yet, apart from what I have already written (of "self"), what follows is about all I can add to it.

Introduction

If this paper were intended for those already acquainted with my works I could have made short work of it. The difficulty, however, is writing for those without this particular background. With no time to repeat what I have already gone over, some people may find this paper difficult reading. Questions are bound to arise that have already been addressed or gone over at length that cannot be repeated here. Realizing this problem, I decided that in the interest of making this paper more comprehensible, I would begin with a statement of its *major premise and conclusion,* and leave the rest of the paper to provide its *minor premises* or *middle terms.*

This syllogistic set-up is not intended to *prove* anything, but is simply a way to understand this paper in light of its *premise and conclusion*. So here, then, is our thesis statement:

Premise: *"Self is the cause of individuation"*.

Conclusion: *"Without Self there is no individuation.*[1]

Individuation

As used in this paper, the term *"individuation"* is to be understood in its philosophical sense and not its more contemporary Jungian sense. Where psychology takes man's *experience of individuality* for granted, philosophy questions the *cause* of this experience – i.e., how man's knows and experiences *his own* individual *"I am"*, *"I exist"*, *"I think"*. Without the experience of *his own being* the entire philosophical question of *"being"* would never have arisen in the first place. So the source or *cause* of *individuation* is first and foremost man experiencing *himself* as a discrete individual being.

From a philosophical perspective, the problem of "self" can be put this way: based on the theory that man (human nature) is a composite of *matter* and *form* (soul), it is difficult to explain how either *prime matter* (which is the *same* in *all* physical things), or substantial *form* (which is the *same* in all members of the same species) could be the **cause or principle of individuation** (individuality). Since neither *matter* or *form* (soul) is the *cause* of "individuation", then neither *matter* or *form* is the *cause* of man experiencing himself as an *individual being*. The question, then, is **"What" is it that causes man's one universal human nature to be individuated**

---

[1] See both my book *What Is Self?* and DVD *"A Passage Through Self"*. Chapters on self can also be found in my book *Essays on the Christian Spiritual Journey*. My first two books (*The Experience of No-Self* and *The Path to No-Self*) were *not* concerned with the true nature of self. The first book solely recounts the conundrum of living *without* the experience of self and the mystery of the **true nature of "what" remains beyond all self** – a question of far greater importance to man than the true nature of self. As to *"what"* lies beyond all self, this is the subject of my most recent book, *The Real Christ*.

into a plethora of individual persons or selves?

Given there is but one *common human nature* and not *many* human natures, different kinds of human nature, or even a *particular* human nature - "*What is common to all is proper to none*" – **the question is how to get from *one universal human nature* to every man being *his own* incommunicable *self* or *person?*** In some respects, this question harks back to the ancient Greeks pondering how the "one" could be many or the many be "one". As a proverbial question, however, it is one for which no answer has ever proved satisfactory. Thus, for example, Plato thought *matter* was responsible for individuating man's *universal soul* into many individuals. Aristotle, on the other hand, thought it was the *soul* that individuated matter – because, he said, it is the *essence* of man's *common* soul *to be one*. For Aristotle then, it is the soul *in-forming* matter that is the *cause* of individuation – i.e., many individual "ones". Of course there were other views as well – the Stoics, Plotinus, etc..

Simply put, my answer to this proverbial question is this: *self is the cause of individuating man's one common universal human nature into many individual selves or persons*. Human differences are not due to man's *common human nature*, but to that particular *property* of human nature man *experiences* as "self" – as "*I am, I exist, I am myself and no other*". Self, then, is responsible for the *experience* of being a discrete entity, a unique individual person. Without self, man would **not** experience himself as an *individual* or *person*, nor as *a being* - a "*who*" or "*I am*". This means that **man's common universal human nature** is **void** of all these experiences, void of any experience that could be called or defined as "*self*". In short, man's one common, universal human nature, is *void of any self.*

Self IS self-awareness

As a mere word, "self" is simply the expression of everyman's **experience of existence** – "I exist", "I am". Self-awareness is not something man was taught or figured out – indeed, within the first year of life infants give signs of being aware of themselves – rather, *self* is first and foremost everyman's *awareness of his own existence*. (For those who get hung up on mere *words*, sign-language expresses the same thing). The reason most people take self-awareness for granted is because, as an "experience", they have *never been without it!* (In truth, one never knows what he *has* until it is gone!) Thus when people refer to their "selves", the usual reference is to their whole being, their very existence and *not* to some idea in their heads, to some bodily organism, or to a disembodied soul. It is because man's awareness of his *own* existence is an autonomous "given", he takes "self" as everything it means *to exist*. So unless otherwise specified, all "self" words refer to man's entire being, more especially, to *himself* as a discrete **individual entity** or person.

All self-words, then – "*me, myself and I*" – are simply expressions of man *experiencing* his individual existence as the independent owner, agent or steward of his *own* being. He is aware that his thoughts, desires, judgments, feelings and acts are *his own* and *not* someone else's. *Self*, then, *is autonomous self-awareness* responsible for everyone being his own unique "person" – person defined as one in possession of himself, or maybe, one who is "self possessed". Since it is *self-awareness* that *individuates* man's universal *human nature*, we **define "*self*"** (what it means and "what" it **is**) **as "*self-awareness*".** As an objective study, self-awareness is called **"*consciousness*",** the singular nature of which is awareness-of-oneself – one's *own* being, *own* existence. Thus "self-awareness" and "consciousness" are synonymous terms for "self" for without consciousness or self-awareness, man would have no experience of "self". There is no self beyond consciousness or any consciousness beyond self. In fact, there is also no such "thing" as "the unconscious" or an "*unconscious* self". What is called "*unconscious*" is merely a term for what one either does *not* know or is *not* aware of, in which case, it has no *reality* for anyone. As for different "levels" of consciousness, they are all *self*. [2]

---

[2] Obviously my use of the term "*individuation*" is not Carl Jung's use of the term. His was a dual notion of self as the *conscious* ego ("I am") and an *unconscious* "true self". What he called "individuation" was integrating the conscious and unconscious, a kind of "self-realization" that constituted an authentic or holistic selfhood. We could say this was his idea of a "whole undivided *person*".

Perhaps it is not for nothing the Greek term for "soul" was "*psyche*". Though the psyche or soul was defined as "life", today, however, *psyche* is just another term for "consciousness" or "self-awareness", which is *not*, however, "life" defined as a "soul". Keep in mind, man's human nature is a composition of matter-plant-animal-and-human *life*. It is because human nature includes the life of *all beings* that the ancients regarded man as a "*microcosm*" of the *macrocosm* (universe). What is unique about the *human* soul, however, is self-awareness or consciousness.[3] Yet, as a *function* of the *human soul*, *self* is *not*, however, man's real or true *life*. If this function (self or self-awareness) were to cease functioning, nothing could be more obvious than that the physical body has a *life* of it own - with no one running the show, no *one* even *in* the body – we call this "*vegetative life*". So too, *sensory or animal life* is *not* human life – plants and animals have no human "psyche", this is solely a human prerogative.

Needless to say, if "self" was *not* man's immediate awareness of his own existence, there would never be an inquiry into "*what*" self is. So given that self-awareness is everyman's *experience*, the concern is not "*that*" self-awareness exists, rather, the concern is "*what*" is it that *every human being knows and experiences as his self*? For most people the simple answer is, "*I experience myself as a human being* – **because that's "what" I am**"! *To be* one's own self, then, is to know and experience one's *self* as a *human being*. The usual reference to "self", then, is to the experience of being a discrete *individual human being*. Indeed, it is *because* in common parlance "self" is reference to an individual human *being*, we get the view that **"self is a being"**. As a *function* of the human soul, however, **self is not an individual being.**

Self is the major Faculty (function) of the human soul

To understand how self-awareness works, it is important to

---

[3] Although the uniqueness of the *human* soul has been defined as a "*rational soul*", there is little evidence for this. Man acts more on his feelings than on reason. The only group in history that warned man that his feelings and emotions *swamped* his ability to use his reason were the Stoics – and they were right. Man has to overcome his affective responses before he can ever use pure reason.

know the difference between "reflexive" and "reflective". The soul's function of self-awareness is *autonomously reflexive*, it is only with deliberate *reflection* man becomes aware of its autonomy. So while man autonomously "knows himself," he does not know he knows himself until he deliberately *reflects* on himself to realize he is always aware of himself – even when he is *not* aware of this! Needless to say, since man never created himself (or even asked to exist), he has no control over self-awareness, nor can he ever get rid of it – even if he wanted to. (To be without any self-awareness scares most people. Since they regard "self" as a reference to their entire being, they think that without self-awareness they would cease to exist!)

The term "reflexive" obviously indicates a *function*, thus the soul's function of self-awareness is like a *contraction* or a bending on itself to know itself as object-to-itself.[4] A bad analogy might be seeing one's reflection in a mirror – "bad" because an immaterial soul is *imageless*. The point, however, is that **self-awareness is a *function*, and as such, it is *the* major faculty (or function) of the human soul.**[5] No man could live a normal life on earth if he lacked this autonomous reflexive function, indeed, without it, there could be no development of the intellect and will – those other faculties (functions) of the soul. The ability to *use* the intellect and will totally depends on a *user* – a self-aware being. Without self or self-awareness "who" or "what" would run the show? – **that's the real question!** Life *with* self-awareness is obvious, but life *without* self-awareness is literally *unthinkable*.

---

[4] Duns Scotus (b.1266), the great Franciscan theologian, held that how the *one common essence of human nature* becomes an *individual* person, is due to what he called a *"contraction"* – i.e., individuals being a *"modification"* or *"contraction"* of man's *"un-contracted"* common essence. Since another term for "contraction" is "reflexion", we agree that the *cause* of *individuation* (individual selves or persons) is the function of *reflexive* self-awareness, a contraction "imposed", as it were, on the *un-contracted* common universal. Thus the *common essence of human nature* is *not* self-awareness, *not* "I am", nor any *individual* being or "person".

[5] Some theologians held that the nature of the soul was nothing more than *its functions*. But if these functions ceased, then man would be out of a soul – lose his soul. Without self-awareness, however, "***who***" would be out of a soul? **No one!**

For anything to *function* there are two requirements: 1. there has to be some *mechanism* in place, and 2. there has to be some *fuel* to run it. Given the fuel, this mechanism is the mind's ability to bend on itself, know itself – know "I exist". In general, people regard this "mechanism" to be in their heads, minds or physical brains – witness people who try to "silence" their mind or stop thinking altogether. What most do not know, however, is that the *fuel* that runs the reflexive mechanism comes directly from the center of their being – physically experienced, at least, just below the navel. Although people are not really aware of this connection, they might notice that when *centered* in themselves, the mind's "thinking" is greatly reduced. This is why, to find God, many people look to the *still* center of their being; yet, *without* self-awareness they could not do this because there would *be* no "*center*" or "*within*" – none! Anyone who can look "within" has a self he can look into. Without reflexive self-awareness, however, there is no *one* to look into and *nothing* to look into. (It is somewhat facetious that people look within themselves to find their "true self" when self is the one looking in!) No question, self-awareness ("I exist") creates a *circumference of individuality that. like every enclosed circumference, has a center.* Without self-awareness there would be neither circumference (individuality) nor "center" – no one to look *within himself* or experience any *interior life* at all.

This reflexive "function" (self-awareness), however, is *never* under man's control, he cannot turn it off or on, he has no say or *power* over it – *not ever*! The "fuel" that generates this mechanism (self-awareness) belongs to no man. Just as man never created himself he can never get rid of himself.[6] All he can do is *use* what he has been given to become the best *person* he can be. Thus every man – for better or worse – *creates his*

---

[6] The idea self can get rid of itself is an oxymoron – as if the created soul could *un-create* itself. The idea of "*getting rid of self*" goes no further than getting get rid of the soul's *self-centeredness* (ego) that people want out of the way so God can be the *true center of their being* – *true center of* **themselves**, *that is*. Nobody wants to get rid of their self-awareness because without it "*who*" could ever be *aware of God or a* "*divine Center*"? **No one!** The early father's saying "*Man is created Theocentric*" is only true so long as man *has* a center. Without self-awareness there is no center, no circumference, no within or without, no awareness of self – or God.

own unique *person* (*"who"* he becomes), even though he did not create or bring himself into existence.

Self as Person

In early Christianity, "person" was defined as a *"property"* of human nature. *Person* was *not* the *essence* of human nature (*essence* defined as *"what"* something is), rather, person is a *property* of human nature – *"property"* meaning *ownership*.[7] So *"what"* every human being *owns* is his own human nature, is responsible for *his own* thinking, own behaviors – desires, pursuits, etc. In other words, he is master of himself, the *agent* governing his own existence – in short, he is his *own person*, his own incommunicable *self* that can never be "another". So while "essence" defines *human nature* or **"what"** all human beings share in common, *"person"* solely defines **"who"** an *individual* or *particular* human being is. *Human nature* (**what** man is), then, is a *"universal"*, while *person* is a singular or *"particular"* (**who** someone is).

Thus Socrates, Plato and Aristotle are of the same identical human nature, but were not the same *self* or *person*. So if the *property* of human nature is *to be* one's own self (a unique *person*), **the common essence of human nature, however, is *not* "self" – is *not* an individual *person* nor any *particular being*.** What makes for *differentiation*, then, *is* self or person and *not* human nature. *"What"* man is, then, is a *universal*, whereas *"who"* a man is, is a particular individual *person* or *self.* Given that *"person"* and *"self"* both answer the question of *"who"* a *particular individual* is, they are synonymous terms.

---

[7] Tertullian (165-220) is credited with the definition of "person" as a *property*. Both philosophically and theologically, however, all *"properties"* of human nature are said to be *accidental* to its *essence or true nature*. Thus an *accidense* (Latin) has no independent and self-sufficient existence, but exists only in another being, substance, or in another accident. As opposed to *"substance"*, *accidents* may change, *disappear*, or be added, while "substance" remains the same. Thus the "faculties" of the human soul are regarded as the "proper" *accidents* of the human soul – meaning, that even if they ceased to function, there would be no change in the *essence* (or *substance*) of human nature.

Were there *no person or self*, then **who** would ever think of asking **"Who?"** No *"one"*! It is because *self* is always a reference to a *particular* individual that the question "Who?" arises. (The idea that human language is based on *no communicable human experience* is absurd. All language is the expression of some experience).

What is *responsible*, then, for the *differentiation* or *individuation* of man's common human nature is the *property* of human nature man knows and experiences as *self* or *person*. Thus, to know the true *cause of individuation* is simply to *"know thyself"*. Obviously, **self is *not* the *essence* of man's human nature, rather, self is the *property* of human nature responsible for the *individuation* or *differentiation* of man's *one common human nature*.**

Individual vs. Individuation

For just about everyone, "individual" refers to a material, physical entity. Even Aristotle defined *"individual"* as a *"numerical one"*. As he saw it, human nature was a composite or union of a material body and an immaterial soul — the soul being the *life* of the body. For him, reference to "individual" (or "individuality") is always to something material or physical — *quantitative*, that is. But if one can count heads (individuals), one *cannot* count human natures — human nature is *not quantitative*. (By definition, no universal is "quantitative"). Interestingly, since Aristotle (unlike Plato) held there was no "soul" without a body, he granted neither body or soul any eternal life.[8]

Since everything that exists is a material individual "something" - atom, molecule, seed, plant, animal or human being — to be an "individual" means to be some discrete *material* entity, and hence, some *sensory object*. As pointed out, however, *material individuality* cannot account for being an incommunicable *human person;* if it did, then every material "thing"

---

[8] For Aristotle, the only thing *eternal* in man was his *"contemplative faculty — "that"* in man that would *eternally* *"contemplate the 'One'"*. Based on the ancient definition of *human nature* as a composite of *body-soul-spirit*, this *contemplative faculty* would be man's *spirit — not* his soul.

(atom or molecule) would be its own independent "person" or "self" - for which there is no evidence. To account for a human "person" or "self" requires something *more* than being an *individual physical* body. Keep in mind, given time, all material bodies become a heap of *undifferentiated* ashes – "dust" the Bible calls them. Since no *material body* can account for *self-awareness or consciousness*, then no *material individual* body constitutes a *person* or *self*. **In short, physical** (material, quantitative) ***individuality*** does ***not*** **account for** ***"individuation"***. **Self is no** ***individual material*** **being or entity).**

Perception vs. Awareness

Just as it is an error to mistake *material individuality* for *individuation* (self or self-awareness), there follows the proverbial failure to differentiate between *perception* and *awareness*. Objects-of-**perception** are solely *material sensory objects*, whereas the sole *object-of-**awareness** is self*. Where the senses can only look outward, the human soul looks inward. For the philosophers, this was the major difference between animal and man, between a *sensory* soul and a *human* soul – "Know Thyself" was a *human* prerogative. Where the senses only *perceive* material objects in the environment, the major function of the human soul is to look inward - to *know itself*. For the soul *to know itself*, however, it has to *be an object to itself, otherwise there would be no "subject" to know.* Thus man only "knows himself" as *"object-of-the-subject"* or *"subject-of-the-object"* – same thing, *subject is "I am"*, *object is "Myself"*. It goes without saying, as an *object*-to-itself, the soul is not some *sensory perceptual* material object or image – indeed, the human soul admits of no sensory "objects" or images. (Where the imagination plays on sensory objects, the human soul is *incapable* of "*perceiving*" sensory objects or images). So keep in mind, "*perception*" belongs solely to the animal *sensory* soul (material objects), and *not* to the *human* soul (which is solely *aware* of itself).

Another mistake is to think that to look outward or inward is just a matter of choice – not so! Man only looks outward *through the glasses of self-awareness*. Though conscious of himself looking out, it is not consciousness that looks out, rather, it is solely the senses. **Self-*awareness***

and *perception* are **two entirely different functions, different natures with totally different effects.** The senses only *perceive* material objects while consciousness is solely *aware of itself*. People, however, regular-
ly mistake "awareness" for "perception" – and vice versa. Because of
this mistake, man has a penchant for projecting *his* self-awareness onto
objects, animals, other people – even God. This is because *he only knows
"the other" according to how he knows himself.* Yet neither animals, objects, nor
God are self-aware beings, this is solely a *human* prerogative.[9] So just as
the senses are *incapable* of looking within (or inward), so too, self-
awareness (or "consciousness") is *incapable* of looking out (or outward).[10]
We could give many examples of contemplatives making this mistake,
one being the idea they (themselves) are really no different than a tree, a
chair, or some sensory object – totally absurd! The point is that no physical, material individuality can account for individuation – i.e., the experience "*I am*", "*I exist*", "*I think*" etc.

Effects of self-awareness

Self-awareness is responsible for man's *experience* of "*life*", "*being*",
"*soul*", "*self*", "*energy*" and all his *emotional or affective experiences*. It is responsible for man's "*interior life*" of being able to *look within* himself and *experience a "spiritual" dimension* beyond his sensory body. Self-awareness is
man's experience of having a *center* in himself, of his being a discrete individual *person* or *entity*, it is even his experience of *oneness with God*. There
are many other subtle experiences due to self-awareness or self. In fact,
without the awareness "I am", "I exist", man *as we know him* would not
exist. As for the true *essence* of man's *universal* human nature, this is "*Universal Man*", Man, however, that **no** *individual* person or self could ever

---

[9] To think God is a self-aware being is to make God into man's own self-image.
As for being "aware" of God, if all awareness is *self-awareness,* then, strictly speaking, man can never be "aware" of God. Man can be aware of **his own** awareness of God, which *awareness,* however, is *not* God. God is beyond awareness,
consciousness or self.

[10] While "self-awareness" is the true nature of *self,* "self-perception" is the definition of a "false self". "*Perceiving*" one's self as a sensory object or image is **not**
to "*know thyself*" at all!

know so long as there is any self (self-awareness or consciousness) remaining. The true essence of man's human nature is **no** *individual person* or *particular* being. In truth, the *eternal essence* of man's common *universal human nature* is known only to *its Creator*, and it is solely this *"Universal Man"* (and *not* any individual self or person) that it eternally one with its Creator. It is this **"Oneness"** of the *unknowable* essence of God and *unknowable* essence of Man that God revealed as everything Christianity knows and calls '**Christ**'.

Man as Spirit

According to the ancients, to Paul, the early fathers and even "scripture", man is a composite of body-soul-**spirit**. That the medieval theologians omitted the *"human spirit"* is the major problem with their theologies.[11] Nothing so keeps man grounded to life on earth as the *faculties of the* **soul** – indeed, this is what they were created to do. Knowing this is why "spiritual adepts" tell us we must have no-mind, no-will (or desires) and no-self – why? *Because they keep a man grounded, down to earth, keep him from soaring to God beyond himself.*

So there is certainly *more* to man than these faculties of the human soul. Holding man to being solely a union of body and soul is totally off the mark. The **spirit** is man's true "spiritual life", his *mystical* dimension *beyond* the souls' *faculties*. While the *spirit* is not God, it is the vehicle by which God is revealed to man, communicates to him, and by which man encounters God not only in himself, but in all creation. A *spiritual* man, then, is really a *contemplative* man, the *spirit* raising him *beyond himself* to a dimension of existence apart from all he knows as his "body-

---

[11] Western Theology literally did away with the "spirit". Its theologians divided the *intellect* into a *higher and lower* part – the "higher intellect" supposedly taking the place of the "spirit"! This is one reason the Eastern Church ignores Western theology. For the East, *"mystical theology"* is the only "theology" it recognizes – i.e., a theology based on man's *experiences* of God and not on his *intellectual* prowess – as the West does.) If Western theology were totally scrapped, the only ones to miss it are those who *depend* on their intellects *instead* of their "spirits" for the *Truth*. The spirit is *"that"* mystery in man that truly sees and knows God and, in eternal life, shares in the *essence* of the Godhead's *Triune eternal life.*

soul-and *self*. It is this mysterious *spirit* in man that longs for and is *drawn up* to "*That*" which alone can fulfill his entire human nature – whatever that may be. He does not know "*What*" It is that draws him, he only knows "*That*" It is.

This *spirit* is not a soul, not a self or a body; it is also not an "energy" or anything man thinks is a "spiritual" energy. It is *because* man's **"spirit" is non-experiential** it is a *mystery*. Yet it is this mystery in man that contemplates (sees) and knows God, and is the medium that unites the infinite and finite in eternal life. Where the 'eye of the *soul*' is solely on *itself* – i.e., "*the eye with which I see God is the same 'eye' with which God sees me*" – the **eye of the spirit**, on the other hand, **is selfless** – sees neither subject nor object (self or God). Man often wonders "*what*" it is in himself that sees, knows and unites him to God, he wonders because he knows it is **not** his mind, intellect, will-power or even his self. He only knows this mystery is "that" in him that is most akin to God. St. Paul explained that just as the soul has *its own physical* body, the **spirit has its own spiritual** body, and it is this *spiritual body* that is resurrected into eternal life in God.

There is nothing *eternal* about the *functions* of the human soul - nothing eternal about self-awareness, consciousness or "self". God creates no person, self or particular individual, God only creates "what" man is – i.e., his one *common human nature*. It is each individual that creates or develops his *own person* – "who" he is and how he lives his life. But in the end, God is no respecter of *persons* or "*who*" someone is. It is how man has fulfilled *the human nature* God created him *to be* that matters, for this alone has eternally life with and in God.

Conclusion

The true nature of "self" is **the** major faculty (or function) of the human soul. As the awareness of *his own* existence this function is responsible for individuating man's common human nature into individual *selves* – every man knowing and experiencing "I am", "I exist". So the *function* of self-awareness or consciousness is to **individuate** man's universal human nature into individual persons or selves. As human beings, *all are alike and no different*, but as individual selves or persons, *none are alike and all are different*. So while "human nature" defines *every* human being, "person" defines "*who*" a *particular* individual is. Thus we could define **"Self" as the *state of being an individual person*** – "*person*" being what it means to be *unique, incommunicable – different*. While no man created *human nature*, it is how he **uses** the faculties he has been given that c*reates* or determines the *person* he becomes – "who" he is.

Self, then, is obviously not a "being", not just a "word" or cognitive construct, and certainly not an "illusion", rather, self is everyman's *experience* "I exist" – simple as that. It is this self-awareness or consciousness ("*I, me, myself*") that *causes individuation* – i.e., the simple awareness of *one's own existence*, of being *one's own person*. **Without this, man as we know him would not exist.** The importance of "self", then, is that without it, this planet would be only fit for animals – *sensory* beings, that is.[12]

There is really no great mystery about "self" or man's self-awareness. The real mystery is the true nature of "*what*" remains when it is gone – has ceased to function. With the cessation of self-awareness, all the *experiential effects* it generated are gone in the blink of an eye. And what *were* these effects? They were the **experience** of "*being*", of "*life*", "*soul*", "*energy*", "*mind* and *will*", "*interiority*" (within-ness), the "*affective system*", even the awareness of "*being one with God*" – all these experience are suddenly blown out and gone forever! Now there is no center (God) and no circumference (self). In truth, this "blow out" (or cessation) is the only *death-experience* man will ever experience – could ever have, in fact. So take away self-awareness with all its *experiential* effects and the real question becomes **"*what* is the *true nature* of what remains *beyond***

---

[12] As already pointed out, everything in existence is some *individual* material "thing", and thus, it is solely an *object of sensory perception*. *Material individuality*, however, is not *what individuates* - matter alone cannot account for any experience of self or self-awareness – in fact, nothing man *perceives* is eternal. The question, of course, is if there is anything man is "aware of" that is eternal?!

all self." This is the real *mystery of man and* the *real question* he needs to have answered.[13]

No idea in the mind could ever come up with a satisfactory answer to this mystery, only God can **reveal** the true nature of *"what"* remains beyond all self and individuation. Since only the Creator knows the *true essence* of man's *common human nature,* only God can reveal *its eternal oneness with God.* I have written a book about this *revelation,* its title being *The Real Christ.*

THE END [14]

---

[13] The reason I never had an interest in the true nature of *self* is because the simple awareness *"I exist"* is a human *given* – obvious, simple, *undeniable.* That this awareness (*"I am"*) is **eternal,** however, **this** is a whole different question and one man should **really be concerned about!**

[14] **Food for thought:** Some time ago, listening to the quiz show *Jeopardy,* one of the questions was *"What is the name of the German Psychiatrist who had a patient say to him,* **"Doctor, I have no self**'? No one on the panel knew the answer - which turned out to be *"Doctor Alzheimer"*. For people who want to get rid of their "self", this, at least, is one way to go.

/ 15 /

THE PATH

THE PATH

NO-SELF OR CONSCIOUSNESS

Christ Revealed

INCARNATION - Reverse of the Ascension: coming down from Glory or heaven to the human condition. (Many difficult years adjusting to ordinary life).

GOD AWFUL VOID - of the Glory of God.

ASCENSION - Body (whole being) dissolves into divine Air – Glory.

PENTECOST - The "Cloud of Knowing" descends: Truth (God) as It exists beyond self or consciousness. All experiences of God had been self - self is the experience, the experiencer and the experienced). God, however, is beyond all self or consciousness).

RESURRECTION – All form is void of God. The void is absolute. The void **is the Absolute,** the Logos, the eternal "Form of God", source and true nature of all form. This is what remain beyond all self or consciousness.

VOIDS OF VOIDS – non-relative, absolute

NO-SELF - No Consciousness: 2 steps: 1. Cessation of reflexive mechanism 2. Extinction of center -the inner Divine Flame. No Center = no circumference. No "within" = no "without." "Pure sensory perception" remains. Looming question: "What is the true nature of 'this' that remains beyond self?" The answer can only be revealed.

Unitive Consciousness
The Marketplace

EGOLESS GIVING AND LIVING – Spontaneous, automatic way of life. No need of former practices. Seeks challenges. Joy in suffering. Sees God in all things: people, nature, situations. Outward looking. Nothing in life for self – a *"Dark Night of Self".* Inner Flame (Center) is consuming self - God increases as self decreases. (John's "I die because I do not die.") When there is nothing left to consume (no fuel) the divine FLAME WILL GO OUT.

IMPERATIVE TURNING POINT Inward journey is finished. The movement turns around and MOVES OUTWARD to test and manifest the new life of Union. Transient glimpses of a further state wherein there is no self, only the glory of God. Since heaven is not yet, there is full acceptance of one's humanity just as Christ accepted it. And just as He emptied himself of glory to take on our humanity, so too we FORFEIT ALL EXPERIENCES OF GOD to serve Him selflessly. Determination to live the human potential fully and fearlessly. God goes underground – so to speak.

FIELD OF CONSCIOUSNESS OR SELF

Transformation
"Passive Night of the Spirit"

UNITIVE REVELATION of a permanent, abiding oneness where God is our deepest being ("true self"). No longer dark but Light. With this revelation there is the instant sense of being a new person, new being; utter freedom; beginning of a new life, certitude of Union - the mature state of man. END OF THE INWARD JOURNEY--cannot go deeper than the Deepest.

MID-POINT IN THE NIGHT Hit bottom of the empty center where there is peace, stillness, and seeing God in the darkness, the deepest Point of our being. End of interior pain. From here on all aspects (movements) of self are passively integrated around the immovable diving Center. This is the "Little Way" of surrender, an integration that is God's doing, not our doing. This is the making (or re-making) of a new consciousness, new self, a new life around a new divine center.

NO-EGO. The Center of being (the ego)—where we had experienced God's presence—suddenly falls away. Two steps: 1) Descent of "Cloud of Unknowing" (the mind is shrouded). 2) A bottomless black hole appears at the center where, to then, we had seen and experienced God. "That" which experienced God is gone, yet it seems as if God is gone. This is John's *"Passive Night of the Spirit"*, the ONSET of Unitive transformation - an irreversible predicament (no turning back). Experience: INTERIOR VOID, emptiness, nothingness (all relative). No known path; struggle to become passive, submissive to the Unknown. Deep spiritual pain (not psychological). Seeing into this darkness is a "third eye" (painful at that).

Ego Consciousness
Practice

"PASSIVE NIGHT OF THE SENSES" - being weaned from delightful experiences of God. Increasing prolonged periods of dryness, aridity, darkness, emptiness. A test of determination and selflessness to love God for His own sake and not for our sake. Must let go expectation and desire for experiences (all ego-oriented) and blindly surrender self to God.

CONVERSION EXPERIENCE A Revelation. Leaving all behind. The ego (will, energy, desire) gives up everything in pursuit of God -Truth and ultimate Goodness. Test of endurance, perseverance, determination. This is the process of REFORMATION, (not transformation) and John of the Cross' *"Active Night of the Senses"*. An "ascetical path"- our own doing.

Searching

PRE-PATH Doubt, inquiry, study, disunity, testing the waters, (different practices off and on).

68141634R00170

Made in the USA
Middletown, DE
27 March 2018